ANGKOR
The
MAGNIFICENT

To a fellow Orientalist —
Helen C. Candee

ANGKOR THE MAGNIFICENT

Wonder City Of Ancient Cambodia

HELEN CHURCHILL CANDEE

Featuring:

LIFE'S DÉCOR:

A Biography of Helen Churchill Candee

RANDY BRYAN BIGHAM

DatASIA, Inc.
MMXI

DatASIA PRESS
www.DatASIA.US

© Copyright 2008 DatASIA, Inc. - Holmes Beach, FL 34218
Paperback edition © Copyright 2011.

All rights reserved. No part of this book may be reproduced, stored in a retrieval system, or transmitted in any form without prior permission.

2011 Edition Notes
This volume contains the full contents of the original 1924 first edition issued by the Frederick A. Stokes Company, including all text, 79 photographs and one map. This new edition also contains a biography of Helen Churchill Candee, additional photos, bibliographical information, an appendix and index not found in the original.

Production Credits
Editor: Kent Davis

Assistant Editor: Kathi Rolfe

Design and Illustrations: All cover, graphic and text design by
Kristen Tuttle, Tuttle Graphics, Sarasota, FL.

Special thanks to Trey Ratcliff for the rear cover photo of modern Angkor Wat.
To see more of his work visit www.TreyRatcliff.com and www.StuckInCustoms.com;

Phillip Gowan for photos and historical information relating to
Helen Churchill Candee's biography section, *Life's Décor*;

and to the Fund for American Studies (www.tfas.org) for the photo
of Helen Candee's home at 1621 New Hampshire Avenue, Washington DC.

For more information about this book please visit:
www.AngkorSecrets.com

For more historical information about Titanic and her passengers please visit:

Encyclopedia Titanica	www.encyclopedia-titanica.org
Titanic Historical Society	www.titanic1.org
Titanic.com	www.titanic.com

ISBN 978-1-934431-02-3 (paperback)
Library of Congress Preassigned Control Number: 2010941517

Candee, Helen Churchill
Angkor the Magnificent: Wonder City Of Ancient Cambodia
Includes bibliographical references and index.

Printed in the United States of America

PUBLISHER'S INTRODUCTION

It is with hesitation that I mention the larger ladies of the carvings, the Tevadas or sacred dancers. I am made shy in their presence, while they remain unperturbed. They are so many to know all at once, and their character is to me unfathomable.

Helen Candee
Angkor Wat, 1922

Helen Churchill Candee was a modern woman who the *devata*, the sacred Daughters of Angkor Wat in all their glory, would have certainly welcomed as one of their own.

She was remarkable for so many reasons that it is truly difficult to articulate her life in a few statements. Although best known for surviving history's most infamous maritime disaster, the sinking of the *RMS Titanic*, that event was a mere coincidence in the context of Helen's self-determined destiny.

This independent woman not only walked with kings, presidents, the wealthy and the powerful…she entertained, charmed, influenced and educatedthem. She supported herself and her family, out of necessity, in an era when women were expected to depend on men. She championed feminine equality and fought tirelessly for women's rights. And as a single woman she traveled the world with a keen eye for detail, an inquisitive mind and a sensitivity for local culture.

Angkor the Magnificent, Helen Candee's most acclaimed work, is far more than a tale of early 20th century travel to an exotic Asian destination. Helen's insights never disappoint as she relates the history, culture and context of ancient Khmer monuments in an elegant style that is both enlightening and quite readable. By her hand, we have one of the first significant works on Cambodia in the English language.

As editor, it was unimaginable to change a word of her prose, so I present it here, intact, as the author intended. Helen Candee based her research on contemporary expert sources, however the experts themselves were mistaken at times. Her text remains unchanged with a few corrections added as footnotes.

The author employs British spellings (colour, defence, honour, storeys, etc.) and foreign words in Khmer, Latin and French are italicized. I've added definitions for a few particularly obscure words. Archaic terms are intact to maintain the classic flavor of her text: *Civa (Shiva), Civaism (Shivaism) Tevada (devata)*, etc. I confess to changing *Tcheou-Ta-Kouan* to the modern transliteration *Zhou Daguan* to help readers find the brilliant book Peter Harris issued in 2007, giving Anglophones the first direct Chinese to English translation of this important 13th century work.

Graphic designer Kristen Tuttle has improved our book by designing original graphics, enhancing faded antique photos and increasing font sizes. Our goal was to make this edition friendly for "English as a Second Language" readers around the world. Not to mention for aging readers, like me, who now reluctantly peruse thick tomes packed with 10pt type.

Helen Candee earned considerable praise with her book, returning to Cambodia in 1929 to receive an award from King Sisowath Monivong. In 2009, her work was again featured in a royal ceremony when US Ambassador to Cambodia Carol Rodley presented His Majesty King Norodom Sihamoni with this new edition as one of her official US gifts. So, it can truly be said that Helen Candee's book is "fit for a king!"

This modern edition expands the author's original 1924 book with a reprint of her personal report of the sinking of the *Titanic* and, for the first time in print, a biography of Helen Churchill Candee herself by journalist Randy Bryan Bigham.

Next to living great adventures, reading well-written personal accounts by those who have lived them is the next best thing. I wish all readers an enjoyable journey with this most admirable woman, Helen Churchill Candee. May she look favorably upon my humble effort to share her tale with new generations.

Kent Davis
Anna Maria Island, Florida

TABLE OF CONTENTS

PUBLISHER'S INTRODUCTION... V

LIST OF ILLUSTRATIONS... X

ANGKOR THE MAGNIFICENT

A FORECAST... 5

I. HONG-KONG HARBOUR... 9
The Captain's brief trip to Canton. The Captain's story. The conflict at Canton. Pirates in the Pearl River. A refugee abnormally unfilial. The Captain's charmed life.

II. ABOARD THE PAK HOI... 22
The Captain's wife. Thieves. Leaving Hong Kong. Deck passengers. The Mate. The story of the Russian Fleet. The Southern Cross.

III. SAIGON... 36
The Captain's vacation. Cap St. Jacques. Saigon docks. Coaling by Annamites. Native women. Cafés and streets. Nectar from the cocoa palm.

IV. UP THE MEKONG.. 47
Mytho. Phnom Penh, the capital of Cambodia. The royal palace. George Groslier and the Museum. Off again via Tonlé Sap. A late arrival.

V. FIRST VIEW OF ANGKOR VAT.................................. 62
A walk across the moat. The outer enceinte. The Causeway and the Park. The Cruciform Terrace. Investigating the first and second galleries. The grand entrance. The central group. Five towers and the Sanctuary.

VI. STILL ANGKOR VAT..... 81
Reviewing the enceinte. The outer gallery on first story. The bas-reliefs. Historic subjects. Story of the Asuras and Devas, The pageantry of the army, Hanuman, Pure ornament in reliefs. The motif of human figure. Tevadas and Apsaras.

VII. A NOCTURNE..... 103
The dance.

VIII. A SURVEY..... 114
An elephant ride. Royal Angkor Thom. A hint of the power of the Bayon. The public square. The Terraces. The Eastern Gate of Victory. The Devas and Asuras on the bridge. Back through Angkor Thom.

IX. THE BAYON..... 127
Civil of the priests. Building to create fear. The bonzes as guides. The bas-reliefs. Destruction of the temple. The towers of four giant faces.

X. ANIMALS..... 138
Naga, the prince. His legends. His use in art. The lion of Khmer sculpture. Whence comes he? Elephants of importance. Garuda the fabulous. Monkeys and little beasties.

XI. THE TERRACE OF HONOUR..... 147
Its grand stair. Garudas as caryatides. The Tevadas called sacred wives. Elephants hunting along the Terrace. The Terrace of the Leper King. A boy by the wayside. Maidens of the Terrace. The double wall. The sculpture of the Leper King.

XII. PHIMEANAKAS..... 165
Extracts from a Chinese diary. Zhou Daguan as a historian. An audience with the King. Pictures of palace life. When the King goes abroad. Reconstructing the palace.

XIII. THE VILLAGE OF SIEM REAP..... 181
Investigating the natives. The Artist athirst. The search for cocoa-nuts. A typical shop. Native girls and a bracelet. Trying to buy silver. A crop of babies. At last a drink. Blake at the Bungalow.

XIV. SMALLER TEMPLES..... 195
Bak-Keng. The approaching stair and the plateau. The temple and the oxen. Investigating the Baphuon. On to the Buddha of Tep Pranam. Small towers near the public square. The elephants of Pra Pithu. Ta Keo as a hanging garden.

XV. THE BUNGALOW..... 210
Sleep and a marauder. New arrivals. After déjeuner. The native guide-chauffeur. A quest for Néak Pian. Almost an Adventure.

XVI. BANTEAI KEDEI, TA PROHM... 224
The Queen-Mother. Prowling among the carvings. The three great temples outside the city. The gate at Ta Prohm. Civaism and the tower. The personnel of temples. Lodgings. Sacred dancers. Life in religious retreat.

XVII. WATER.. 239
Hydraulic construction. Moats. Pools and reservoirs. The two Barays.

XVIII. PRAH KHAN, NÉAK PEAN.. 245
General plan. The confusion of ruin. The charm of nature. The imprudence of monkeys. How to discover Néak Pean and its beauties. Its unique pedestal and setting.

XIX. FOR THE CHARMINGLY UNINFORMED................................. 259
Questions answered. The mixture of races. Chinese influence. Where vanished the Khmers? Chiseled writings. Legends of religion. The line of Kings. The jungle.

APPENDIX I

LIFE'S DÉCOR: A Biography of Helen Churchill Candee................. 277

ABOUT THE BIOGRAPHER... 317

APPENDIX II

INTRODUCTION TO "SEALED ORDERS".................................... 319

"SEALED ORDERS" by Helen Churchill Candee.......................... 322

BIBLIOGRAPHY... 342

INDEX.. 348

LIST OF ILLUSTRATIONS

ANGKOR THE MAGNIFICENT

The Authoress, the Beguiler and Effie.	2
Angkor Vat — General View.	4
Between India and China; Malay Peninsula and Indochina (map).	8
Pirate Junk Near Hong-Kong.	11
On the River Mekong.	13
Palace Enclosures, Phnom Penh	15
Nagas and Lions on the Stair Leading to the Summit of the Phnom	17
The Museum and Art School at Phnom Penh.	25
Angkor Vat from the Inner Causeway.	27
A Building of Symmetry and Beauty Called a Library.	29
The Park, Angkor Vat	31
The Cruciform Terrace, Angkor Vat.	39
The Front Line of Rooms to a Sequence Following the Line of the Façade.	41
A Corner of the First Gallery	43
The Cruciform Terrace	49
The Gallery Joining the First and Second Galleries, with Pool in the Foreground.	51
The Gallery Connecting the First and Second Stories.	53
Detail of Carving.	55
The *Tevadas*, oh, the *Tevadas*!	65
View from the Second Gallery.	67

The Second Gallery Before Clearing Away the Brush.	69
Detail of Door and Windows of the Second Gallery.	71
The Grass Court Between the First and Second Galleries.	73
The Beautiful Paved Court Leads to the Entrance Stair of the Central Pile.	75
The Gallery of the Second Story.	83
The Third Gallery.	85
The Entrance to the Sanctuary.	89
The Portico of the Enceinte.	93
To Right and to Left Stand the Ruins of Two Symmetric Buildings.	97
The Khmer Builders Gained Architectural Magnificence Through the Device of Long Galleries.	99
Embrasure of a Window Covered with a Close Carving that is Akin to the Pattern of a Woven Cloth.	101
Royal Dancers, Phnom Penh.	103
Prince and Princess Saluting Before the Dance.	109
In the Center of the Great Design Sits a Four-armed Deity, Vishnu of God-like Calm, and the Men Fall Both Ways from This Point.	117
The Great Army of the Khmers Passes in Review.	119
Much Space of the Bas-reliefs is Taken Up with Combats of the Gods of a Fierce and Complicated Nature.	121
The Mount That Thrills is the Splendid Elephant.	123
The Figure is That of Vishnuloka the King.	129
The Cruciform Terrace, Angkor Vat.	131
The Head of the Serpent is Like *Naga's*, Polycephalous, and the Giant Who Holds It Is Also Many Headed.	133
North Gate, Angkor Thom.	141
Bramanic Face, Bayon.	143
The Gate of Victory, Angkor Thom.	149
Devas or Demi-gods Holding the Sacred Snake *Naga*.	151
The Bayon Occupies a Point in the Exact Center of the City, Angkor Thom.	153
One of the Fifty Odd Towers of the Bayon Which was Built in the Ninth Century.	155

Bas-relief, the Bayon.	157
Bas-relief, the Bayon.	159
The Towers of the Four Faces on the Third Story of the Bayon.	167
A Tower of the Bayon.	169
Dancing Figures on a Square Column of the Bayon.	171
The Vat Shows Him Superb, Triumphant, Lending His Upright Heads to Welcome All Who Approach.	173
On the Way Across the Gardens to the Central Temple of Angkor.	185
Naga, Angkor Vat.	187
Lion, Phnom Bak-Keng.	189
Lion on the Cruciform Terrace, Angkor Vat.	191
Terrace of Honor Upheld by Caryatid *Garudas* and Topped with *Naga* Railings and Lions.	199
The *Tevadas* Are Dressed with the Richness of Princesses. They Are Called the Sacred Wives of the God-kings	201
The Elephant Terrace, Angkor Thom.	203
Procession of Elephants Hunting with Archers on Their Backs.	205
The Elephants at the Corners of the Terrace.	211
The Terrace of the Leper-king.	215
The Terrace of the Leper-king.	217
The Statue of the Leper-king Smiles Among the Jungle Trees Above His Terrace of Court Beauties.	219
Phnom Bak-Keng.	227
The Baphuon.	229
Pré Rup.	231
Prah Pithu.	233
Ta Kéo, on the Outskirts of Angkor Thom.	243
Prah Khan, that Pitiful Ruin which Nearest Approaches the Great Vat in Size.	247
A Fallen Stone of Graphic Eloquence.	249
The Four Faced Tower of Civa Overgrown by the Jungle.	251
Ta Prom's State of Ruin is a State of Beauty.	253
Ta Prom — A Pilaster.	255

Reflections in the Pond of the Bonzes.	263
One of the Four Pools in the First Gallery of Angkor Vat.	265
Prah Khan.	267
There Are Delicious Shady Spots in Which to Stay Still.	269
Néak Pean.	271
The Wild-fig Tree on the Centre Island Completely Enfolds the Little Temple in its Grasp.	273

APPENDIX I
LIFE'S DÉCOR: A Biography of Helen Churchill Candee

Helen Candee - Circa 1908.	276
Helen Candee - Circa 1901.	280
Helen Candee - Circa 1905.	283
One of Helen Candee's Washington DC homes.	285
Candee interior design showing her Italian country taste – Early 1900's.	289
The *RMS Titanic* at Southampton before her maiden voyage – 1912.	294
Mr. Edward Austin Kent 1854-1912.	295
Titanic Monument.	296
The New York Times, April 16, 1912.	297
Helen's cameo of her mother Mary recovered from Edward Kent's body.	298
Collier's magazine.	300
The Tapestry Book – 1912.	302
Gobelin's late 19th century tapestry from *The Tapestry Book* – 1912.	303
Helen at the head of the National Woman Suffrage Association's "Votes for Women" parade in Washington DC.	305
Jacobean Furniture - 1916.	306
The Italian Red Cross "carri da letto.".	308
Helen Candee passport photo – Circa 1920.	309
Holyroodhouse, where Helen gave a command reading of *Angkor the Magnificent* to King George and Queen Mary.	310
Harold Candee.	310
King Sisowath Monivong on his coronation day in 1928.	311

Helen at Angkor Wat with Effie and "The Beguiler"......................... 313
Helen Candee in her garden at the Clock House in Stoke Poges, England....... 314
Edith Mathews and her children – Circa 1923............................. 315

APPENDIX II
"SEALED ORDERS" by Helen Churchill Candee

Titanic Embarking — April 10, 1912...................................... 318
RMS Titanic sea trials April 2, 1912...................................... 323
A first-class cabin aboard the *RMS Titanic*................................ 324
A view of *Titanic's* Grand Staircase...................................... 327
Titanic's first-class smoking room.. 330
Lifeboat 6 with Helen Candee and Molly Brown upon rescue................ 332
Titanic Sinking by Willy Stöwer 1864-1931............................... 334
The *Women's Titanic Memorial*... 340
Titanic's bow as seen from the Russian MIR I submersible 341

Angkor The Magnificent

Wonder City Of Ancient Cambodia

HELEN CHURCHILL CANDEE

First Published By
Frederick A. Stokes Company
New York
XCXXIV

The Authoress, the Beguiler, and Effie

TO ALL VISITORS AT ANGKOR,
THE BEGUILING GUIDE,
and
SCHUYLER L. MATHEWS

Angkor Vat — General View from the park the distant towers thrill and mystify.

A FORECAST

The tale of it is incredible; the wonder which is Angkor is unmatched in Asia.

We think we have exposed and investigated the secret places of the whole round globe, when there comes word of a new one, and not only a secret place but a place full of secrets.

In Cambodia lived and developed a mixed race - Malay, Hindu, Chinese - whose history began five hundred years before the Christian era. Improving in all matters which go to make a nation, this race arrived at a period of high development in the eighth and ninth centuries. They became implacable warriors, ambitious artists, exponents of wealth and luxury. Under direction of ambitious kings they built throughout four centuries one of the most grandiose cities of antiquity, Angkor Thom, and added to that incredibly magnificent temples through the surrounding country.

In these precincts, the race called Khmers lived a life of luxury, pomp and display which has not been exceeded at any time in any part of the world. And all of this was at a time when Europe was sunk in the dull apathy of the Dark Ages, when France was a savage country, England uncivilized, Germany a hinterland of barbarous hordes. In Asia the Khmers were known, envied, feared. China sent her Ambassadors there, wise old China that has never slept, never has had a period called Dark Ages. But Europe took no cognizance of the growth of the wealthy Asiatic kingdom, for Europe was not travelling in those centuries.

To maintain the wealth, the Khmer kings had to protect it against invading nations of the Indochina peninsula; also, to forestall jealous attacks, they gathered together their own magnificent army and aggressively marched forth to make terrible war. For centuries the Khmers were the victors, enriched with treasure and captives. Then came the inevitable turn. The Khmers lost, first to the people on the east, then in the hour of their depletion they fell completely into the hands of victorious Siam. This final and conclusive overthrow was late in the twelve hundreds.

What happened after then was incalculable. It is still a mystery, still a secret of Angkor. When overcome the population was enormous, magnificently housed, following the gracious arts of a cultivated taste. A million souls lived within the walls of the royal city. Their temples and palaces were of a grandeur and of a number which made marvel all who saw them. Then all at once the whole thing was blotted out, this entire high civilization and all its works. The jungle, with no hand of man to arrest it, rose like a tide creeping up foot by foot and covered, completely covered, all the work of the centuries. The Khmers disappeared, the temples and towns were swallowed by the relentless sea of verdure, and the places thereof were by both God and men forgot.

Angkor was of the past. Cambodia existed as a quiet country of dark-skinned jungle-people and fishermen. Angkor left no history: it simply passed. Asia forgot it, and sleeping Europe had never known of it.

Thus it was when Cambodia with other countries of Indochina fell under the protection of France.

One day a French naturalist penetrated the jungle, as a boy fired with curiosity penetrates the forest on a farm. He came upon the towers of Angkor Vat. He who had found for days of travel nothing larger nor more recondite in construction than a bamboo hut, saw before him thrusting through the jungle the magnificent pile of architecture. In an ecstasy he sprang forward to meet marvel after marvel. It was unbelievable. He thought himself translated to some other planet. Such beauty, such grandeur, could not exist on earth unknown. He questioned the brown natives. They said the temples had always been there, the gods had built them for their own habitat, and proved it by legends.

The man, in a trance, flew back to the coast and told France of his discovery. France with her instinct for art was thrilled, excited to ecstasy. But hold, go softly! The territory of the marvelous ruins, although formerly belonging to Cambodia, now belonged to Siam. Before letting the world know of its *trouvaille**, France must get possession. And she did. Some political hocus-pocus was managed, Siam was given a *quid pro quo*, and France received into her capable hands the inestimable treasure of the ancient ruins of the Khmers. This transfer was accomplished as recently as 1907.

But for all that Angkor has passed into the hands of new owners, she keeps her secrets. Savants, artists, archaeologues are working at them, prying into the conduct of life in the temples, peeping at the hours of leisure of princes, reveling in conventions of the sacred dancers, and are giving us bit by bit an idea of the fascinating civilization that died in 1295. But so much is left to do, so many mysteries are unfathomed, that decades more will be needed to decipher the writings on stone in a little known tongue and in Sanskrit.

Meanwhile the news is leaking out to the great world that loves a new sensation that there are secrets to be pried open in Cambodia, and special marvels to be seen that even the greatest museums of the greatest cities cannot show. More than that, one can go as a discoverer to the mysterious land and find things for oneself, and one may make deductions with a daring mind. One may even add a bit to the growing history of Khmer civilization through a study of the carvings and thus feel the same proud ecstasy that thrilled the exploring French naturalist when he re-discovered Angkor Vat.

* *trouvaille* – Fr. feminine n. A lucky find; ingenious idea.

Between India and China, Malay Peninsula and Indochina

Chapter I

HONG KONG HARBOUR

When you have longed to go, with a longing such as youth knows, and with a poignant hopelessness such as maturity accepts, it is hard to realize that you are really off, that the journey to the land of delight is begun.

The fantastic towers of Angkor had for months risen before my imagination, with their magnificent upward thrust above the tallest jungle. I could see their exotic silhouettes piling serrated points against a radiant mass of cumuli glorified by the low tropic sun as though the clouds copied them.

I had long been mad to revel in keen sensuous lust-of-the-eye, to feast and feast upon Angkor's tree-embowered palaces, upon lily-embarrassed moats and orchid-decked courts.

What I wanted with all the force of a holy curiosity was to wrest from the quiet brown people of this land of Cambodia some of the secrets of the ancient ruins. Who were their builders, the Khmers? Are they themselves, these gentle forest people, are they the remnant of the great race? Or did the last of the real Khmers who built the world wonder of the Angkor group, assemble his legions, and with band and banner, elephant and chariot, march magnificently away into never-never land to be seen no more, leaving the world to guess and to divine what they could from the splendid structures left behind?

If the quiet pleasant people of today's jungle could not answer the riddle of why so much of magnificence was deserted in splendid estate, then I wanted to search and prowl, to haunt the deserted city in frank noon and mystic twilight, and find out secrets that the archeologue had missed, that had slipped by because he looked with the eye of science while I should absorb with sense and soul, an open and receptive soul. He reads the ancient script of the age-old stones, but much of the story is sure to linger in the land about Angkor and among the present Cambodian people. So I add a divining rod to the tourist equipment.

"But why go to Angkor — it is so far off the beaten track?" asks petulantly the globe-girdler who keeps dates with his encircling steamer.

"That is why. You have said it. Because it is so far off the beaten track. I go there with a piqued interest, because it is the fruit so hard to pluck." More than that, one who knows not Angkor is but ill informed in the art of ancient peoples.

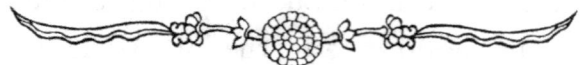

At Hong Kong one changes steamer for Saigon, the big French port of Cochin China. It is not always that one makes close connection with the Saigon ship. It is a variety of vessel that rarely advertises in the columns of the pages of misrepresented news that compose the various Hong Kong dailies, and one never knows when it is to start. There are the big occasional ships of the French Messageries Maritimes, but those are avoided by the traveler who thirsts for novelty.

Pirate Junk Near Hong Kong — "The only way now is for two junks to close in on the ship in lonely waters."

Down the harbour toward Portuguese Macao a fleet of disreputably small steamships lies tethered. No dock receives them, no godowns* of mammoth signs yawn to shelter their priceless cargoes. Whatever wishes to travel thereon, either freight or human, will find no official tender for conveyance. Each must provide his own, a sampan, a launch, and get stowed on board at his own initiative.

This modest little fleet, looked down upon from the pathway at the top of the Peak, compares with the fleet of giant ocean liners anchored near Kowloon as water spiders compare with floating swans.

They are the rice boats, and their first province is to take cabbages to Saigon and bring back rice to Canton. One of these was to start in three days.

Now an impatient traveler, one eager to reach the mystery land of Cambodia, cannot possibly spend three days seeing Hong Kong, up the funicular to the Peak, a half-hour's gaze at the astounding view at sunset, and you have finished, and then sink into the noisy loneliness of hotel life.

But Canton — there was time for a glimpse of that, while the Pak Hoi slipped off her rice and rolled on her cabbages. And Canton was bristling with danger, for war, red war, was running through her streets and stabling in her sacred temples. That lifted her at once from the low level of a tourist's show place, a town where catchpenny trifles and gaudy shawls are made for all the world of money wasters.

It added a sauce piquant to know that two armies were hustling through the crowds of Canton, both eagerly awaiting the arrival of Sun Yat Sen, when they would begin in earnest to annihilate him or each other or whatever appealed to their boyish fancy — shopkeepers perhaps. There is a special fancy for shopkeepers as a quarry, by the soldiery of China. The army belongs always to some great general who commands it for the delicate purpose of keeping for himself the pay of the troops. When at last the soldiers feel the pinch of hunger they turn to the shops as a child to his parents and appropriate the needed food

---

* In India and East Asia, a warehouse, especially one at a dockside.

On the River Mekong — Every native hut is like a bamboo birdcage set high on stilts to fend against floods and tigers.

and funds. There is a reason for everything in China if you will search for it. The richer shops in Canton were closed and barred — because of these possibilities.

Choose well your captains in Hong Kong harbour, for a sampan or for a trans-ocean ship. The British resident of Hong Kong with a gesticulate wave of the arm directs your gaze to the terraces all up the mountain, to the astonishing array of arcaded palaces mounting the cliffs. Truly their building was an achievement. But the Beguiling Guide pointed out to me that these are but as shells on the shore, or nests of gulls on the rocks, compared to craft on the harbour waters, and that the captain is here supreme, the great deity who feeds all, who governs all. There is a lot of class distinction among the captains not dependent entirely on whether a man commands a coaster or a river boat, a junk or a sampan. Here, as all over Asia, the white man regards himself as conqueror, giving to Asiatics the place of a subject people. But why? But why? All they have conquered is wealth through commerce and Commerce is a filthy sister of the arch-fiend Industrialism. In the Orient, at least.

The caste of captains, then, depends on race and Hong Kong's favourites are the British, irrespective of the craft they command. And who gets better sea training than they? Before the mast as lads they are turned into men of oak and iron, men strong to meet the terrible storms of the tropic sea, to quell a mutiny-or to play blithely a set of tennis at Happy Valley, shiny with soap, boyish in white flannels.

"Take the river-boat of Captain McIntosh to Canton. Here is a card to him and here is one to a Saigon ship." And thus these fine British seamen pass you on from one safety to another.

The Canton boat astonished by its size, suggesting with its lavish white paint a summer trip up the Hudson or through Long Island Sound. Millions of Chinese were on the pier getting on, and all were detained by a baggage examination more thorough than polite. Their pitiful belongings showed humble worthlessness as they were tumbled

Palace Enclosures, Phnom Penh — In the center is the Temple of the Silver Floor.

out of bundles and bags onto the planks of the dock. I had not heard that duty existed between Hong Kong and Canton; and I saw none collected from the examined passengers. Yet the officers relentlessly searched. We were to hear why later on.

Once started, the captain sent for us to come to his generous quarters. Mounting to the hurricane deck, we found half-a-dozen armed soldiers, bayonets fixed, pacing like sentinels, eyes sweeping the sea or piercing the intent of passengers.

Across the deck, entirely isolating the navigating apparatus, the boat of the Pearl River wears a barrier like prison bars, with a big fan of vicious points extending out beyond the extreme edge of the deck. A locked door gives access to the captain.

"Are they afraid you will escape, Captain?"

"That's on account of pirates," was the reply given without emotion. Short, stout, ruddy, he defied such stuff as emotion. As we wound among the beauteous islands and slipped between river shores the captain grew more diffusive, warming to the Beguiler's receptivity.

"Maybe you don't know," he said seriously, "that piracy is a profession here. It is taken up not like the ministry exactly, but like trade. It passes from father to son. Why it's only a little while ago that a pirate always wore a red coat to show he was a pirate. There's plenty of them in these waters. The Pearl River is full of hiding places."

"Are we in danger?"

"No, not you. I'm the one they want." He chuckled richly in his short throat. "They came for me two weeks ago. But I got through all right. We were in a quiet place like this we're in now, no traffic about, only some fishing sampans, no thought of trouble with the watch scanning the waters and reporting nothing. The mate was passing through the big saloon where the Chinese passengers travel when he noticed a nice respectable Chinese woman stand up and throw a look over the crowd. She was one of those kind-faced Chinese ladies dressed in black, with a smile that children like.

Chapter I: Hong Kong Harbour 17

Nagas and Lions on the Stair Leading to the Summit of the Phnom

"All at once she raised an arm and fired two pistol shots into the ceiling. Then another. Quick as a flash everyone was on his feet, pistols came out until every man was armed. They were disguised pirates, everyone of them. Away they all went for the passengers. It was hands-up all over the ship. Up in my quarters I knew nothing of it until two men pressed pistols against my head and told me to take the boat into yon quiet river. There lay a lot of sampans and a junk. We were coming down from Canton, you see, and in a place like that are completely hid from sight.

"My first duty anyone could tell you was to protect my passengers by ridding the ship of these thieves. But in my hasty necessity I decided that a dead captain was no good to them." He twinkled an eye-flash. "So I accommodated the gentlemen and slipped the boat up into the river and hid her there. Then all the devils swarmed on board from the sampans, took every bit of value from the passengers — they got a mighty haul — and told off the junk to fly with the treasure.

"But before they took the cold steel from the vicinity of my head, a small company of them came here to this same room, and very smiling, very polite, lots of bows, told me I was plenty good captain and they wanted to give me *cumsha** on parting, a token of friendship as it were. Then these funny Chinks — no one in the world like 'em — with more bows they gave me a handsome gold watch and chain that they had looted from some passenger! And blamed if they didn't think they had done the handsome thing, what the French call 'Noblesse oblige.'

"The only way now," continued the captain, pouring tea with slow chunky hands, "is for two junks to close in on the ship in lonely waters, and to swarm aboard both sides at once and shoot up the ship. But first they go for the captain. Some day my Scotch blood will get the better of my discretion and then there'll be no captain left to tell tales. We have the passengers all searched for arms now, all their luggage too. You may have noticed. No more sweet-faced old Chinese ladies firing pistol signals. No more pirates as passengers."

* China Coast Pidgin English for a tip or alms.

Half jocular he was, which made all the pluckier his life on the isolated bridge, a life which might end on any mile of the River.

A day at Canton with the Cantonese. Everyone knows that the place is obnoxious, with its vile smells, its overcrowding; and all know that whatever Chinese individual is of ill-repute in the Western world is a native of that overworked city, a place where too many people work too hard for too many consecutive hours, a thin, mirthless people weighed down with misery, mostly the animal misery of hunger, fatigue, dirt, disease.

It was true that armies were in possession. What they possessed in the main appeared to be a bare dry hill outside the town — once sacred — and most of the temples in the town. In the courts and outbuildings they stabled their rough little ponies, and built against temple walls the little fires that cooked their rice — with the resulting impious litter of rejectamenta*.

Soldiers were everywhere in the streets, and a helpless populace accepted them patiently like a castigation from the hand of God. They were absurdly young, with faces like round fresh apples. Most of them could not have been more than schoolboys. Streets were too crowded for them to walk in military formation, so they made their way single file through the crowded narrow streets, and Canton took no notice of them.

But the Beguiler and I, not being of an Asiatic fatalism, shivered at noting that each apple-faced boy carried a Mauser, cocked, ready for instant use. Therefore on the judgment or the caprice of a boy we depended for permission to continue our lives, lives which the sights of Asia had greatly increased in value.

Chair porters at last landed us in Shameen, the clean British concession. There we snatched creature comforts and a silken embroidered shawl of gorgeous flowering, and were glad to trail along the quay that led once more to the Canton-Hong Kong boat and its brotherly captain, the bluff scorner of danger.

---

* Things thrown out or away; especially, things excreted by a living organism.

The returning boat was an hour late in starting. I filled that hour with an intimate gazing at sampan life from the deck. All sense of shame lost, I stared at private life with the searching directness of a sunray.

Privacy polite, it seems, is limited to one's own race. And so I stared entranced at cooking, at thieving and at toilet making as practiced on the tiny boats.

Canton is left. Pagodas begin. If asked to define one I should say it is the Finger of God. In all ages and countries nothing more purely beautiful has ever been erected than the tall symmetric tower, housing nothing, an appanage of nothing, but standing alone and perfect, in a bit of desolate country, or rising from uninhabited heights. It must be pointing to a spiritual heaven. Now and then one appears on the shores of the Pearl River, in a lonely distant spot; always it thrills, it inspires.

The trip down the river was made friendly by two quiet grey craft which, as they kept our pace, never left us. Junks and sampans showed great respect for them by scuttling away as fast as wind and flood permitted. They were painted the ugly grey of warships and evidently belonged to a navy, but with their antique build and Chinese flags they had the aspect of large toys.

The captain seemed not to hear when I suggested this. Instead, he began to relate a happening of the day in the dull tone of one who knows it to be without interest:

"An hour before we left the dock at Canton a thin little Chinese fellow came on board hot-haste and must speak to me alone. I'm not seeing Chinese alone since that affair of last week, but I said they could bring this man up, put him by my bars on the deck and I'd hear what he had to say. So he came up.

"He was a young chap. Began by begging to come inside the iron bars. No, Sir. Then he said his life was in my hands for what he was going to tell. He said he was a pirate. His people had always been pirates. His father was a Number One pirate. But he hated the profession and was going to give it up. Would I help him? I waited to see what else was coming.

"There was a lot of money on board, he said. Two Cantonese together were flying from the seat of war with fifty thousand dollars each, before looters should take it, and their wives with them were dripping with pearls, diamonds and jade. Pirates knew of this. A plot was prepared, an attack was to be made half way down to Hong Kong, an attack headed by the boy's father, the Number One.

"Now his life was in the good captain's hands after this confession, and he begged him to lock him up in the securest closet in the ship and deliver him safely in Hong Kong.

"He talked so earnest I did what he said. I saw signs on the way — an hour back — that pirates had made big preparations; you probably didn't notice it.

"And I made some defences myself," he emphasized drily. "Perhaps you did not observe we've travelled all the way with a gunboat escort." But we did!

A fine type, that British captain, modest, brave, efficient, with a heart that beat for the golf links at Repulse Bay and for his kiddies at Kowloon.

CHAPTER II

ABOARD THE PAK HOI

The Pak Hoi, sailing for Indochina, sat regally in Hong Kong Bay indifferent to docks or drays. She was an autocrat to whom all men and all goods must come in small boats, as she scorned the Hong Kong docks and rested far out on the water. Around her majestic sides was a jostling flotilla of sampans and flatboats. An occasional motor-launch came alongside. That meant a rich passenger.

The Scotch captain leaned from his deck and commented dispassionately, "There come the thieves." It was true. Thieves board every ship, and so cleverly that none sees them. Their little sampan looks like the brother of the fruit vendor's boat and quite as honest. Their methods are simple but effectual. They clamber from one sampan to another until they achieve that one lying next the long line of steps which runs up the ship's side. They linger long enough to seem to belong to the flat-boat discharging cabbages, then they spring softly upwards to the deck. Once there, the most vigilant never sees a meek slinking man pick up the bits of rope, the iron nails, the misplaced tool or the tin of food which represents his day's quarry — his "bag," as he is a true hunter and of adventurous spirit.

Confederates down below throw him a rope over the stern, he draws up a basket, fills it, lowers it to his confrère, and empty-handed slouches impassive among the crowd and steps innocently down to the boats again.

Pak Hoi slipped away — little boats bobbing farewell courtesies — slipped past the imposing palatial buildings holding tight to the mountain's steep cliff, past Repulse Bay and on, on among the enchanted isles which strew the way to the southern ocean. Clouds and sun and golden haze conspire to make sunset and afterglow an unforgettable dream. On the way to Angkor! It was but fitting that the path was half of glory, half of mystery.

The next day, and the next and the next the Pak Hoi pounded her reliable little engine and slid down the map in the thousand-mile stretch lying along China and the coast of Annam. Saigon was our port.

The Captain, the Beguiler, and a Chinese gentleman were at table when I sat down to breakfast. But where was Mrs. Captain? I had heard a man at Hong Kong ask the skipper if his wife were aboard, to which he had answered drily, "She always sails with me." We held our peace, for breakfast at sea is a ticklish time, a feast which ladies oft renounce. But I was distinctly desirous of meeting the only other white woman aboard.

Should one make fifty journeys on a rice-boat down the Annam coast there would always be keen interest in the ship. The deck passengers make it. Here is a vivacious variety which keeps even the Captain, seasoned old mariner, leaning over the forward rail of his quarters in his hours of ease.

When we Europeans travel — even on a rice-boat — we have each a cabin to ourselves, a servant to fetch and carry, a bathroom, and three rousing meals in the saloon prepared by an able cook and served by two deft waiters. We have beds and pillows, chairs and rugs.

But the Chinese travel not so. They pay one-twelfth of our passage money, and have nothing, save what they bring on board. Their object is purely to get their mortal frames set down in Saigon — or Cholon, its Chinese neighbour. What that frame endures in discomfort on the way is of no consequence.

This is what we look down upon.

The centre of the deck below is taken up with a hatch. On either side of this is a field of cabbages packed in baskets hermetically sealed, and piled high against the taffrail* with a narrow aisle on either side of the hatch. Forward of this are two sheep-pens, one to right and one to left, each with twenty bleating sheep. Nearby are bales of hay on which to nourish them, and also nearby are ducks and fowls in wicker baskets — short-lived passengers who will never reach Saigon except in the form of vitality imparted to some Chinese.

Besides these few things on the deck there are people, people, people. All Chinese, of course, and apparently poor and lowly. But no, some are rich, many prosperous. They actually like that way of travel. The man of Canton would fly into atoms and disappear in thin air if he were not banded by a crowd. No, the Chinese of the South like herding or they would not so universally live in packs. The sage in the forest, the hermit on the mountain so often depicted in marvellous old Chinese paintings, he, I think, died shortly after being portrayed.

Five hundred deck passengers the Captain said the Pak Hoi carried. And I thought we were to be the only ones on board! Among the hundreds the first to stand out brilliantly was a Chinese girl of fifteen, placid, silent, pretty. Hatless, of course, her long black hair plaited but bound round at the nape of her smooth neck with a silken band of a scarlet that burned. Her childish cheeks were skillfully rouged, jade earrings dangled, gold rings and gold bangles made gay her hands; and one band was around an ankle over the silken stockings — black satin coat and trousers and embroidered shoes. Her brows were straight and smooth, her eyes soft and shy, herself all wonder.

*The rail around the stern of a vessel.

The Museum and Art School at Phnom Penh

Beside this pretty article of commerce stood her vendor, a Chinese lady of the sort one would choose for one's daughter's protector, respectability and all the cardinal virtues glowing from her face. Graying hair and a self-respecting aloofness completed her disguise. We lost the pair when the sea roughened, but at Saigon got another glimpse, each lady set deep in the hood of a pousse-pousse, being rapidly drawn away. The grey-haired lady looked more exclusively good than ever, the maiden more serenely wondering.

The Captain's wife — ever an *ignis fatuus**. I caught the Oriental perfume of her once, a sweet and pungent odour of the tropics; yet a Chinese cabin boy who passed before used scent.

The monsoon was but a gentle breeze, so all China stayed in the open, loafing on top the piled cabbage baskets whenever permitted, and thus two gamins got near us and talked merry sign-language. But with the constant activity of housekeeping leisure was rare among deck passengers. Somewhere among the sheep and fowls and cabbages and hay was a deck kitchen where hot water could be obtained, and rice already cooked.

Hot water is for tea. And for washing.

The personal dirt of China is distressing to him who loves not the Chinese and to him who does. The people are a dirty lot. No one can deny it. But would not any people be dirty who could not obtain water? On the ship I saw efforts at personal cleanliness that equaled those of the fastidious — supposing the fastidious were limited to a small hand basin and a small corner of the open deck.

One happy custom is the use of hot water-cloths of Turkish towelling dipped in and passed steaming to those travellers who are journeying far. It is the most refreshing way of using a cupful of water if one have but a cupful as his allotment, this steaming wet cloth on face and hands.

If another philanthropist such as Rockefeller should give big gifts to China, may he see fit to make water possible to her people.

---

* A Latin term for; 1. A phosphorescent light that hovers or flits over swampy ground at night, possibly caused by spontaneous combustion of gases emitted by rotting organic matter. Also called friar's lantern, jack-o'-lantern, will-o'-the-wisp, wisp. 2. Something that misleads or deludes; an illusion.

Angkor Vat from the Inner Causeway

Tea. Everywhere and always tea. A nation's drink. The wine of the country. This they drink and do not forget the law, which cannot be said of the wine of certain other countries. One is expected to ask for a pot of tea at any moment of the day, travelling or at home, steaming, fragrant restorative. Thus the supply of boiling water is all ready in the cook house on the deck, ready for the hot washings and the tea drinkings.

Over the hatch, almost the length of the deck, stretches a wire. The importance of this wire to the deck passenger can scarce be known to those who sit at meat at the Captain's table and spread their kit in a cabin's space. The hatch over which its fine straight length extends is full of men, each one occupying a self-allotted space the size of his person. When all the occupants are there and tucked in for the night there is not a spare inch empty. What to do with umbrellas, baskets, bags, drying food, and all things unnecessary to slumber, would be a problem without that wire. So from it depends a row of miscellany most ill-assorted. A bird-cage swings easily, a new hat and a big umbrella hold light tenure, a basket of food threatens overweight; but the prostrate men below sleep on with such quiet that one is reminded of sprats. Such utter quiet, such muscular control, such economy of space. By seven o'clock in the evening the mass is resolved into even rows, each man wrapped in his blanket, a blanket insufficiently warm, and having taken his place keeps it lest he disturb his fellows.

Nothing could better illustrate the sweetness of temper of the Chinese than the amiability with which they travel herded together as deck passengers. All is harmony. No pushings or shovings, no plaints. As for sounds, there are occasional gentle laughs during the snuggling-in process, which may last an hour, but after sleep descends from the stars above them there is not even a snore. And thus they spend the night in the open.

They are waked in the morning by the raucous voice of a humorous shrew. She has on deck a pet parrot of small parts but loud notes. Some man slips off the hatch and provokes the bird. Its cries reach even to the

Chapter II: *Aboard The Pak Hoi* 29

A Building of Symmetry and Beauty Called a Library

lower regions where the women sleep and hide themselves most of the day. At once appears the small brown woman to protect her bird. She shrieks at the waking men monosyllabic maledictions, and in return gets better than she sends until the Chinese sense of humour wakes and bantering jests begin. The woman is a wit, a sharp one though merry and her voice is like her parrot's. The men chuckle, unroll from their blankets, and day begins with a laugh.

No other women come in sight. Not even the Captain's wife. We are on the second day and she has not appeared. At tiffin* we asked for her and were told drily that she was feeling the weather. The weather! It was made of polished opal. The sea was a moon-stone in flux. We were floating down the coast of Annam as in a dream. Rosy mountains lifted rocky heads as far as the eye could see to north and to south, the sky above was a mass of filmy decoration on a ground of blue.

We were lying on the deck dreaming things historic and poetic, with all this as a setting, about Timur and the great Moguls, and Marco Polo the luxury lover. The mate stepped into the picture. He was a little man, dark and old, but with the eye and the activity of a boy. He seemed nervously on the lookout for something unpleasant.

"I can't stay a minute," he said, and his voice was a joy to listen to, deep and smooth. "I wanted to have a hammock put up for you. I'll tell one of the men. Hope you're comfortable. I must be going." He stepped about all the time he was speaking, looking forward and aft with eyes too restless to dwell on his audience. He tipped his cap. "The Captain mustn't find me here," and he was off, but threw me a parting look over which to wonder. It was an appeal, distinctly an appeal though it had a sparkle in it.

Presently the Captain came onto the deck with his dog, the kind of dog whose indifference is almost hostility, but whose loyalty to his master expressed itself in contact. If the Captain walked, the dog's nose touched his heels, if he sat, it rested somewhere on his person.

A mind for talking, possessed the Captain. "Is this coast habitable?

---

* A British term for a midday meal; a luncheon.

The Park, Angkor Vat — looking west toward the gallery of the enceinte from the Cruciform Terrace. Libraries on either side.

Have you had occasion to stop anywhere along?" asked the Beguiler to provoke ship's tales.

"You see how the water stretches in behind this land we are sailing near?" he asked, thrusting out a masterful hand to indicate. "That is Cam Ranh Bay. Below here, down the coast a ways is Phan Rang, another bay. You remember the war between Russia and Japan. When that was going on I carried a man on this ship who by his own telling had a finger in that hot pie. His name was Pettus, and he was a reporter on a big Manchester paper. A good deal of a man; had stuffin' in him."

"You mean about the Russian Fleet?"

"That's it. It got lost. It sailed from the Baltic Sea, made the passage out, came around through the English Channel, through the Mediterranean, by Suez to the East. It was known to have passed Singapore, but it had never got to Hong Kong. So it was lost somewhere in between those points.

"Pettus' boss cabled him to find it. Funny, wasn't it, to set one newspaper reporter to meddling with the war, and to go on such a mighty errand? They chose their man well. He could do it. The third day out from Hong Kong we were sailing along the coast just as we are now. Pettus had been using his glass on the open sea all day. He grumbled that his eyes were tired with it, and he turned to enjoy the sunset. He saw the mountains with the light behind them and watched the clouds all gold and pink.

A wisp of grey cloud began to rise right up against the sunset.

" 'Skipper, what mines or factories are there on the shore just here?' There aren't any, of course. As for mines the French won't let any be worked unless they get all the ore, and as for factories there are no people here to work in them. It's all wild elephants and tigers along this shore.

" 'Smoke, by God, the smoke of big ships — the smoke of the Russian Fleet!'

"I thought he'd burst with joy, his face got so red. 'Put me off at the nearest port!' That, of course, wasn't possible. The ships of my company make no stops between Hong Kong and Saigon. It was hard on him.

"So he went down to Saigon, and fell in with the French marine officers stationed there. He tried to get information. They wouldn't give it. He tried to telegraph to his paper in England that he suspected the lost Russian fleet was at Phan Rang. The French refused to send his messages. Blocked he was.

"After all, he thought, he had not accurate in. formation. He must go to the place and see for himself. He walked the long docks of Saigon looking for a vessel. Nothing stopping nearer than Hanoi, which overshot the mark by hundreds of miles. At last a little Chinese boat was found which would drop him nearby.

"When he got there, he was set down at a lone pier jutting out into the water. No town, no village, just a pier, at two o'clock in the morning. Dark, of course. He sat on his travelling bag and waited. Tigers in the woods. No food. When morning came he found a road, walked until noon, found a likely-looking house, knocked on the door — which was opened by an English lady! They got chummy right away, and he told her his errand. She refused information, but, bless you, he could see for himself by climbing a little hill. The whole fleet lay before him smoking little clouds such as he had seen from my ship. There is a wire at Phan Rang. He jumped to the station to send word of his great find to his paper. He alone of all the world could tell the world where lay the lost fleet. It was tremendous.

"He did it. And his paper printed it. Then what? In two days they wired him they didn't believe his despatches. That if it were true he would not be the only one to know it. He wired back that it was true, he could see the smoke of the battleships as he wrote, with a glass he read their names. Meanwhile the press of the world was jeering at his paper and at him for trying to pass off a fake. This, his people at the home office wired him.

"Then something happened. He woke one morning to find the Beet had gone — slipped away in the night. With his quarry right at hand, it got off. The home office was right, he didn't know where the Russian fleet was hiding.

"It was no easier getting away from Phan Rang than getting there. The coast is all mountains, bad ones, nothing lives on them but elephants and tigers, but a map marks a thin scarlet line which shows a road running north. And by that map Cam Ranh Bay should be but thirty miles away.

"Pettus felt himself good for that thirty miles either in a bullock cart or on foot. He had thought out probabilities. The fleet's friends at Saigon had sent them word that an English newspaper man had spotted them, and their move was to find another berth. Pettus guessed at Cam Ranh as their likeliest shelter. For three months they had been in safe hiding, they were surely not ready to be pushed out to the open sea and inevitable combat at such short notice. The chances were they would slip into one of the deep, protected bays nearby.

"Cam Ranh is one of those hiding places that would fool anyone sailing down the coast. It is a wide bay, lying between mountains with a generous island to block the ocean view. But that is by no means all. The real bay is an inland sea thirty miles long, its only entrance being a narrow gut opening in from the bay that curves in from the ocean. The best spyglass on a deck could not suspect that inland sea was there.

"Pettus' guess was a good one. The fleet was there. He covered his thirty miles in two days, and from a turn in the road came upon the whole picture at once. It was a pretty sight, the fleet at harbour on smooth waters. Prettier than ever after having once got away from him.

"All the way back to Phan Rang he went to get his telegraph wire. And he made it hum with the enthusiasm of his discovery. Here was the fleet of a big European country lost to all, but he alone knew where it was.

"Pretty big business.

"His messages rang with force to his doubting editor man. They would have to believe him now. The line went to Saigon where messages were repeated to Singapore and then on to England. The office at Saigon refused them! No reason given, but they refused point blank. So he sent them in cipher. No cipher would be sent to England that the French governors could not de-code.

"To be baulked now was unthinkable. Time was passing and he must prove his news true and get it printed before other reporters had investigated the Annamite coast.

"'Might he send despatches to Hong Kong?' That was allowed. So his cipher went, and was sent from that British port to England.

"That time Pettus was believed. The news flew around the world and was verified by other venturers who followed Pettus," the captain finished.

The end is history, the fleet with its hiding place discovered to the enemy steamed out into the high seas and made for Vladivostok, the Japanese catching it in the narrow Straits between Japan and Korea and wiping it completely out.

That night the heat fell on us like a benediction. From my bed I could hear the soft slip-slop of straw sandals. The ship seemed gently awake to the beauty of the night. I left my room in a light wrap and sought the open, standing beside the port taffrail. The sea was flowing smooth, we undulated in rhythm. But the world of reality was the world of the stars. For the first time I saw the burning constellation of the Southern Cross. In its light I wondered and pondered over the ideals of men. Why was it considered an admirable thing for a man of a neutral country to deliver a navy into the hands of the destroying Japanese?

Chapter III

SAIGON

Here is a matter for delicate wonderment. It concerns the Captain. He is going to take a vacation. He left his home on the Isle of Man twenty years ago, and is now going to return to it for two months. He has been amassing money for this wondrous pleasuring for many years until he has a fine purse of twenty thousand dollars "Mex."

"Is that enough?" he asks naively. "I've been sailing a ship on the China coast all these twenty years and I don't know prices."

"Ridiculously much, unless your wife buys heavily in London."

"I don't take my wife. She goes to her people in Tokio. She is Japanese." There was no mistaking it, he clearly stiffened whenever he mentioned her. And in all this time we had not seen a flutter of her garments. One could easily believe she was a myth. He said affectedly, "The poor little thing is tired."

But about the Captain's vacation. This is what he was going home to do. Not to see his boyhood friends, not to see the wonders of London. To buy a small boat and fish all summer off the Isle of Man! And this as a change after twenty years of uninterrupted sea life. Where was his sense of humour?

As for the mate, he continued to pop in on us from time to time, appearing on the deck as a stable dog appears in the house, timid, agitated, nervous.

Once I asked him skillfully about the mystery of the Captain's wife. It frightened him so that he fled muttering, "He mustn't catch me here. I must be off." Irish he was and temperamental. Too old, he said, to get a ship of his own or even a mate's position on another, although fifty-five ought to balance the advantage of youth by its sagacity. Why do he and the Captain stay together hating each other?

Saigon tomorrow morning, was the Captain's announcement. It was just before twilight. Like a huge planet glowed the light on Cap St. Jacques. Just below is the mouth of the Mekong and we shall turn into the river's smooth-winding way to disembark on the morrow.

Cap St. Jacques looked lonely. The light and the keeper's house are built on a rocky spur of the mountain, its feet washed by the sea. We could see the white line of wavelets pushed up against the rocks by the monsoon. A high masonry wall was built across the spur, a wall against the pitiless forest neighbours. Last month a tiger had scaled it and had killed the keeper of the light. The hard, lonely point was a hideous place to ask a man to live. Before him the sea, behind him a forest of ferocious beasts; one little boat on the rocks his only means of communication with his fellows, and the nearest habitation many miles away.

Saigon was to be a distinct surprise. What had our life of the ship, our nearness to a terrible coast, to do with a French port where luxury, pomp, dissipation, made a world more effete than any spot in Europe?

The Chinese deck passengers were restless with quieted excitement. At dawn, the soft, warm dawn of the tropics, the larder baskets were opened down to their lowest tier and the last meal eaten. Pressed duck — flat as pressed roses but less poetic — dried fish and dried cabbages were taken down from the wire line and packed away. And each individual had lost his indifference and inertia and was dressed to a degree of elegance. They all filed off the boat, joyous as children, a kindly, amiable crowd.

Then the French officers of the Protectorate ordered them into a sort of pen for examinations as to their fitness to enter the port (an Asiatic port, and they were Asiatics!) and there the crowd wilted under the pitiless sun until after tiffin-time, five or six hours.

We being Europeans — a race distinction only — were allowed to disembark at pleasure, take a rickshaw — a pousse-pousse the Saigonese call it — and wheel softly down the long dock-front to the town.

But on the way we passed the coaling yards. If one could alter the slavery there, if one might protest against the wrecking of youthful bodies, it were worthwhile to experience the pain of seeing how the work is done under the French Protectorate. Otherwise it were well not to watch the grimy crowd of sweltering children and their tiny mothers staggering under the yoke of coal buckets. It is a sight that sticks in the memory, that comes to mind in the moments of night-waking, and it provokes reflections on the cruelty of the European toward the Asiatic. These people are not slaves, these Annamites, though so regarded.

Saigon is an important port. It can brag of the immense amount of tonnage sailing from its river harbour. All of the ships that enter are coaled here at request. And all are coaled by tired, thin little women and their girl children down to nursery age. The ship lies on one side the road, the coal yards on the other. Each carrier fills two buckets, hung on either end of a shoulder pole, and thus overloaded carries the black burdens throughout a day of twelve burning hours.

These little women and children of the Annamites dress always in black, a single long garment of black cotton which gives the effect of mourning. When the terrific day's work is over, they walk into a shallow of the river, dressed as they are and wash off the hateful coal-dust from skin and gown. A dry gown on the shore makes them modest and fit for the walk home — if they have homes. The price paid for this crippling labour of women and children is a few cents a day.

The big cafe on the square near the Theatre Municipal is a shady place for cool drinks and a contemplation of Saigon's citizens. Many

The Cruciform Terrace, Angkor Vat — Palms of excessive height, crowned with languid fronds.

of them pass noisily in motors, many more in *gharris**. I resent motors in Asiatic towns. The *gharri* suits the climate. It allows a pretty woman to assume a graceful pose, to spread her light draperies, and to group around her the dressy babies. And the ponies who draw it are leisurely enough to let one see the beauty of the ensemble in passing.

An hour of lounging at the cafe reveals the surface of things in French Indochina. It shows the French as unhappy exiles, miserable in the work of colonizing. Every man and woman there lives but to return to France, and lives in a bitter imitation of Paris.

All the requirements of a French town are found in this far Asian city. There are boulevards wide and umbrageous, their sidewalk cafes dressed with iron furniture, plants, awnings. And any drink found in Paris is found there.

There is a huge municipal theatre and a cathedral; there is a palace for the governor general — veritably a palace, in modern French architectural grandeur. Other palaces are for each high official among the French. Commerce has also erected its palaces and the law has its Palace of Justice.

The Rue Catinat has shops that would not disgrace Paris. Jewellers display the latest devices in precious gems, perfumers sell Houbigant and Coty novelties, booksellers have the newest novels and reviews, and — delightful touch to complete the illusion of a Paris street — the name of the great purveyor, Felix Potin, rises over a shop filled with his choice goodies and wines. A big department store dresses its many windows with everything needed for house or person.

Through these streets of elegance and variety slip the slim little Annamite women all in black, humbly wondering at the ways of the people who have come to set them an example in deportment and in dress. Three or four stop before a corner window. It displays the bathing costume as worn at Deauville. Five wax manikins of pinkest flesh are posed in coquettish attitudes. Each wears an "Annette Kellermann" which that famous swimmer would be ashamed to wear. Above the waist,

---

* An Indian term for a small horse-drawn cart or carriage.

The Front Line of Rooms to a Sequence following a Line of the Facade

a couple of straps, below the waist but little more. And the smiles of the naked wax ladies are of such enticement as to dress them completely with indecency.

Before this window stand gazing four young Annamite women, pale, serious, wearing their modest national dress, a close slip of black reaching from throat to foot, with sleeves to the wrist.

What parallels are they drawing? I think of the ladies of the French colony swimming in these green and red scantinesses, and contrast them with the begrimed little slaves of the coal yard bathing after the twelve-hour labour in their long black gowns.

The Annamites are beings I should like to know, really know, their animus, character, legends. For is not this one of the races intimately concerned with the Khmers of Angkor? Under the name of Champas they did heavy damage to the brilliant civilization I am approaching and which lies up this great river Mekong.

But these people about the streets of Saigon have all the ways of a subject people, not the jubilant carriage of the free. The men are the porters and the servants. They also become clerks and dress in pyjamas for street wear. But it is the Annamite women who pique the imagination.

No matter how many you see they are all the same age, all young, and they all dress alike, though quality varies. Also they are all the same size. How this result is achieved one may not know without much closer acquaintance than a traveller is like to get. At first their faces seem too flat, but soon one sees beauty in them. Charm is their birthright, charm in the sad quiet visage, and still greater charm in the slight symmetric figure.

The Greeks drew nothing more lovely in outline than the woman of Annam. Watch one coming along the shady quay by the Hotel de la Rotonde. She is a lady of means for she is all in silk. The little head is poised above square shoulders on a line with the narrow hips. As she walks she thrusts forward her foot with a graceful freedom which outlines the length of the straight and supple leg. The effect is of drapery

A Corner of the First Gallery — A few moments' pause lets the imagination people it with the king and guards of other days ranged in Oriental magnificence before the temple.

blown back by the wind and revealing an intoxicating symmetry.

The black dress has true chic, yet is purely native. The long robe is fastened at the side, Chinese fashion, and is slit from hem to waist over the hip. Thus are revealed the straight trousers of whitest silk, below which show white silk stockings and black sandals. A white silk kerchief is tied over her head, and the close-sleeved arm upholds a parasol of heliotrope. She is all reserve. Aloofness is her guardian. She never looks at you — but how hungrily you wish she would. She walks alone as is the Annamite woman's way. But no one speaks to her, nor breaks her reserve.

Opposite the hotel, along the water-front is an open woodyard, which adjoins the docks whence sail the riverboats for Phnom Penh and Angkor. The tram or train to Cholon passes here with frightful shrieks and heavy clankings. Especially late at night. Also night is the time when the hotel dining-room and sidewalk are turned into one vast French cafe of excessive gaiety and noise. Therefore one is wakened from time to time during the warm dark hours.

And every time I am wakened I rise and promenade the enclosed balcony with which each bedroom in Saigon is fitted. And often I hear the low long cry of a child being hushed by its mother. The sounds come from the woodyard.

Early morning before sunrise again I view the world from the balcony. On the sidewalk is a public watertap, and at that thin, running stream a black-robed Annamite washes her baby. Thus I stumble on the truth that many of the natives cannot afford, under the head-tax of the Protectorate, to own a home. This little woman who looked the essence of all that was delicate, must seek the shelter of the woodyard for her baby's nesting.

Coolies who draw the pousse-pousse live with equal sketchiness. The shabby little vehicle they let with their muscular legs is also their house. Often one sees the shafts propped high in a shady corner and the owner curled up sleeping within.

Food is ready at hand for the homeless if they have the pennies with which to buy it, for the ambulatory kitchen steams on every corner, and the stuff to feed the system is always ready.

We look on the sallow nostalgic French and then on the impoverished native and wonder why the combination was ever made. In the interests of civilization and modern progress, is the proper answer. But really it is the greed of those who exploit Asia for the benefit of the West.

At Saigon one may gain pleasure by intimacy with the cocoanut. Here it is found in its tenderest mood. It is a nut that plays a varied part in the commerce of the world. It is known as copra and is turned into olive oil and soap. It is known as "shies" and goes to the successful shooter. But here in the tropics in midwinter, it is a nectar and a poem.

All along the broad walk of the Quay, before the shops where Hindus change money and natives sell pottery and cottons, sit quietly and intermittently the cocoanut vendors. The nuts are green, the pulp just hardening to the thickness of a quarter inch. The small brown hands of the Annamite woman wield a murderous hatchet with which she hacks away the thick green covering bit by bit with astounding skill until the whole brown nut is revealed sitting in a cup of green. But such skill has produced not a hard globe of our Western ken, but a tender flexile orb which yields soft and pliant to the touch.

After the wondrous thing has been in your delighted hand and has given a plea for tender handling, a disc is cut on top the brown dome, a disc which reveals a white purity within, unequalled in the world. And this pure chalice holds your drink, a soothing draught cool, poetic, fragrant. Not from a cup, mind. Drink straight from that pure well and receive the balm to your spirit that lies in the hidden chamber of the big brown cup. But to know the joy to the full, one must know first the tropic heat and that heat's thirst.

It was the chief engineer of the Pak Hoi who taught us the trick when he encountered us in the Saigon streets. He was one who knew how to find simple delights. "How is the Captain's wife?" we asked, while sipping the cocoanut.

"The Captain has no wife." He looked serious. "You touch on the weak place of the Pak Hoi. The skipper is an A1 skipper, but for one thing. He thinks he has a Japanese wife aboard and is fiercely jealous of the mate because of her. So the ship company is sending him home for a vacation. You may have heard him speak of it. It's bad for a man to stay too long in the East. Some of us can't stand it."

Five days in Saigon leads one to think that its greatest attraction is the big river boat that sails up the Mekong. It lies beside the floating dock and looks not unlike the lightly made white boats that take travellers up the Hudson.

We go on board at the hour when Saigon is beginning its joys. Men and women in fresh light dress are being drawn through the beautiful embowered streets, by ponies or by men, in the attitudes of luxurious ease which the tropics make natural. Dinners are going on at clubs and in the palace-like homes, where the discussions run on Sunday's race-track, or on costumes for the coming ball. At the restaurants scores of men and women are gathering for a long evening of play and forgetting, forgetting they are not in France.

But in the soft dark I hear the whimpers of the babies, the crooning of the Annamite mothers, as we pass the open woodyard before the boat's quay.

Chapter IV

UP THE MEKONG

The long, slow way is the overture to the Angkor drama, the quiet preparation of the mind for overpowering scenes.

If Angkor Vat and its group were accessible to the tourist loafer at Saigon, if one could take a rickshaw or a *gharri* from the quay or the public gardens, and in a few minutes reach the ruins and hastily scramble over their bewildering terraces — one of the world's greatest wonders might fail to thrill the souls of such hasty audience.

With consummate art of progress the approach is prepared. After the heat and noise of the French city of Saigon, the deck of a river steamer is a refuge of cool repose. And after the night on board, one awakens to a tropic country and already appreciative of such strange customs as morning coffee at seven, and tiffin at eleven with a long siesta to follow.

We awoke to Mytho the first stop, Mytho which seemed only a pierful of chattering Annamites, baskets of green cocoanuts, bananas, pineapples — all against a park-like background of tropic trees splashed with bougainvillea. From that on, one floats all through the fragrant day on a wide, wide river of yellow water, while gradually wise, mild nature changes the itineried traveller into a tropic idler.

We were in another world. We were among European tourists who were intriguing even as travellers. There was, for instance, a Boston maid of astuteness who decorated the world by the big splash of colour which was her gown. There was a splendid beauty so evidently an ex-diva that one could see a music-hall around her and hear the rustle of programmes. She held a sad husband by the leash of delicate health. He was tall, loose-hung, dejected and rich. He had made a famous slip in honesty. That this had saddened him was the rare and interesting point in his commercial character.

And there was Priscilla, full of charming inconsistencies. Like a neat wren, only always in white. Puritan by every visible evidence. And pretty with the neatness of a porcelain figurine. She had the hardihood to travel alone to Angkor, and was chummy with the Diva and her husband.

Besides these, were two French priests. Lest the words conjure up a picture of the usual "corbeau," examine them. One was insignificant. The biggest wore a long yellow beard frizzing down to a point almost as far as a layman's lower waistcoat button. It wagged as he talked in manner Shakespearian. He was fat as Santa Claus is fat, and red of face and bald of pate — tonsured by nature's barber. His dress was not a *soutane** at all but a long black garment in the Chinese shape fastening across the chest, and on his head a white cork helmet. Such is the dress of the thousands of priests to whom the French have delivered the souls of the natives throughout French Indochina.

All these folk and many more were going to the great world wonder of Angkor. Two journalists from Nice came later, also Blake, but these in the nature of flagellants to the other travellers.

Such a river as it is, the Mekong, slow, wide, keeping itself muddy by constantly licking off the clay of rice-paddies, with no banks higher than the heads of the brown children who play at its edge. But traced on

---

* A French feminine noun for a vestment.

The Cruciform Terrace — The steps are made to force a halt at beauteous obstructions. There is now the Cruciform Terrace forming plateau of elegance before the principal door of entry.

the map it runs right away free of the French Protectorate and finds its independent way through terrifying gorges in China, gorges which are crossed only by perilous wires on which the most hazardous of peoples hang during the crossing of the canyon from cliff to cliff. Further away still this indomitable river has its source-in impenetrable Tibet whose melting snows provide its first floods.

Here in Cochin-China it is the big waterway for junks and sampans, feeding Saigon and carrying rice for the return cargo of the Pak Hoi and her kind.

This is not all of its tricks. It grows so low in the dry season as to cause even a sampan to look to its plumb-line, while during the summer rains it rises to the point of inundation. The effect of this is to make it desirable to visit Angkor between November and January.

Flat, flat, all is flat. "It is just like the savannahs of Florida," announces Blake aloud to nobody, ferreting the world with his prismatics, The sky line is made of palms, nothing but palms. One thinks of the Bible, of the opera of "Aïda," of "Enoch Arden" and one lies down to pleasant dreams at siesta time.

All day, and all the long languorous evening, it is the river. Delicious monotony of scene. Every native hut is like every other native hut, a bamboo bird-cage set high on stilts to fend against floods in wet season and against tigers in dry season, for wild beasts lie in the land a very few miles back from the river on both sides, tigers, cheetahs, elephants.

Around each native hut is a banana grove, a bunch of those poetic utilitarians, the cocoanut palms, and around the boles of these the naked brown babies play hide-and-seek with the passing boats. And between each house are the wide stretches of the rice paddies. It is interesting to know that Khmer civilization followed the course of rice. Where it grew, there also grew the intellectual progress of the mysterious race which flamed and faded.

And thus gazing at the shore and gazing at fellow passengers the day passes, night comes, and tourists pack themselves away with cabin

The Gallery Joining the First and Second Galleries, with Pool in the Foreground

doors left open that they may see the stars of the tropic night.

Morning and Phnom Penh. All pilgrims to Angkor are interested in the Cambodian town from the journey's start because of its name, a strange name of unlikely spelling. Spelling of names in Asia is a lesson in phonetic writing, for each European country spells the Asiatic sounds according to its own custom. Also one finds here all the "h's" which have been lost in England.

At first blush Phnom Penh is a smaller Saigon, with fine French buildings facing a long quay, shaded avenues and public gardens. But scratch the surface and one finds more of the native. The French here seem less *ennuyé** than in Saigon, and the natives less cowed.

Cambodia announces itself, though it wear a French veil. This is the capital of Cambodia in that the Royal Palace is here where the king has residence. It was a clever move, to leave the king and his court while establishing a Protectorate, for it avoids a lot of dissension, perhaps of rebellion, among the natives. If they do not like the laws established by the "Protectors," they have their king to whom to look.

The king, however, is a lion with drawn claws. He lives in a gorgeous, shabby palace with little privacy, as it is ever on view to accredited visitors. The palace is almost barbaric in its treasures, as for instance a life-size statue of Buddha made of solid gold and ornamented with diamonds of prodigious size. Also it has a large hall furnished with a floor of pure silver tiles engraved. In another building the Sacred Sword is held inviolate. The palace has its department of the dance, quarters where live the many maidens who dance before the king to the music of a native orchestra. The monarch has also his herd of elephants on which to ride in ancient magnificence on occasions of state.

But the court exists without vitality, a sort of shady circus which sketchily reproduces a dead grandeur for the amusement of those who buy tickets of admission. Alas and alas for kings, in these days of democracy!

---

* A French adjective for annoyed, worried or bothered.

The Gallery Connecting the First and Second Stories — Columns everywhere, square gray columns.

Yet Sisowath, the King of Cambodia, amusingly interested Paris when he paid his first visit to France after the Protectorate over Cambodia had been established. *Le Roi de Cambodge* was flattered and amused during his stay, was exhibited and honored through a dazzling week. Then he was packed off to Marseilles to take ship for his kingdom of Cambodia, his royaume, barring the fact that the French Governor General was the real ruler.

But the king preferred Paris! So he accepted the official adieux with Asiatic expressions of regret at parting, and then from Marseilles he flew back to Paris. Much consternation!

By now he knows his place. As an example, examine his birthday honours. He receives an annual salary for kingly expenses, but when his birthday arrives he is visited by officers of the Protectorate to whom he is obliged to make gifts. They give him congratulations; he gives them a quarter of his income. This miserable play is the residuum of the ancient glory of the Khmer monarchs whose royal seat was Angkor Thom.

Phnom Penh has a park, a pretty place of trees and lawns, where French children play. Within it is a hill with an ancient temple on the top, approached by a flight of steps in true Khmer fashion. *Naga*, the serpent, forms the stair rail and lions stand guard. One begins to lose France and to feel Cambodia.

Near the palace is the Khmer Museum. It is quite worthwhile, even to the most casual skimmer of surfaces. It is a bit of Angkor. It is an opening wedge to the European brain which lets in the new art of which Angkor is the highest expression. It is a preparation, but, after all, one should see it after the visit to Angkor to know what it really means.

Here are collected wondrous bronzes and sculptured stones, jewellery and implements of war, dug from remains of the classic period of Khmer art, and one is puzzled and charmed with strange beauty.

The courtyard is like a cloister with buildings all around the square,

Detail of Carving — All is subdued, subservient to the architecture.
Blossoms are dissected and petals re-arranged in new conventions.

buildings open to light and air, in which young Cambodian students are being trained in the arts of long ago that native art may be kept vital.

This museum, this school of art, are the life work of George Groslier. He elects to spend his life preserving the art of ancient Cambodia and in giving to the world an understanding and appreciation of the Khmer ruins. He is the apostle of Angkor. Shut in his museum, far from his loved France, he studies, works and writes that he may bring the world nearer the ancient work of a forgotten people. Does one wish to know profoundly the souls of the Khmers, those wild, luxurious conquerors, he should turn to the big French volumes of George Groslier, president of the museum at Phnom Penh.

For some reason the boat of the French company, the *Messageries Fluviales*, sails from Phnom Penh at night, just as does the boat from Saigon. After a French dinner with French wines and food, at a French hotel, one goes on board. One finds the same little cabins opening on the deck, and beds without sheets or covers.

The stern deck, upstairs and down, is covered with deck passengers, each recumbent, each surrounded with mats and pillows and baskets of food. Unlike the Chinese on the Pak Hoi, men, women and children form the crowd; and, as to kind, they are Malay, Hindu, Annamite. On the dock, women with hats like parasols eagerly reach up their wares to sell, breadfruit, bananas, and the satisfying green cocoanut, besides unmentionable things made of fish and meat.

We move off gaily, dropping the fine-railed gangplank into the river, and start on the last étape of the journey, which is taken on the Tonlé Sap, a river which here joins the Mekong. So we leave the poetic river which starts as a chilly brook on the frozen uplands of Tibet to widen into a flood of many deltas slipping through tropic savannahs into the China Sea.

The stars and the sound of water chained me late to the deck. Night is the time to be abroad. A native woman of extreme loveliness was in a deck chair, a lap-dog by her side. Over her dark hair a scarf of chiffon, which blew across the large eyes and frequent smile. On her feet shoes of sophistication; on her person the Annamite dress, but of soft French gauzes. She rested in the chair, as perfumed and languorous as a worn flower — until, alas, a sharp whistle came from the French captain's cabin. She obeyed the call like one accustomed.

When finally I went to bed, Blake was snapping his torch light over the prostrate crowd of deck passengers and letting it linger on the women.

Priscilla's cabin was next to mine, both opening out to the hot night with only a narrow strip of deck between us and the taffrail. She, being a true Puritan, had her door shut, but I nearly stepped on a bundle before it. It was the Hindu manservant she had chosen in place of a lady's maid, lying like a dog fast asleep on a mat before her door. How worshipful are the ways of inconsistency.

The *Messageries Fluviales* assured us we would dine in Angkor next night. We did nothing of the kind. Instead we stayed on board far longer, as a chrysalis stays in its case, quietly accepting a transformation of the soul. We were gradually loosening the adhesive that bound us to a world of commonplace, we were listening to a long overture or intermezzo which prepared us for the strange world of the ancient Khmer. A pity 'tis the day is coming when the pilgrim will be whizzed in motor cars from Saigon even unto Angkor, and thus will arrive with mind dizzy instead of with mind calm, with thoughts of modern inventions and not of ancient intrigue.

While the Mekong flows away for Northern adventures, the Tonlé Sap turns gently and changes from a flat, muddy line into an opalescent lake, a lake so wide that land is lost. Through the greater part of the day one watches white herons along the shore, big buffaloes cooling by the banks of the farms, so deep in water that only their muzzles and branching black horns are seen. Palms everywhere — and palms mean poetry to the Occidental.

Then all at once the lake, Tonlé Sap. The unrippled spread of it is broken only by our big, white boat chugging along with scarce perceptible speed. The water gets low in January and should a high-spirited and impatient boat ram well into the mud, there'd be no help for it until the wet season came to float it off. They say that before the rain begins to fall the Grand Lac becomes only a grand mudflat.

Thus the captain proceeded with caution through the shallow opal flux, while outside his door the pretty lady of Asia, with accessories of Paris. played with her lap-dog and smiled entrancingly on all whom she could catch up with a glance.

At twilight life grew so calm that we lost all sense and were mere spirits floating in an exquisitely coloured ether. Then dinner came and illusion went by the board.

It was a slow and sleepy evening. The boat had abandoned shore stops when it entered the lake. Instead it stopped at odd hours in midwater at the strange cry of a boatman who stood off in the dark in a tiny sampan with a single faint light. Precarious passings over the rail of the lower deck took place, persons getting off, persons getting on. All mysterious, when there seemed no place to have come from, no place to go to except a far waste of water.

One open sampan received from the steamer an Annamite woman and her baby. The mother spread her square of matting on the little boat's floor and nested the child. Sad anxiety and patience under difficulty – Mary's flight into Egypt repeated in Cambodia.

The sampan waited for another passenger. He came bustling, vociferating, important. It was the big priest with the beard of Jove. He was helped safely into the sampan, he tripped heavily over the cowering mother and babe without consideration and possessed himself of the only comfortable rest. Then the little boat vanished. At last a new star on the night, a lamp fixed high for mariners. The journey's end! Little lights on the water, voices, sounds of rowers. The boat stopped, we missed the engine's thump.

The sampans stole alongside, not showing they were there until over the rail, on to the deck, leaped dozens of dark men, half naked, headed by a superb creature clad in khaki, who dominated and commanded all. He shouted in Cambodian to the too executive coolies and directed in French to the voyagers.

We were a silent crowd, half asleep, and we were a timorous one. It looked foolhardy to exchange present safety for a tippy sampan manned by howling savages at midnight on a wide sheet of unknown water. The Diva baulked, and effectively threw her beautiful plump person onto the bosom of a husband who took the assault with limp arms and a face of disillusion.

The orange-yellow Boston maid took the lead with youth's spirited agility, while the brown man in khaki hurled unknown Cambodian curses at his sweating henchmen tugging at the baggage, and passed to the task of directing us, the sacred goods of the *Messageries Fluviales*.

He straightened his great figure for a mental effort and addressed the timid petulant huddlers, which we had become.

"Une zong-bong pour les touristes!"

"Une zong-bong pour les bag-gages!"

Very staccato, very imperative.

We slipped away in the perilous dark on the "zong-bong" for an unguessable haven, our faith pinned to the light of the feeble lantern we had seen from the steamboat, for the only man who could instruct or spread confidence was on another boat with "les bagages,"

We had to learn that one lives a year of sensations between the steamer and the ultimate stop. The overloaded sampans were sculled across the waters it seemed for hours, with no sign of land. Constellations above reflected in the lake and no sky line showed a break between sky and flood. The burning stars seemed the nearest haven.

When a change came it was not land we met but a forest of spreading trees having water as their element instead of earth. Through their branches we saw the stars, below them the same bright sparks were sprinkled, and from the foliage came the music of birds that call at night.

On and on through this endless enchantment. We no longer feared. Beauty was all there was in the world and it was ours. The stalwart boys who stood high at bow and stern propelling with long oars began to croon snatches of native songs with deep, sweet voices.

Out on the warm silence spread a melody familiar. "Marching through Georgia!": Yes, the song of the Civil War in America.

"Hurrah, hurrah, we shout the jubilee,
Hurrah, hurrah, the flag that makes us free!
And thus we swell the chorus
From Atlanta to the sea!"

There the air stopped, wandered off into bars of strange notes. Then it returned to the refrain — not the words of course. Strange. Does it mean that the boy caught it from a tourist or is it a musical accident of coincidence?

He stopped it as we casually reached a shore. We had forgotten there was a shore or any element save water. In a moment the Diva was screaming for her twelve pieces of luggage, Priscilla, the competent, was selecting hers with the Hindu, and we were being packed away in motor cars. Incredible! Motor cars at the end of three days' and nights' journey up a wild tropic river into the jungle! Faithful, ubiquitous Henry Ford awaited us.

If one has never been in a jungle, and if one has read Kipling's stories of the animals one has a feeling it is full of menacing wild creatures, as well it is. Seated in a small open car rolling through the thick black forest, one can have many a thrill. I watched the roadside foliage for blazing green eyes. I watched the roadway for coiling cobras. Ten miles lie between the landing at Siem Reap and the Bungalow hotel at Angkor. I was on the alert to spy death before he saw me, all that long black distance.

But had I satisfied a tiger, I myself was first feasted on beauty. The stars above the road were such as I had never seen, the birds; I heard were strangely sweet, the air which flowed around me was balm perfumed by a million flowers high on the forest trees.

The Bungalow. The manager as affable as though it were not 2 a.m. gave us all big rooms with baths and netted beds. Sleep settled down over that section of Cambodia. But not until we saluted the Southern Cross low on the southern sky.

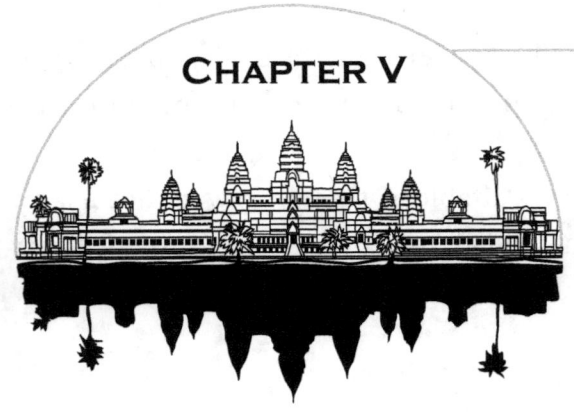

Chapter V

FIRST VIEW OF ANGKOR VAT

Not one knew that before us stretched the great temple Angkor Vat. Next morning we rose, bathed, dressed, in a dreamy apathy of fatigue, thinking no further than toast and coffee. Then from each bedroom a figure stepped out upon the tiled verandas which serve as corridors and proceeded over the grass of the big square courts to the front.

Raising our eyes, the great temple seized us.

Sitting in majesty across a flooded space, it claimed us. It held out spirit arms and embraced us. The soft morning airs blowing from its grandeur baptized us into a new worship. The light glowing on its five distant towers illuminated our consciousness, our very souls. We stretched out our arms and stepped towards it in ecstatic forgetting of physical sense.

We were not prepared to find it thus at hand.

We had not been told it would greet us like the sun at early morning. We had planned to journey further to find it. We had even thought we would choose to see first the lesser beauties of the Angkor group, and save this famed marvel for the final joy.

But we were thrown before its beauty unprepared, unshrived, unshorn.

A hundred yards of turf shaded by two or three huge trees end in a stone coping which tops a seawall. Below this a lake, only that the lake is a moat. Beyond this a long columned structure of one impressive storey with gates to pierce it. Far beyond that the reflected marvel of the Sanctuary, the five central towers. The glory of the morning was behind them, the eastern sun glowed on piled clouds affiliated with the temple's highest points which invited heaven itself. The tower of Babel, built to touch heaven's high dome, carried man no nearer God's throne than do the uplifting towers of Angkor Vat.

With faces alight we gazed, ecstatic, speechless. With lowered heads we seriously turned away and took up the tasks of living. It was a silent breakfast. A tyrant is the digestion, demanding fuel while mind and soul want but to blend with the spirits of the gods and men who built Angkor.

Those who like to chatter formed groups after breakfast, found a guide in khaki to lead them on. There are but two male costumes for civilians at the Bungalow — one is brown khaki, the other is brown skin and a *sampot*.

The gradual sloughing off of the kind of person really deserving of the name tourist left a charming loneliness. The two or three who were left eyed each other with distrust and withdrew to completer isolation. Even the Beguiler.

These few solitaries the Vat had seized and marked for its own. Each was under its spell; the wondrous temple called each to worship it alone. "For I am a jealous god," spoke the Hebrew Jehovah, and the gods of the Vat say the same.

When sure that none would join me I started out to explore the mundane base of the celestial towers. The water must be crossed. The way was obvious, a stone causeway the entrance to which was down the road a hundred yards, such a beautiful entrance as made one pause and wonder over the grand style of the architects of "the savages" as the Diva called the Khmers. Wide steps led to a generous platform, half a dozen steps all across the front, and on the sides the grassy slopes lowered the height to but two steps. Later on I knew this was done to make easy the way for the hesitating elephant.

Away from the plateau of entry the causeway stretched over the moat, a veritable avenue to the temple walls. It is balustraded with *Nagas* on either side, it is thirty-six feet wide, and its length is the unbelievable width of the moat, over two hundred meters, nearly seven hundred feet. A moat with us means a grassy cincture sunk around a castle — twenty-five or thirty feet might span it. The moat of Angkor Vat has no such niggard measure. It is a lake in width, it is enclosed in masonry, and it measures about three miles around! Superb! Few architects think in measurements as big as that.

This moat is filled with water on which waterweed floats and lotus blooms. Were it not for the corps of workers who pull up the masses of succulent weeds the water would be entirely obliterated by the heavy growth. Industry keeps it like a lake. This outer ring of the most stupendous temple in the world here lends itself to the uses of the simple native life with touching condescension. Instead of being awed with all that pertains to the Vat, these pleasant, quiet people use the moat as children take liberties with an august parent. A party of boys are bathing in the far corner by the concourse, women of the huts along the opposite shore are washing their scant linen and a pair of elephants are luxuriating in a cumbrous bath.

Slowly walking across this concourse which bridges the moat, one faces the long front of the outer wall, the gallery which the moat encircles, in itself a sufficient reward for the long journeying from Saigon. Here the pointed domes of the Vat may not be seen, they are shut away by the superb erection of the outer gallery with its grand entrance. Any architect would thrill at the harmony of the facade, an unbroken stretch of repeated pillars leading from the far angles of the

The *Tevadas*, oh, the *Tevadas*! — I am sure I heard a humming chorus of musical calls from them.

structure to the central opening which is dominated by three imposing towers with broken summits.

Half way across the moat it stops you by its very grandeur. Then it commands your approach, and you hurry on to the entrance that you may satisfy a sudden need to look within this outer rampart of a temple where no guard stops your eager feet. The steps mount importantly, though worn and broken, and put upon you the vow of silence. You are coming within an atmosphere of mystery, the great mystery of the Khmers and their strange gods.

The mounting steps are dressed with perrons* on which were placed the lion which guards all Khmer temples. To right and to left is another entrance, another passage through this enclosing gallery of the great Vat, but one takes the central opening lying in the straight path.

Within are great stone chambers, lofty in height, grey, damp, malodorous. Impressive and bewildering it is, but repellent also, not for what the builders have made but for the conditions that time and neglect have wrought. A long vista between columns opens on either hand, a vista so long as to seem impossible to accomplish with human feet. The impulse to go on, to penetrate the central temple, draws one away from the long galleries to the chambers beneath the tower. One must get on to the wondrous group of the five domes, companions of the sky, sisters of the clouds, and determine whether or not one lives in a world of reality or in a fantastic dream.

Its fresh vision strikes hard the consciousness, the big door of exit from the enceinte** frames the distant Sanctuary. The Vat rises in fair majesty against the heavens. All the ancient power of the temple and its gods is puissant still. It surrounds those who look upon the wonder. The eyes sweep upward over the rising storeys, up, up, to the mounting towers, to the pure firmament, and pause subdued.

It is ever thus. Some power overcomes, some mysterious spell is cast, one can never look upon the ensemble of the Vat without a thrill,

---

* An archaic term for an out-of-door flight of steps, as in a garden, leading to a terrace or to an upper story. It is usually applied to mediæval or later structures of some architectural pretensions.

** A French feminine noun meaning a fortification, wall, fence or ring shaped enclosure.

View from the Second Gallery — In the foreground is an entrance to the First Gallery. The twin libraries on either side of the causeway and a corner of one of the ponds are seen in the park. In the distance are the towers and inner wall of the enceinte.

a pause, a feeling of being caught up into the heavens. Perhaps it is the most impressive sight in the world of edifices.

The causeway that crosses the moat continues from the immense gallery of the enceinte — cincture, if you like — for hundreds of yards more to the temple porch, a broad way paved with stone upheld by an embankment flanked with columns. It passes through a park of interest and charm, for here are palms of excessive height crowned with languid fronds, and here are two independent buildings of symmetry and beauty denominated libraries. Whatever books they may have held to make the name appropriate, they are now but the *bibliotheques* of the cicada and the lizard. Time and vandals have so emptied them that one may not securely guess their purpose.

Also in the park are pools, one on either hand, and near the northern pool, the yellow-clad bonzes have built a shelter. Another evidence of the paternal spirit of the Vat which tolerates its children's trespassing.

It is this first walk over the grand ensemble of the Vat that introduces one to *Naga*, the sublime serpent. One knows at once he is filled with attributes quite other than those which make a snake a thing of horror. He is majestic more than fearsome. He raises a fan of seven heads with such grace that the long body trailing after seems to undulate with natural effort.

If Khmer art had originated no other decoration than this, it should be honoured for ever in all countries. Here on the stone causeway *Naga* is seen at his best. His group of lifted heads meets all who mount any of the approaches from the park, and his extended body, finely chiselled, forms the long balustrade upheld on carved stone supports. He makes all other hand-rails seem mere expedients. None have produced better than a flowing moulding ending in an ornamented curve. But the *Naga* has dignity, the interest of legend, the beauty of line and richness of ornament, besides which his long, round serpent body makes in life the very curves and extended distances required by architecture. The ornament of the grouped cobra heads, so fine, so intriguing, robs the

The Second Gallery Before Clearing Away the Brush

motif of all repulsiveness. Even without knowing the legend which makes *Naga* and Indra's daughter the Adam and Eve of the race of Khmers, one feels the charm of this marvellous decoration.

Step by step something of interest is found on the causeway and everything arouses wonder. There is a light streak on the stones, which makes one ponder. Presently a party of workers on the ruins passes, their bare feet following the light streak. Ah, it is the path worn by their soft padding steps.

There are deep ruts in the stones, as of wheels, many wheels passing that way. Later the bas-reliefs of the temple suggest they were worn by the chariots of the mighty who came to worship the Mightiest. In the bright hot sun approaches a brown lad carrying on a shoulder pole a number of cylindric vessels filled with colourless liquor. Did he draw water in the temple? A scrutiny of the tall, tall palms showed the font from which his liquid came, it was palm-sap drawn by men high up among the waving fronds. Ladders showed plainly, nailed the height of the trunks.

The cruciform terrace next. One never enters a temple of Angkor directly from a pathway. Steps are made to force a halt at beauteous obstructions that the mind may be prepared for the atmosphere of sanctity. It is an unbelievable distance from the first steps onto the causeway the other side of the moat, almost a third of a mile, but one may not yet enter directly the central group of buildings. There is now the cruciform terrace forming a plateau of elegance before the principal door of entry. A few steps lead one up. A few moments' pause lets the imagination people it with the kings and guards of other days ranged in Oriental magnificence before the temple. *Nagas* raise high their curving heads at the angles, and form with their trailing lengths the balustrade.

Mounting still further steps, the portico is reached. Once inside, vistas open to right, to left and straight ahead. One is lost in a symmetry of massed chambers, the whole forming a vast square. High and vaulted are chambers and galleries and all of dark grey sandstone grown darker

Detail of Door and Windows of the Second Gallery

yet in the shadow of the interior. It is hard to grasp at once the meaning of the splendid place which seems but a repetition of unused chambers. Remembering that the front line of rooms were all a sequence following the line of the facade, they become at once the adjuncts of the portico. Turning the back to the entrance, the vista ahead leads to covered steps mounting surely to the temple's central buildings.

But this first gallery must not be passed by without awareness of its importance. Although eager steps stride quickly through it transversely it has a prodigious length. It outlines a rectangular oblong measuring three quarters of a mile around.

Even at the first moment one observes the vaulted ceiling and the narrowness of the chambers, and then comes remembrance that the Khmers with all their magnificence of architectural conception were ignorant of the science of the arch. With sudden determination to find no faults in the wonders of Angkor, we think on Greece which stands for perfection, and she too knew naught of arches. The vault of the Khmers rose from straight walls by means of overlapping stones, each one slipped a little further toward the centre, the top one being not a keystone but a lid, not giving strength but requiring it.

But if large halls, wide audience chambers, vast basilicas were not possible to this kind of vault, the Khmer builders gained architectural magnificence through the device of long galleries. And this lower first gallery of the Vat's central pile is the perfect example. Besides its beauty as a part of the great architectural plan, this is the gallery where are found the incredibly extensive bas-reliefs. But they are not for the first visit. They are not for the novitiate who is learning the grand ensemble. They claim days all their own.

Crossing the space from the first gallery to the stairs which ascend the second is no sudden act. One might rush through if the place was only a part of the grassy court, but as it is, beauty stops one. The plan of this great architectural link between the two galleries is a square marked off into four other squares, deep pools of water with columned

Chapter V: First View Of Angkor Vat   73

The Grass Court Between the First and Second Galleries — A library in the distance.

porticos outlining all. Columns everywhere, square grey columns with the sardonic head of Civa carved lightly near the base. It is a head to make one shiver, so sinister it is, so cruel, so prevalent.

Other carvings press themselves upon you. You cannot hasten, it is impossible with so much to see. The whole place is carved, once you open your eyes to it, columns, lintels, surbases, panels, pediments, jambs of doors and windows. Ceilings are absent. They were originally of wood and stretched below the ogival* arch, but tropic insects have long since destroyed them. Some rare fragments which remain show these too, to have been as rich in carving as famous ceilings of the Italian Renaissance.

We have not yet reached the court of the decorative ladies, for here in the passages the ornament is light and playful, a display of flowers bent to new groupings. Blossoms are dissected and petals rearranged in new conventions, lotus, rosaces, and all the tropic blooms are used to make a field of pure decoration. Yet all is subdued, subservient to the architecture. The carvings alter the texture of the stone but make no sharp contrasting shadows as would occur had the chisel cut deep. All is low and delicate. It is said they were painted in bright colours long ago. I am glad of their delicate grayness now. They better suit the phantoms that float invisibly among the splendour of the columns.

Straight ahead lies a stairway, rising not in one big sweep, but in storeys, and these are roofed in grades. A pause on the first step, and a quick glance about shows what I have missed in courtyards, in pools sunk in massive basins, in *Tevadas* — oh, the *Tevadas*, I am sure I heard a humming chorus of musical calls from them. But by this time I am resolved to bring a rug and a biscuit and dwell ascetically in Angkor Vat until they become mine, so I can afford to hasten past them now.

Up three grades of steps to the second gallery.

Here is repeated the interior of the portico of the first storey, in size, divided like that into several chambers. A huge doorway opens into each, but devoid of doors. Possibly rich fabrics were let down in golden

---

* Derived from the English word ogive meaning; 1. A diagonal rib of a Gothic vault. 2. A pointed arch.

Chapter V: First View Of Angkor Vat 75

The Beautiful Paved Court Leads to the Entrance Stair of the Central Pile

lengths to form the screen instead of doors, or possibly the voracious tropic ant has eaten all the wood.

Stone door sills remain, and these to stop the weary. The door-opening is a perfect thing, like a silver frame to a photograph, the bottom line as important as the sides. The sill is a good two feet high and is also wide, so that one must mount the stiff barrier and then descend. Forty of these are crossed in making the tour of the second storey. Two dozen more are possible if one is eager to view the terrace below at the angles of intersection. Feat for an athlete, yet one does the greater part of it without demur, being under the spell of the Vat and breathless to see it all, all that very first morning.

There is a belief that those whom the spirit of the Vat chooses as its own, are drawn by the ancient puissance that lies within the central chamber of the pile and that rest is impossible to them until they have reached the ancient heart, where sat enthroned the great Brahmanic god.

The second gallery takes cobwebs from the mind. From any of its openings one can step outward and learn a little of the plan of the great ensemble. Here one sees below the grassy court inside the first gallery, and looks upon the two smaller buildings constructed toward the west, libraries, which term conveys little, as not a page nor yet a letter is contained within. One sees also that the grassy court is higher than the park; and looking from an opposite window one sees that the court of the second gallery is higher still. Thus built the Khmers in ever higher terraces or storeys, each one smaller than that below.

Onward, ever onward, neglecting the Buddhist treasures of the long galleries, impatient for the central pile. From the paved courtyard of the second storey one can see it in its surpassing grandeur, aloof in its separateness from the other buildings. To support its tower stones of prodigious height are laid in carved beauty piled high and higher to form a surbase attained by perilous stairs.

Before, across the paved court, rises the entrance stair. Its height, its width, its perrons at the side, where once rested the challenging

Khmer lion, but above all its steepness, make it an awesome approach — awesome yet attracting. One must mount. Each step is high, and too narrow to let the foot rest straight upon it. Half way up one is ready to rest a finger-tip on steps above for better balance. Eleven other stairs make the ascent from the paved court to this third storey, but of such steep construction that none attempt their use.

Up to the top, and then the view. One steps out on a projection of the portico, and like a bird surveys the world below. Conscious of great shadows one looks upward. The five enormous towers of the central group rise like mountains, symmetric mountains of ornamental stone. Looking down, one sees the roofs of the second gallery and of the first — roofs long and narrow, arched over the spaces under them and covered with tiles and beautiful carved eaves. The roofs are lovelier than one would think a roof can be, marvels of effective workmanship.

Beyond them the palm trees of the park, dressing with green plumes the beautiful austerity. Beyond the park the walls of the enceinte seemingly miles away; and all the world else, as far as the eye can see — the jungle, the captivating sea of the jungle which flows in waves of green across illimitable space. Kings who came here to worship the great Brahmanic Trimurti, on turning from the high altar to descend, met this same view, and with it fortified the spirit.

From this high level of the Vat rises the grand dome of the central tower, far higher than the four other towers of the central group, two hundred and thirteen feet from the level of the park. Within this tower, in its exact centre, is the habitation of Vishnu, the god to whom the whole edifice was dedicated.

It is but a small stone chamber, a cubicle, a cell, yet it is the heart of the great Vat, that most perfect of all the Khmer constructions. It is the Sanctuary, the holy of holies. It is the sacred penetralia* that none may look upon but the king and the highest ministrant. It is reached by long physical effort, while the mind is being prepared for psychic things

---

* An English plural noun meaning; 1. The innermost parts of a building, especially the sanctuary of a temple. 2. The most private or secret parts; recesses.

by gradually leaving the world during the passage from the high road to the water, through the wide quiet park of the first enclosure, through the porticos, up the stairs, and finally mounting the sharp acclivity of the last perilous flight of steps to the upper halls.

The small spare chamber in the centre of the pile inspires awe. Tradition long said one might not step within and live. Four corridors from the four points of the compass approach it, each one ending against the huge stones which form its sides. The way inside was blocked for centuries. Legends grew up about it. Perhaps they are true in part. One says that this holy cell contained a wondrous statue of Vishnu carved from precious stone, and that the last king of the Khmers sought sanctuary here when the conquering Siamese set upon him in their final battle, He entered the sacred refuge and stood beside the statue while trusted soldiers followed his command to wall him in. There he died, while outside his armies were destroyed and his country fell never to rise again.

Perhaps this legend kept the people of Cambodia in awe throughout the centuries, and deterred them from the profanation of opening the holy casket. But when the French took over the country they were held back by no such superstition. Alas, ancient stone gods have a commercial value outweighing their religious worth in these days of wide collecting, and this one was reputed to be of emerald.

But when the holy of holies was penetrated the exploring French found nothing of importance, shadows and emptiness, damp and chill.

But wandering in the Vat I have evolved a theory of my own; no material thing was ever put within that sacred chalice. High priests, deep thinkers, know that God is spirit, not matter. He is not of the stuff that can be touched, and seen. The Holy Spirit, Brahmanic or Buddhist, would better occupy a space left empty for His divine abode, empty because things of the spirit are immaterial. It may then be that with the great Vat as a setting, the chamber for the Guest was left for Him to fill at will.

Lingering in the Vat one imagines the great Khmer king going to worship on the eve of battle. The great bridge is guarded with soldiers, is gay with banners. Inside the park twelve thousand guardian soldiers with their shields and arms make resplendent the concourse. In the covered ways between the first and second storeys of the Vat are gathered the ladies of the court, magnificent in jewels and silks. The warm sun shining on them flashes back colour and perfume. An orchestra taps and tinkles in the corridors. In the last courtyard are gathered the favourites of the king, princes and great generals dressed as for war, attendants holding high the parasols of rank, the golden fans and swaying fly-brushes.

The king mounts the steeps of the last great stair of the central mass before a cortege of high priests chanting praises to Vishnu. All the temple, from moat to towers, is stilled while the king approaches the Sanctuary. At the top of the stair he turns and with arms outstretched looks over the gorgeous scene burning in the sunlight, then with figure erect he passes within the shadows of the galleries. Here he leaves attendant priests. Not even the highest may go with him into the sacred penetralia. He enters alone the little stone cell still and dark, the highest mortal to meet his highest god, and there in the shadowy silence he lets his spirit mingle with the Infinite.

It was not my wish to commit sacrilege against the ancient god or an ancient people's religion. After my vision I looked down the shadows of the corridor and felt the solemnity of the place, then turned away for something human, some palpitating evidence of common life.

I found it on my descent to the first gallery, where I seated myself on one of the two-feet-high doorsills for a rest and a cooling. It was the Lead King, the disillusioned husband of the Diva. He advanced listlessly with wobbly feet, still carrying opened the pongee umbrella with which he had defeated the sun while crossing the long stone causeway. Its green lining cast a horrid pallor on his flaccid face. Poor man, to have lived so long only to find life worthless!

To cheer him I passed the time of day. The melancholy remained. Moreover, his eye wandered to such extent as left no conclusion save that I bored him. So I let him go, but as he reached the angle of the wall his whole face altered and he threw me back a commonplace adieu with the light of rejuvenation flashing.

I rose and stepped to where I could see him saunter down the long gallery of the bas-reliefs. But he had gone only a few steps. The reason for his smiles was close at hand. It was the Puritan Priscilla. Exquisite she was in freshest transparent white, prim, demure, cool in aspect — but flirting rapturously, and with skill, with the Diva's husband.

Chapter VI

STILL ANGKOR VAT

After the first run over the Vat, questions hurl themselves upon a wondering curiosity. Then is the time to study the scheme of the ancient builders. Simply put, the Vat is a dominating central tower around which is constructed a series of concentric squares in ever-enlarging size, all these enclosed in a wide moat. Or, it is a pyramid rising in three stages enclosed by wall and moat. But when details are taken up, details of both construction and ornament, one can give to them a life-time of devotion as does George Groslier, the head of the Museum at Phnom Penh. Or, one can take them as play, with a delightful and disgraceful lightness, merely vivifying them with bits of Asiatic history and religions.

To know the Vat, one should start at the outer gate and capture it, square after square.

The moat comes first. That gives no cause for study, only for wonder at its great extent. The long reaches of the enceinte — one falls unavoidably into French in this land — seem particularly for scenic beauty, and can be looked at and enjoyed with the happiness of tropic languor. In one way it is but the wall of enclosure to the park in which is set the temple group of galleries and towers.

Unless one is examining the enceinte exhaustively, the portico is the only part one studies. This does not mean that this outer cincture is not ever and always a stimulating delight to look upon. Its daring extent awes and attracts from the very first. It seems to separate the Vat from the world at large and give it a celestial country all its own. The facade of this outer enceinte is a double row of columns.

The portico greets the wanderer as the causeway across the moat is ended. A terrace of earth skirts the wall between the moat and the building.

The way in which one passes through the portico is never agreeable because of damp and bats, but from outside one sees it is crowned by three huge towers, damaged relatives of the towers that rise from the Vat's centre. They make of this portico a building so impressive that were it the sole remains at Angkor it would be worth a visit. Inside, to right and to left, are doorless openings showing a long series of empty stone chambers grouped to form a *gopura**. The doorsills uncomfortably high are explained by the probable existence of wooden floors nearly on their level, floors which a few hundred years of tropic climate might have obliterated. The rest of the gallery is a long veranda, columns on the face and an unbroken wall at the back.

It is in the portico of this outer enceinte that one first falls under the charm of the marvellous decorations carved in low relief that humanize this greatest of temples. Infinite in variety, abounding in grace and in originality they introduce one to an art strange and compelling. Surbases, door-lintels, panels, columns, are covered with a close carving that is akin to the pattern of a woven cloth. The *rinceau*** of the Renaissance in Italy is a not uncommon motif, and, side by side with this, use is

---

* A Sanskrit term for a prominent feature of South Indian Hindu temple architecture consisting of the rising tower at a temple entrance, often quite tall with ornate carvings.
** A French term for an ornamental foliate or floral motif.

The Gallery of the Second Story. Before a curtain of carved lace the sacred maidens walk in a smiling trio.

made of preposterous little human figures as the centre of the design. All over the Vat the human figure is a prime motif for pure ornament, and except for the calm ladies or priestesses which we shall see later in bewildering loveliness, they are gay little sprites showing an exaggerated joy of living.

On either side, far from the main portico, are two smaller entries. They may not be important in effect, but their purpose thrills the Occidental. They are the gate of passage for those who come in chariots or on elephants to the temple.

That is the reason for their being on the level of the ground, while the central entrance demands the climbing up of steps and then the marching down. The massive beasts convey an idea of magnificence greater than that of chariots. After languid passage of the gate they crossed the park and then stood along the side of the temple's surbase which was just the height of the howdah*, and here their elegant human freight was deposited. Elephants in the East, one expects to see, but architecture made to fit them is an idea most inspiring.

It was during the visit of General Joffre to Angkor that an effort was made to reproduce the old splendour. Great elephants to the number of a score or more were harnessed and howdahed and led across the great causeway in a procession which could not fail to cause thrills to even the least imaginative.

But how must it have been in the days when the Khmers dominated Indochina, when gold and gems flashed in the sun from the elephants' *caparison***, when chariots rolled up the way and thousands of armed soldiers were ever on guard in the great temple.

Through the portico and into the park, another view of the walls is obtained by looking backward. The beauty of repetition is the beauty of this inner facade stretching into the distance. Columns are on the western face, but here towards the park, the wall is broken by a line of balustered windows. The frequent use of stone balusters,

* From Urdu *haudah*. A seat, usually with canopy and railing, on the back of an elephant or a camel.
** Ornamental covering for a saddle or harness; trappings.

The Third Gallery — From the courtyard it rises in surpassing grandeur, aloof in its separateness from the other buildings.

at times covering a false window, at times letting in the light, makes one wonder if they were not a detail left over from the time when construction was of wood.

From the portico to the first gallery of the temple is a long distance. Sauntering over it in the sun one looks over the reaches of the park and wonders if the whole great square in which the temple is set were not laid out in wondrous gardens such as those of Kashmir. But one is satisfied now with the palms which grow here to enormous height and surpassing beauty. Far to right and to left stand the ruins of two symmetric buildings seen before. Ask anyone, guide or tourist, what is their intent, and the answer is ready and assured, "Libraries." But one may have obstinate mental reservations.

The concourse itself is worth a better scrutiny than is possible on the first running over of its sun-struck length. It is about ten feet from the ground, is faced with stone and upheld by a line of large round columns, making as imposing a way as ever was planned. It is interrupted at stated intervals by flights of steps descending to the gardens or park below. It is paved with large stone flagging and is bordered with superb *Nagas* supported on low cubic balusters. At each interrupting stair *Nagas* terminate in rearing heads, and one seems to pass from point to point under their directing in a way that lessens monotony on the long promenade. *Naga* here does not threaten, he greets, but with lordly hauteur.

To the left is a grove full of the sounds of life. Little homes are seen, of bamboo construction set high on stilts, and one hears low singing, monotone chants. It is the bonzerie* of the Buddhist priests who haunt the temple, who worship there indiscriminately the gods of Buddha or those of Brahma.

A mirror of water nearby is called an elephant pool. Another is on the opposite side of the causeway. Perhaps in old days the elephants bathed here, but now the pools seem like accidents of the rain and not conceptions of an architect.

---

* A Buddhist monastery, derived from bonze, an archaic English term for a Buddhist monk (more properly known as bhikkhu).

And now the temple in all its concentrated grandeur stands before, and we know that it consists of three squares set one within another, each on a higher level, and that all are but frames to the glory of that heart of spiritual mystery which is the Sanctuary.

If it were but possible, one should start the examination of the Vat from that high point, taking a bird's-eye view of the whole construction set in the jungle's sea of green. One could then descend the magnificent stairways, capturing gallery after gallery until the last was reached, and there rest on the imposing cruciform terrace of its entrance. But convenience directs one, the galleries are investigated on the way up and one arrives at the top too hot and exhausted, too sated with beauty, to absorb the full plan of the builders.

The Cruciform Terrace is before us, which splendidly approaches the lowest gallery of the three. It is the locale of the famous bas-reliefs. There is study, for only erudition can smooth the tangle of their many scenes.

The portico is magnificent in a way not unfamiliar. One is at once in harmony with the plan. Nothing exotic about it, nothing that shocks Western traditions, simply grandeur and dignified beauty as we know it in our own architecture. The plan of the outer enceinte is nearly repeated, a central group of chambers, and then long open galleries stretching to right and left, and indeed entirely around the square, which is not quite a square but an oblong. These galleries have an unvarying construction of high, unbroken wall of limestone on the inner side, and a double row of square columns on the outer face of the building, the space between being more like a corridor or a veranda than a chamber, and the whole is roofed with the narrow pointed vault of the Khmers.

The unparalleled sculptures are graven on the plain, high walls where light falls on them from the open side, between the square columns.

At each corner and at a point half way between are architectural interruptions to the wall, perrons at the corners, doorways between, opening onto the grassy court which lies between the first gallery and the second. The view of the wall from this court shows the same elegant use of balustered windows that made interesting the inner facade of the enceinte.

The first storey of the Vat is a place one can never leave, or, leaving, one must ever return to study Khmer life and Khmer myth as pictured on the great bas-reliefs extending themselves for hundreds of feet — two thousand square yards of carving.

You may take the place according to your temperament and your taste. Priscilla and the Diva's husband took it as lover's lane, not a bad substitute, for the long, columned walk stretches far and shady and looks out upon the most gracious and lonely forest. Young Boston took it as an art school and in the brightest of dresses illuminated the sober stones while copying Khmer designs. She had annexed an aspirant, and the two played at art and another game with lightsome touch.

But the bas-reliefs will not let themselves be taken too carelessly. They pique and they challenge with an erudition that eludes all but the scholar. One is ashamed not to know the meaning of all these vivid scenes.

By their beauty they first attract, by their strangeness they hold attention. In parts they portray an art not understood by Europeans, an art so primitive as to suggest an undeveloped race. Remembering the grand perfection of the Vat one cannot accuse the Khmers of being a savage people; remembering that their graphic art is largely one of fixed convention, its peculiar style is understood. Certain drawing, certain personifications had to be as they had ever been.

Looking through Italy's galleries we understand the long faces of Byzantine madonnas which stray far from nature's lines, for we know the Church imposed that convention upon the artists. If eyes and mind hasten to accept the conventions and legends imposed upon Khmer artists, delight in their work comes quicker to the student. Student? Yes, that must be the word for the Westerner, as we are not brought up by

Chapter VI: Still Angkor Vat   89

The Entrance to the Sanctuary — Across the paved court rises the entrance stair. Its height, its width, its perrons at the side where once rested the lions, make it an awesome approach.

priests of Brahma and do not recount glibly the books of the Ramayana and the Mahabarata whose scenes are here depicted.

The general effect is most alluring. The endless chiselling impresses one as a decoration, suave and softening, giving the hard stone wall a covering as of tapestry. Then all at once one is drawn by the absolute beauty of a single figure. The figure is that of Vishnuloka, the King, seated on a throne above his generals to whom he is giving orders to assemble the army for one of the great Khmer conflicts with the Chams of Annam or the Thais of Siam.

The subject is historic not religious and I am sufficiently daring to like it better on that account. It gives delight to ferret out the customs of the mysterious race of the Khmers, a race which has left no literature save what is found graven on the ancient stones. In this picture we learn the fashion in royal dress — a few bands of gold and a few bands of fabric, quite sufficient for a hot day at Angkor. Around the king are those evidences of sacred rank, the umbrellas.

On China's most ancient stones umbrellas cover the heads of highest personages, the top of the stone *dagoba** is finished with one, and today in the streets of Peking they are a feature of ceremonials. It would be interesting to know their history and why this Vishnuloka directing his generals is shaded by eight of them, pictured like a full-blown lotus inverted.

Having once started to find definite meaning in the groups, the bas-reliefs become irresistible. The figure of Vishnuloka represents a type. He is often found and is always a person high among the gods or high among men. He is the perfection of manhood, a strong, graceful aristocrat, ready to lead, powerful to conquer. Sometimes he appears in elegant repose among court beauties, sometimes mounted on an elephant going to give battle, sometimes tensely active as in the portrayal of Rama, who kills with a bow his enemy, Maricha, who has come to him during the chase in the guise of a deer — a marvellous golden deer with horns of emerald.

---

* A Sanskrit term for a type of Buddhist mound-like structure found across Asia. In Southeast Asia the Pali word is more common; stupa.

We may take this glorious being as the ideal man of the Khmers. What Apollo was to the Greeks this man of beauty and intelligence was to the Khmers. That he was real, that he lived in duplicate, that he was a splendid type in this old city of Angkor there can be no doubt.

When I passed the easel of the red-frocked Boston girl she was fixing him on her canvas. She, too, had fallen under the spell of his vital charm. She had selected a scene on the southern gallery depicting the condition of bliss of those who ascend to heaven. Three chambers are the setting for each group decorated with lace-like carving, and in the centre sits the demi-god while his lovely ladies offer him refreshing fruits and feminine wiles.

In this part of the gallery the reliefs are taken up with the long succession of scenes which picture in infinite excruciating variety the tortures of inferno, and, in rather monotonous sameness, the delights of heaven. The imagination of the sculptors was endless when it came to depicting hell, but futile and saccharine in treating the heavenly regions, which makes one wonder if the life of subordinate chisellers was not one of misery infinitely varied, with which they were well acquainted, while heaven about which they could know little, seemed to belong only to the rich and mighty, their patrons on earth.

In the relief picture the torments of hell extend in a long band below, with the pleasures of heaven in an equally long band above. Between the two is a decorative line of *Garudas*, delightful monsters.

In the southern gallery is a scene that arrests by its daring, by the way it thrusts upon the beholder a world of imagination found only in fairy tales and in the Oriental mythology. Looking up, one sees on the wall figures of a far larger scale than elsewhere, two opposing rows of men with arms around a mammoth snake pulling his body as men pull a rope in the physical contest of a tug-of-war. Drawing back far enough for a general view one sees that the head of the serpent is like *Naga's*, polycephalous, and the giant who holds it is also many-headed, and that half way down the two rows of men a similar giant lends aid to the contestants. In the centre of the great design sits a four-armed deity, Vishnu of god-like calm, and the men fall both ways from this point. Below the entire picture is the sea represented by a mass of tumbling fish.

The story is of the churning of the Sea of Milk by the *Asuras* and the *Devas*, a work which was to secure for them a coveted immortality. To attain this end they used the serpent Vasuki as a rope which they twined around the base of the fabled Mount Mandara. By pulling first to right and then to left, the mountain moved and churned the sea into tides. Vishnu most accommodatingly changed himself into a huge tortoise on which the mountain rested and the work went on throughout the centuries. Other gods appeared from time to time with their attendant dancers, the celestial *Apsaras*, and at last arrived the elixir of immortality.

But all was not well even then. The line of gods, the *Devas*, and the line of demons, the *Asuras*, immediately fell into combat to possess the divine elixir. Meanwhile Vishnu seized and drank it, thus securing for himself the immortality coveted by the half-gods. This legend is depicted elsewhere in the Vat and in the Bayon. It is also the probable inspiration for the bridge outside the Gate of Victory where ugly giants are ranged on one side, with benign gods on the other, and the great serpent lies in the laps of both.

It is too stupendous as a decorative motive to be required to furnish any explaining, but a story is a diversion well liked outside of nurseries.

The great army of the Khmers passes in review in another picture, decorating the gallery of history with one of the most vivid reliefs in all the monuments left by ancient races in any part of the world. Much space of the bas-reliefs is taken up with combats of the gods, of so fierce and complicated a nature as to lack interest, but here is a procession marching in the nice order of military troops and leaders which can be understood by any boy who has pushed his way to a curbstone front-line to see a holiday parade. Khmer history, as far

The Portico of the Enceinte — The huge ruined towers make the portico a building so impressive that were it the sole remains at Angkor it would be a worthy visit.

as we know it, shows no interval of peace long enough for inutile processions; theirs were always bellicose in intent and were eagerly marching to meet a foe. Cambodia in the centuries of its wealth and power was ever at war, either to subdue and possess its neighbours, or to defend itself from attacks of envious nations.

We see here to our delight "the warhorse who smelleth the battle afar off," curvetting in a manner spirited and powerful. He is like the horses of the Romans and bears himself with a pride not excelled even by the general on his hack. The old convention of the Roman sculptors is in use, multiplying the outline of a well — drawn horse to indicate more than one. From whence came these splendid horses and whither they fled is another mystery, for the horses of today in Cambodia are funny things, as small as ponies, as quiet as cats.

But in this long army passing by, the mount that thrills is the splendid elephant. We can stand and watch him with all the rapture of a child. He is an elephant transfigured by dreams of triumph, and lifts his head to throw high in air his curving trunk. He passes us entirely conscious that he carries on his back a god-like leader standing, not supinely seated, as he goes forth to war. One foot is planted on the animal's croup, the other is on the saddle, and about him are the umbrellas of rank. And the file of soldiers who march behind him extends an immeasurable distance, proud, stalwart men dressed in close-wound *sampots*, and shouldering arms with which they are sure of winning the victory. And overhead the whole long procession is shaded with trees of a most charming convention. Palm trees, no, but instead umbrageous leafy trees like maidenhair ferns grown mammoth.

One is charmed into watching this procession go by an hour at a time, noting headdresses, arms, musical instruments. There is a band, of course, and men are keeping the stepping time of this splendid army by the regular beat of the tom-toms. There is also an engaging group of such servitors as follow any army, workers and ladies of light allure. These last are springing forward with the grace and spirit of a Botticelli maiden, draperies clinging, feet tripping. Even they are jubilant over anticipated victory.

And so one may pick out spots in the half-mile of bas-reliefs that are easily understood for no other reason than that the Khmers were human even as we. But in those sections of the bas-reliefs dealing purely with the complicated mythology of Brahmanism, both mind and eye grow weary in an endeavor to untangle gods and devils and know the reason for their fantastic conflicts. All the gods of the Hindu Olympus are madly mixed together over large spaces. Those who are really interested can discover them all, each one mounted on the animal he has chosen for his own. But it is a puzzle that needs patience and erudition.

The large space given to the battle of the mono key-men shows the importance of the myths which have Hanuman at their head. They are given a place with the gods, and the romances of Bali and Sugriva, of Hanuman and Sita, his adored wife, are fully portrayed. But for us these creatures are monkeys and the story fails in effect. To us a monkey is a curious animal in a cage or attached to a hand organ. We have not lived for generations in a land where monkeys hold a prominent place in theism.

I turned away and sauntered to a corner. Priscilla was laughing prettily while the Diva's husband, with a languid arm, pointed out a picture for her notice. The sad and disillusioned one had chosen a scene in which Cupid plays an active role. Here he is called Kama. He is provided with a bow — but note the poetry of it, the bow is of flowers, the bowstring is of honey-bees and the arrows are of sugar cane. In the bas-relief Kama is aiming at Civa, who sits aloft in ascetic indifference, a kneeling lady at his right hand, and on his left an attendant with his symbol, the trident. Civa is, of course, impervious, but a recent victim of Kama's sweet arrow lies on the ground beside him with his head in the lap of his inamorata.

Perhaps the Diva's husband is not sad today. And perhaps he has caught some new illusions.

Those who like to linger in this wonderful gallery of bas-reliefs will always be made happy by new discoveries and will return as often as other joys of Angkor will allow. Taken as a promenade alone, what could be lovelier than this shaded walk lifted three or four yards above the turf, from which one looks out on the green shades of the deep forest, with occasionally an opening in the trees leading far, far away to the line of the enclosing enceinte.

Around the temple and down the long walk are gangs of native workmen continuing the work of drawing the ancient structures from the oblivion into which tropic vegetation had thrown them. Five hundred of these men are toiling all the year through at the work of excavating lost stones and replacing fallen monoliths. They seem like a bit of the old life come back again, the life of the toiling slaves who built the splendid Vat and the kingly city of Angkor Thom. These men are brown and bare, splendidly powerful in their slow, determined movements, and one looks on them from the gallery of the bas-reliefs and unites them with the people of the graphic carvings.

It is not alone the large surfaces of the bas-reliefs which give delight. Exquisite pleasure is given by the figures of pure decorations which are sprinkled over the Vat as though a spirit of joy and beauty had laid them there. They are matters of *fantaisie* and bear no relation to the high and rounded carvings used to create an emphasis.

They are carved with so light a touch that the eye is never diverted from the strong architectural lines which they adorn. They are distinctly of two classes, those composed of motifs made from vegetation, flowers and vines, and those made up of human figures.

The great surbases in the Vat lose none of their grandeur from the fact that they are exquisitely chiselled in a fine low relief of vegetation, flowers in conventionalized form. Free hand drawing is but little used apart from the great historic bas-reliefs, for all decoration is conventionalized. Even figures are *stylisés*, which binds the artist in decoration to a repetition most happy in effect however it may hamper

Chapter VI: Still Angkor Vat 97

To Right and to Left Stand the Ruins of Two Symmetric Buildings

him in depicting nature as it is.

An irrepressible passion for decoration is let to flow freely over the stones, but note with what superior skill it is restrained. It is like a filmy lace thrown over splendid outlines — it dresses them but does not obliterate. The whole great structure is softened thereby. Its courts, like those of the first and second storeys, are thus made almost lovable. The awesome grandeur of the great structure is thus humanized.

The little people who appear unexpectedly among the decorations make one sure that fairies were accepted among the ancient people who habited Angkor. As is proper with fairies these diminutive human figures are set in charming arrangements of flowers and curling leaves. In one place they occupy each circle of a rinceau formed by bound reeds or vines, each one buoyantly active as though from joy of living.

In another placing, we see tiny deities or worshipful ladies sitting within the shelter of a single leaf, hands together, holding a lotus bud, or arms outstretched, lost in a leaf. Of all the minor carvings this one has the greatest charm. The entourage of this lovely figure which is not more than five inches tall is a wealth of volutes*, of curving, curling leaves cunningly composed to form a point, at the apex of which sits the enchantress. The design is repeated to cover an entire pilaster beside a door, and it forms in wider aspect a tall panel of verdure with a line of dainty beings peeping through in a line down the centre.

Alas, and alas, beauty is not always a blessing. It cannot be an accident that in pilaster after pilaster the gracious heads of these tiny seated ladies have been removed, knocked off, while the equally frail volutes are left intact.

It is with hesitation that I mention the larger ladies of the carvings, the *Tevadas* or sacred dancers. I am made shy in their presence, while they remain unperturbed. They are so many to know all at once, and their character is to me unfathomable. Coming into the court where they abound is like being shown into a room full of living strangers. They give the illusion of being sentient, as real as the girls of the village

---

* A spiral scroll-like ornament.

The Khmer Builders Gained Architectural Magnificence Through the Device of Long Galleries

of Siem Reap, but far, far more lovely. They have the ease of those to whom self-consciousness is unknown, the air of the rich aristocrat. But best of all they have unvaryingly happy tempers. They are not mad with joy as are the little dancing figures which meet us at every turn, but their attitudes indicate the repose that marks the highest caste.

The famous smile on the face of Leonardo's "Gioconda" is not more enigmatic than that with which these Khmer ladies greet the visitor. They stand in groups with arms affectionately interlaced, or singly, upholding a flower or an end of the strangely draped *sampot*. Gauze and silk clothe them, and the sun has taught them to be half naked yet unashamed. Jewels adorn them and headdresses create wonder. These friendly, pleasant ladies are placed against a gracious background carved as though by a goldsmith, so patient and so talented are its infinitesimal details. They stand and look at one across the chasm which ever separates beings of differing race. It is not the years that part us, it is the opposing point of view which holds apart the West and East to the heavy loss of both.

In another part of the Vat one comes on the dancing figures, mad, joyous beings. You know these are fable. The girls — *Tevadas* you may call them — are human, but these lightsome dancers are too happy to bother about hearts or souls with all their appanage* of serious thoughts. Their mission is to enliven, to divert. Religious dancers they are called, but one questions why. In dress and ornament they are not unlike the *Tevadas*, the enigmatic ladies, but in attitude they are fascinatingly acrobatic. No more exquisite entourage was ever made than the frame for these figures, a flowered scroll which gracefully widens to accommodate the active knees, narrows for the slender waist, swells again for the head, and forms altogether a vase-like outline.

The fabled *Apsaras* are kin to this figure, ancestors perhaps. One feels that the court of Angkor must have abounded in dancers like the one dancing within her frame, but *Apsaras* are of the gods. They are the maddest, merriest beings on the Hindu Olympus. They are always

---

* An English noun with multiple meanings; 1. A source of revenue, such as land, given by a sovereign for the maintenance of a member of the ruling family. 2. Something extra offered to or claimed by a party as due; a perquisite. 3. A rightful or customary accompaniment or adjunct.

Embrasure of a Window Covered with a Close Carving that is Akin to the Pattern of a Woven Cloth

in battalions, always high in air above the actors in a scene played by gods or demi-gods. No human could be so abandoned to joy as these heavenly acrobats, the sales of whose feet are lifted to the sun, fairly spurning both earth and heaven can they but dance between.

Untellable are all the varieties of pure decoration, but still another is always taken away in the mind's depository of photographic films. It is the delicious parade of little men who perform ecstatic antics on the backs of the strange mounts they are riding. A frieze of them runs above the groups of winsome girls, just over the balustered windows of the courtyard. Each mount, a horse, an elephant, a rhinoceros, is rampant, each rider is as joyously acrobatic as the lady of the circus on her trained stallion. And all is done, not as an exhibition but because some inward spirit demands a wildly reckless expression.

Fascinating, demanding beings, these of the Vat, with whom one could play for many a day. But one must carry on, for there are many things to see at Angkor.

Chapter VII

A NOCTURNE

There is dancing tonight at Angkor Vat.

All day there has been unusual activity along the road which runs beside the flowered waters of the moat, an activity vivid though soft and noiseless.

Chattering groups of little women pass, speaking their Cambodian tongue gently as always, and guests at the Bungalow look up to see them come along the way from Siem Reap and vanish under trees near the terrace which is the splendid approach to the causeway of Angkor Vat. Occasionally one bears a nude brown baby astride her hip, and even he is keen, alert. Some are old and very thin, and these are revivified with what is coming.

Boys go by, full of importance, keeping to the road after the manner of men, nor once running to the stone coping which edges the moat where frogs and turtles swim fascinatingly. The boys, too, feel the thrill of belonging to an ancient tradition, of sharing the stirring duties it imposes.

Even the bullock-carts are deployed from stone carrying, and the men who drive them have a holiday look of jaunty swagger.

The carts, the bullocks, the half-nude workers make pictures which have been repeated from generation to generation throughout unfathomable centuries, The ancient artists so chiselled them twelve centuries ago, and time finds them still unchanged.

This time the carts bear unusual freight, not stones, not upturned earth for temple restorations, but a burden of long, green cylinders, torches confectioned with subtle skill from forest treasures of spicy odours and wrapped with fragrant leaves. Such candles as these not only light a scene but send out clouds of incense smoke most grateful to the Spirits of the Air.

Then there are village girls, moonfaced, shy, extremely young, perhaps fifteen, perhaps seventeen. Among these are the dancers. But not now distinguishable from their freer friends who will soon be taken as brides by splendid young boatmen who scull the sampans on the Tonlé Sap.

Dancers from the King's corps are there. The superb brown Buddha disguised as hotel porter brings news to the Bungalow that the village is arranging a dance; and he is full of quiet delight. Two of his sisters are numbered among the dancers of the King and are making the village the yearly visit accorded them by their royal master. They are taking the leading parts tonight, they are setting the standard of perfection for the village troupe to follow.

Seven years ago when they were but eight years old they were taken to the palace at Phnom Penh by father and mother and offered as gifts to the King. By bullock cart and sampans they made the journey with this most precious freight, the prettiest among their offspring. Even thus had their ancestors offered their loveliest little maids, not only at the palace, but also at the great temples, that they might be trained for the service and delight of the monarch and of the gods.

The parents return to their village proud in the acceptance of their

Chapter VII: A Nocturne

Royal Dancers, Phnom Penh—The childish face is shadowless as a moonlit disc.

sacrifice, but the little maid remains to endure the long-extended training which shall fit her to dance before the King when her time of maturity arrives. The tradition of generations is being carried on; she submits to it with the quiet patience of all who have gone before, inspired by the hope that is in the heart of every little maid of the palace, to find favour before the King, favour above that of her fellows who are many. Do we not read that the Khmer monarchs of centuries ago had thousands of women in the palace enclosure? Even the late king. Norodom, was pleased to see about him as many as five hundred; but the present one, Sisovath, finds the palace fully furnished with seventy.

Trainers of the dance are old *premières*, women who themselves were trained and know all the necessities of grace. Classic poses make strange requirements of the articulations. The little hands must be made to turn back at the wrist with shorter curves, and taper fingers must easily take the lines of reversing that they may look like petals of the open lotus.

The dancer must be able to stand balanced on immovable foot for minutes at a time while she undulates in wondrous rhythm the entire body, the shoulders, arms, fingers, with the softness of flowing waters; joints are unjointed, articulations are nil, in attaining such plasticity and grace.

But the little maids under the relentless trainers know the anguish of fingers snapped at being turned backward, of elbows cracking in their disjointing and of sitting long hours daily in the heat at these and other trying exercises, pale, though upheld by the inward spirit, a pride of legend.

For years the training continues, the little girl may not see her parents nor her home, but lives the life of palace attendant. Then comes a glorious time when she is called nearer the person of the King, perhaps to sit among the women who surround him in hours of ease, and wave a silken flybrush or a feathered fan. And by that time she is put among the troupe of those who dance in the King's pavilion.

A preparation for an appearance is the dressing, that marvellous dressing of the old tradition wherein the magnificent past is continued. This, too, is in the hands of the old women who adhere inexorably to the old form. If the girl to be dressed is among the *premières*, her face is whitened, blanched with powder mixed in oil, for white means purity and the race of kings. The childish face is shadowless as a moonlit disc, the monotonous life of petty trial having not yet traced its evidence. The full lips are held for a dash of red pigment, the placid front is presented for a delicate penciling of the brows.

The dress for her who takes the post of a princess is a silken *sampot* pleated in classic folds and held with a jewel in front, its length falling to the ankles. The heavy hand-made *sampot* of the old convention is hard to get now, and imported silks are used instead. Over chest and shoulders is hung a narrow drapery falling square and flat down the back in a long line of grace. Jewels without limit are then loaded on the childish dignity until the young maid is all a-sparkle with scintillant colour.

Tradition demands a wide collar of gems, over which are many chains of gold. Arms are circled with bracelets both above the elbows and at the wrists. Ankles also have their weight of ornament. The fingers, curving in semblance of flower petals, sparkle as with dew in sunlight.

But the headdress works magic. Poised on top the young head, the whole figure takes on a greater beauty, a deeper meaning. Maids dressed like this have ever been fair to look upon, and artists wrought their images into the walls of the highest temples, and called them sacred dancers, or better, divine wives.

To the audience, the girls before them are the heroines of old tales loved and never too often told. The dress of the chief dancer reveals the character she plays and each dance has its special roles. The audience seeks no innovation; it knows in advance each movement of the coming dance on the appearance of the principals. Its delight is not in surprise of novelty, but in living again the old tradition, in happily musing on the spirit of the ages animate in their own people.

The dance is always a drama, always the portrayal of a plot. The centuries pass without alteration of plot or costume, and therein lies the calm delight of the women ruminatingly chewing betel and gazing on the actors.

At the Bungalow is less excitement than among the audience already gathered at the Cruciform Terrace far within the park of Angkor Vat. The foreigners cannot know what is before them.

Under the bright lights, people are sitting at little tables slowly sipping coffee, although the boy who passes the bottles of liqueurs knows the sweet impatience that is being excited down the road.

Someone at last arises, says it is time to see the dance that "has been arranged for us, just as it was arranged for General Joffre when he visited Angkor," and with amiable complaisance all arise and drift out upon the road. Steps quicken on seeing lights down the way and twinkling flashes crossing the causeway over the moat.

An army bearing torches, an army of little brown boys, some with cotton jackets, some without, all crowding the steps and the platform. Their soft chatter is like that of birds, but their prankishness like that of boys. On seeing the foreigners arrive each boy dresses his figure, makes serious his face, for he too has a part in the great tradition, a responsibility.

Each boy grasps his burning torch with greater tension, the mass resolves itself into two flaming rows, and progresses slowly over the concourse, following the line of *Naga's* long stone body, keeping their eyes on the feet of those strange beings who wear shoes and must in consequence be infirm of step and needing light lest they fall.

On either side of the causeway the lake-like waters; above, the tropic heavens with strange-placed constellations; before, the dominating outline of Angkor Vat. Sounding over the murmur of the eager little torch-bearers rings the cry of night-birds and the whistling call of little monkeys in distant trees. And clouding deliciously the evening air is the pungent savour of the incense-yielding torches.

Prince and Princess Saluting Before the Dance — The fingers bend backwards like long white petals of the lotus separated by the evening breeze.

Steps are reached, the steps which mount to the passage which pierces the great enclosing wall. The chivalrous boys run softly ahead to light the danger, tapping each step with torches which marvellously drop thereon discs of flame, a fire of illumination, that the foot of the stranger may not fail.

Up the perilous steps slanted by centuries of passing feet, through the bat-haunted gallery, and down steps again to the open. A quarter mile more across the park for acquaintance with the illumined night, *Naga* trailing like a balustrade on either side the long concourse and thrusting upward his many-headed fan.

The Cruciform Terrace is already filled with a quiet audience vibrating expectancy, yet room is rapidly made in the choicest place that visitors may have the best. The right arm of the cross contains the orchestra of fine-singing strings and time-beating tom-toms; the left arm is completely filled with women standing and crowding to shield the dancers who have been dressed and ready for hours. The centre is cleared, and the brown torch-bearers are seated in an arc of lights as an entourage. Above, scarce seen, like a shadowy cloud in the heavens, the dominating protection of the great Khmer temple.

A hush, the sound of tinkling bells and strings, more insistent beatings of the drums, then an arresting stir among the crowd of women and a distant glistening of jewel-dressed heads moving with decision.

Eight dancers advance through the retiring crowd of women to the centre of the terrace, four princes, four princesses. They come with high rhythmic tread, a dramatic pause between each step, a pose almost, as each lifted foot throws the weight. And the magic feet are bare and rest flexile on the pavement, strong to keep faith with balance. Heads are high and steady, arms and body undulate and sparkling eyes tell of nerves alert, though the faces are the serious moon-like faces of children.

The *première* princess is gorgeous in silks and jewels and high, pointed headdress. A tassel woven with fragrant jasmine flowers adds piquancy as it falls beside the rounded cheek. She is buoyant with knowledge of her beauty and skill. She leads her line to the front. She plants firmly an able foot tinkling with bangles; she poises and sways her supple body and waving arms, she sets firmly the head and poses as the *Tevadas* danced before the Khmer kings ten centuries ago. She is the dancer of the bas-reliefs made flesh, the carving made alive, repeating the incredible postures with the plasticity of life.

In her face rest sobriety and aloofness as she looks far out into the dark as to some high, impalpable audience for whom she dances.

Equally beautiful with her lovely head are her marvellous hands. Rounded and firm are the arms like waving branches or swaying like *Naga* himself; but the hands of the Cambodian dancer are like no others. The fingers bend backward like long white petals of the lotus separated by the evening breeze and turn in strange and eloquent grace. Raised high, posed low, or undulating on the level of the shoulder, hands and arms ever sway as the wind of dawn sways the orchids hanging in the trees of the jungle.

No less elegant is the leader of the line of princes. Only in dress does he differ from the princess, but in the progress of the drama his role is apparent. With play and interplay the two lines of dancers hold the happy attention of the wide-eyed torchbearers, of the crowd of men around the musicians, and the beaming women.

Then on the stage appears a new figure, one which thrills deliciously even those who know him well. He is the King of the Giants and his coming means an interference with the love-story of Prince and Princess which has progressed with grace. There is a hush as the Giant advances. At sight of his terrifying mask the torch-bearers grip tight the lights. He comes slowly, with measured step, but elastic, a malignant presence, puissant, magnetic. He throws his head quickly as though looking where to strike, he moves in flashes with cruelty present in every nervous movement. He stands a moment with knees bent outward and heels off the ground, and defies the world — evil made flesh yet beautiful as a god.

If his entrance seems a challenge, the *pas seul** which follows justifies his confidence. Thrills of cruel joy pass over his body. He is animated by spasms of wicked triumph and his muscles stiffen as by repeated electric shocks. With no word spoken, with no aids of the theatre, this lone dancer in the jungle night strikes deep into human emotions.

The other dancers resume and the thread of drama continues. The Giant steps aside and glowers. At a lovely moment when the Prince is claiming his Princess from her swaying companions, the evil one thrusts forward an agile arm and seizes her, possesses her.

He thrills with the triumph of it and with the humiliation of the Prince. From that moment he dances with increased inspiration. Holding the captive lady with one hand he places his steeled body between her and her lover, and in a series of thrusts and parryings defends his stolen quarry. Almost the audience can see blue flames around the magnetic figure. For long he is victor while a huddling crowd of lesser princes and princesses look on confounded.

The Prince is vested with the virtues; he is bound to win. After long aggression and tireless thrusts, he catches the King of the Giants in a weak moment and draws from him the tender prey.

The Giant is vanquished, yes, but he scorns his failure until it appears as a triumph. Pride and insolence animate his step and bearing. Thus holding himself he first dominates the audience, then passes proudly out of sight.

The reunited lovers end the dance by leading in a joyful series the swaying lines of slender maids. It is incomparably beautiful. And the setting for so simple a drama before so simple a people is of a grandeur indescribable.

The dance ends. The weird orchestra stops its tinklings, the fifty brown torchères fly down the long way to brighten the path for the foreigners who are the first to troop away.

In the sweet-scented dark the causeway is animate with the village audience making no sound louder than the sibilant whisper of bare feet

---

* A French term for a dance presentation for one person.

slipping over the smooth stone paving. Under the heavy trees by the roadside the bullock carts wait to carry home the humble dancers.

And over all brood the terrifying, inspiring towers of the Sanctuary.

Chapter VIII

A SURVEY

Loafing, dreaming, prowling in Angkor Vat, begets a dread of leaving it. But down the long forest road are wonders and wonders in this enchanted land of the mysterious Khmer.

Procrastination wraps a delaying mesh about one. We are told that the Vat, magnificent as are its proportions, is but a single temple outside a city of temples, and that city we have not yet approached. Shameful delay! But the Vat is a sorcerer without the gate and casts such a spell that one loses desire for all else.

We arose one morning to the tinkling of soft bells, velvety bells of wood. The sound came from under the trees beside the moat. Elephants! Elephants caparisoned for riding, elephants awaiting one's pleasure. Wonderful!

But that is the way at Angkor. You arrive at night a humble tourist, you wake in the morning a monarch, an Eastern potentate, with elephants lounging in the offing, tinkling their xylophonic bells.

And the elephants took the procrastinator to the walled city of Angkor Thom.

Let him who feeds peanuts at the "zoo" to languid elephants think not that he knows the animal. Not until she is mounted does my elephant's sympathetic plastic character reveal itself. With the first padding of her soft steps she tells her rider to be comfortable and unafraid. With the flapping of her gentle ears she reassures that she listens to human desires, and the restlessness of her trunk declares her eagerness to serve.

Only a poet could have shown me so many beauties of the forest, as we progressed to the royal city of Angkor Thom. She showed the blossoms high on the trees, she sniffed voluptuously the heavy perfumes, she swung a rhythmic step at the call of birds, and she halted that a scattering troupe of little grey apes might be better seen. At the end of half a mile we were *en rapport*, and I was taking her view of jungle life and thinking on her ancestors. The mystic powerful race of Khmers arose, wrought marvels, and passed away. Elephants were there when they came, they served the conquering race, then when the last troops of Khmers had vanished like Rishis or *Apsaras* in the sky, the elephant still remained faithful to the land, for he is its real possessor throughout the centuries.

Down the forest road a gate. We had come to the entrance of Angkor Thom. Effie stopped. The silent, small mahout who sat her head was but a summer fly in her esteem and mine. She stopped without his signal, that I might compass the thought of the early builders.

Through the verdure is seen the great, forbidding wall of the city, which extends in a square of about eight miles around.

Following the wall is a moat as at Angkor Vat, a moat that has a width of more than three hundred feet. Figures are dry matter, but without them how realize the size of things not seen — and one may see the length of moat and wall only at great pains. Five gates only make points of entry through the wall, gates such as that before me which is a superb tower pierced by a passage with pointed arch. The gate is a massive edifice, a marvel of strange grandeur, and by its character declares the power and riches of the city it protected.

Above the narrow passage is a mammoth Brahmanic head, probably Civa, above this a heavy tower. To right and to left of the opening, are decorative elephants' heads, their long trunks touching the ground, and above them other mammoth heads or masks in profile. All too strange, too impressive, too unaccustomed to understand at once, just as it is with all choice things and recondite.

We step slowly nearer and within the gate. On either hand are small chambers reached by steps, open and secure. Perhaps for the guard. In other days great wooden doors swung here and blocked the way at night or in times of danger, but now all is open, and where kings' pageants once passed the quiet peasants slip through, or, after dark, the hunting animals of the jungle.

Straight, straight from south to north goes our road, and if one went far enough one would reach the north gate on the opposite side of the square which walls Angkor Thom. Or, on reaching the centre one might turn to right, or turn to left, and find at equal distances the eastern and the western gate. The symmetry of this big plan is altered in one regard; a second gate is placed in the eastern wall, north of the central one. The reason for its placing cannot be told at this point, but later, when we know better the royal uses of this city of the king.

We are within the walls. Here is the ancient city, the capital of a kingdom of such fabulous wealth that it ranked in Asia as Golconda in Europe. It was a byword. Gold flamed and flashed to right and to left, not only on the persons of the rich who apparently considered metal ornaments a sufficient costume, but it was lavishly used on royal edifices and to make more glorious a glorious god, Brahma, Civa, or Vishnu.

While Effie swung me down the forest way with tall, tall trees far overhead, I mused on the writings of the emotional Zhou Daguan, who came on a mission from his Chinese emperor in 1295. Gold and jewels so dazzled his eyes and occupied his mind that his memoirs indicate a

Chapter VIII: A Survey 117

In the Center of the Great Design Sits a Four-armed Deity, Vishnu of God-like Calm, and the Men Fall Both Ways from This Point

weakness for the marvellous wealth he saw displayed. He tells of a tower of gold on the big temple of the Bayon which occupies the exact centre of the square which is Angkor Thom. This may have been gilded, or his language may have flowered too much. He tells of statues of gold, of gold window frames where the king was wont to show himself. That is a conception for a royal architect, to frame in gold the monarch who steps forward to let the multitudes view him.

The long delight of swaying through the tallest forest in the world — or so it seems — carries one to the most terrifying, the most mysterious of ruined temples. It is the great, the cruel pile of the Bayon.

We stand before it stunned. It is like nothing else in any land. Its outer terraces one absorbs in one quick glance, things with which one is familiar, such as steps, columned verandas, low walls. But rising above in domination are terrible grey towers faced on four sides with the gigantic face of Civa. A crowd of powerful gods! Fifty or more of these visaged towers have met together to decide the fates of men. The faces are enigmatic, powerful, heroic as fate is heroic, and relentless. What a conception! Fifty sentient towers shouldering one another in implacable consultation. It is not possible for our minds to know the soul of the great edifice. Man must have built it — even though one is willing now to accept the peasant's belief that the gods were its builders. But why should man erect a building so awesome, so cruel, so terrifying! The clergy of that strange race — ah, yes, it was no doubt by means of the Bayon that the clergy implanted the fear of God in the hearts of a public which must shower gold upon them and the temples.

The ruined estate of the Bayon but increases the terror of the place. The gods lean, and seem to reel in horrid mirth at the pains they bring upon the worshippers from whom they exact adoration and tribute. The stones set up without mortar strain apart and alter the expressions on the great masks, and one can believe all the hideous legends of Civa, most active of the Brahmanic Trimurti, he to whom the Bayon is dedicated.

My new friend, the elephant, sighs heavily. She shifts a foot softly,

The Great Army of the Khmers Passes in Review

and wisely carries me away, for we are taking today only a *coup d'œil** of Angkor Thom and its monuments.

It is the city where the powerful Khmer rulers chose to live from about 800 A.D. During the centuries of Europe's darkest of dark centuries Angkor flamed with a brilliant civilization. Rather an interesting fact on which to ponder while padding through this city of marvels, especially when coupled with the European's self-complacency in Asia.

The road turns about the Bayon letting three sides be well seen. Sun and shadow play tricks on the mammoth stone faces. At this distance they look more benign, the wide full lips seem to smile — but enigmatically, with an unfathomable depth of mental reservations. Nowhere in the world does mutual race understanding seem so impossible as before the great temple of the Bayon, built under two kings, Indravarman and Yasovarman about 889. An art expresses a people's soul. A soul that could be thus expressed is not one that the West could understand. However, there is the stern lovable Vat built by these same people two or three hundred years later.

We are still going North, but in passing the Bayon we pass the very centre of the walled square in which the city is built. Wonderfully exact, these old surveyors, with almost never an eccentricity. We are approaching a place of marvels, a place where one can let fly the imagination and reconstruct the life led here many centuries ago.

For want of a better name we will call it the public square, misfit as that really is. Here the forest desists. That is a curious part of it. For scores of miles, hundreds of miles, the heavy forest is like a green sea. Here it stops. Here is greensward, shallow pools, and clear space. But here, too, are such ruins as suggest the old grandeur of the place, and you wonder if it is not respect for these that has kept a devouring jungle from trespass. It has wrought its ruin amongst the buildings but it has left untouched this public square where armies marched, where ambassadors paraded, where athletes contended, and where kings were borne aloft for multitudes to see.

*French term meaning a quick look.

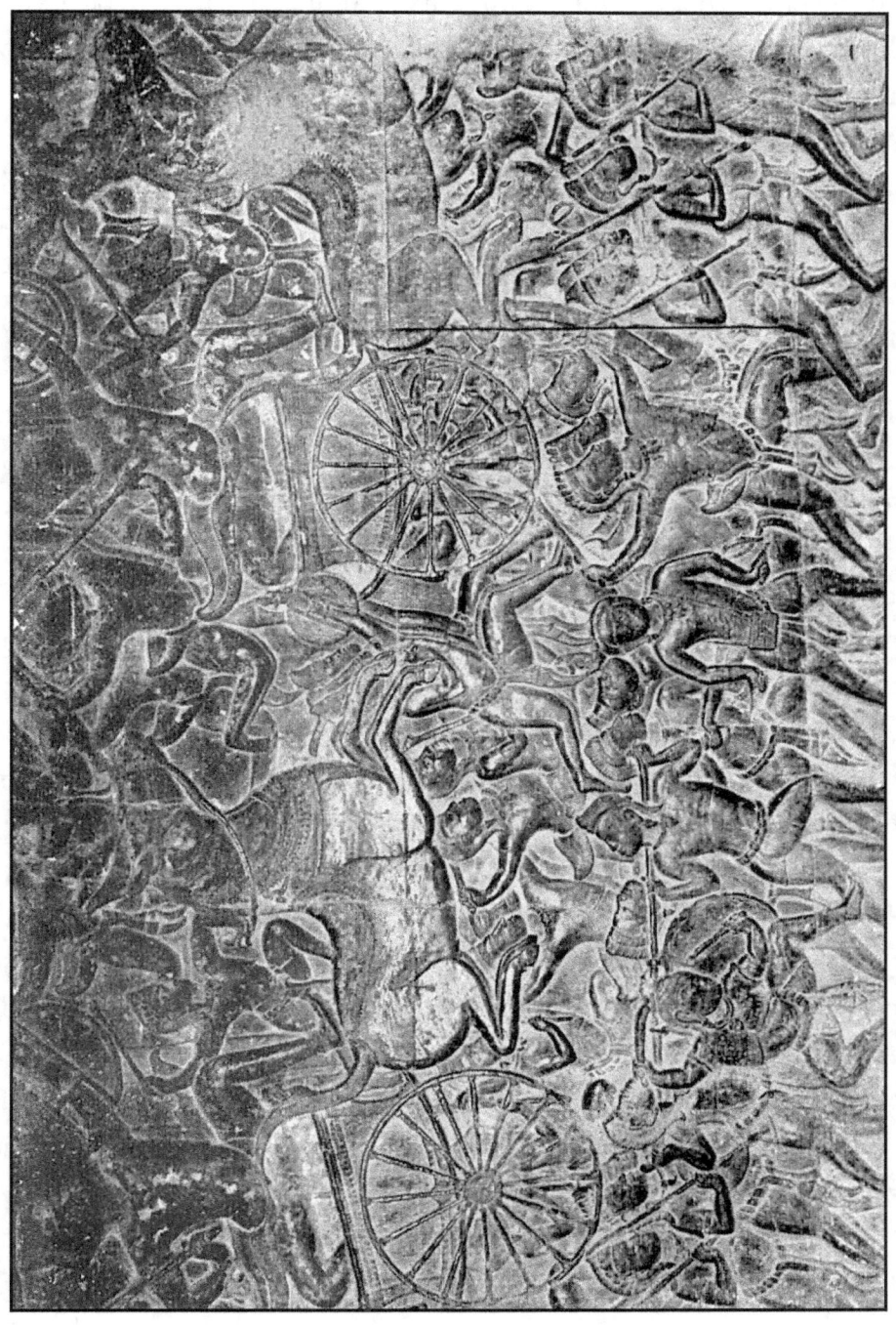

Much Space of the Bas-reliefs is Taken Up with Combats of the Gods of a Fierce and Complicated Nature

To proceed in order I glanced to the left where tumbled stones declare the entry to a distant temple, the Baphuon, saving a closer view for a lesser day. This especial tour was only for skimming the surface, for learning the general ensemble.

We paused a moment. Effie evidently wished me to look down the far length of the open public square, which is an oblong. Innumerable buildings were retiring within the forest all along the right side, before them those lovely mirrors, the grass-set pools, in which white herons plumed themselves and meditatively fed. But on the left was the Terrace.

No one had told me of the terraces. How can one who has seen them talk of aught else? We moved on and I saw their wondrous detail, we moved further and their great length still reached into the distance.

Before them is the foreground of greensward, rising from this a wall of sculptured figures, which wall sustains a terrace of which the forest trees have made an entrancing park. Such in brief is the long scene, but one cannot be brief in visiting it. It is one of the most alluring sights of Angkor, one of the dream-places where one must come again and again and live in imagination the life that made brilliant the court of the powerful Khmers from the ninth century to the thirteenth when their star set.

In the centre of the long face of the Terrace, which has a length of nearly twelve hundred feet, is placed a superb approach, steps leading from the public square up to the level above, an approach made magnificent by three elephant heads on either side, seeming, with their hidden backs, to sustain the weight above them. On the perrons of the steps the challenging lion greeted the arrival of those who mounted, and the *Naga*-parapet reared its heads above.

And this great terrace approach is not only in the centre of its architectural group of the structure called the Phimean-Akas, but with beautiful harmony it also forms the terminus of a long, straight way from the eastern wall of the city.

Chapter VIII: A Survey 123

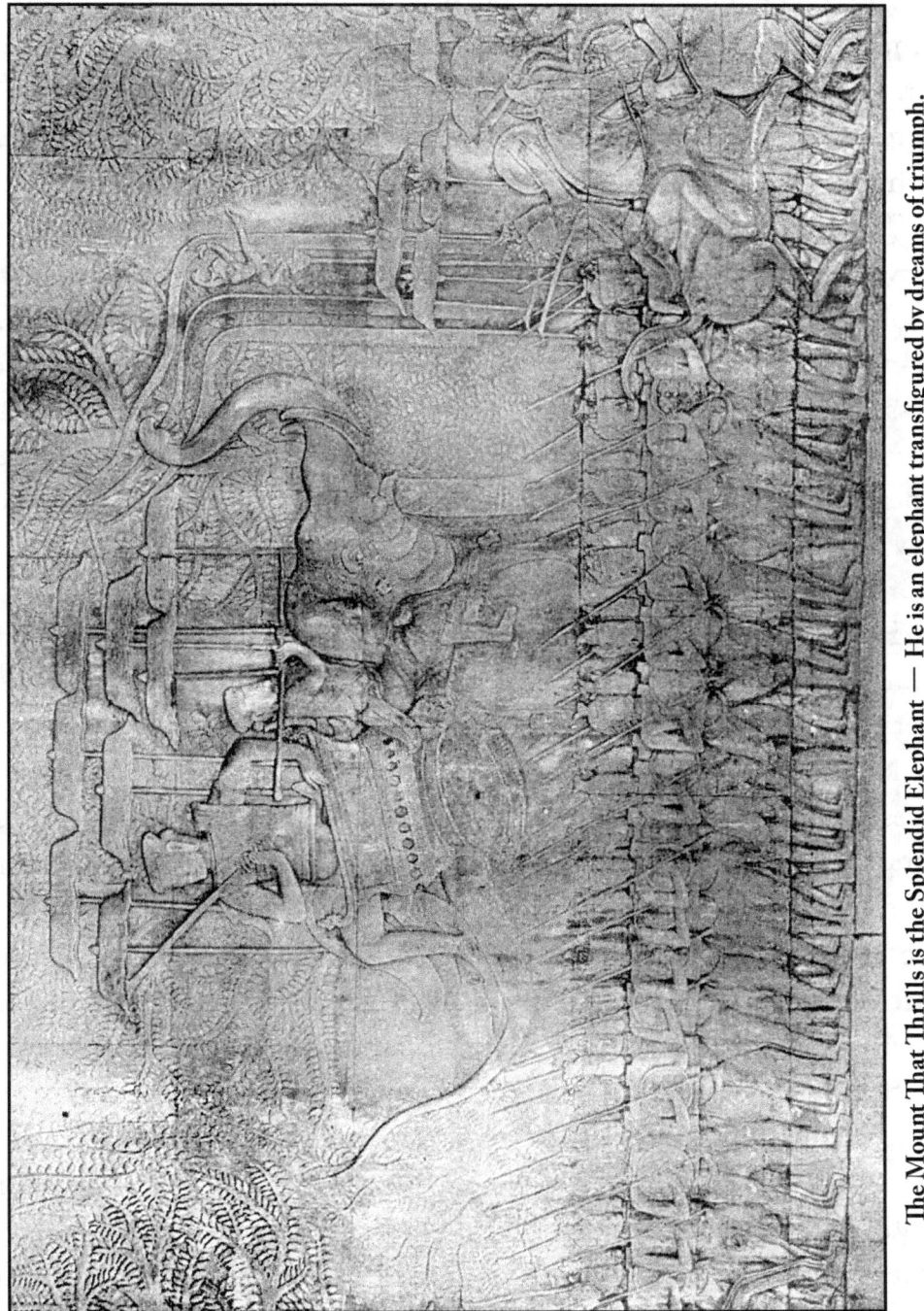

The Mount That Thrills is the Splendid Elephant — He is an elephant transfigured by dreams of triumph.

A closer view of the terrace carvings, of the sections devoted to the succeeding types of caryatides, of the several approaches, all that was for another day. The sentient grey mass under me turned firmly away to the right. We passed between the shallow pools flecked with white herons and re-entered the jungle at right angles between crumbling towers which form a puzzling group.

The love for geometric exactness had laid out the road without a curve. In other days it was crowded with a restless population of a million souls. Now it is deserted but for an occasional group of workers with a bullock-cart. Then it was bordered with buildings of every sort necessary to civilization, houses, shops, shrines. Now the jungle owns all but the roadway and would soon own that also but for the vigilance of the French-directed band of foresters. Penetrate where you will the heavy vegetation, and there you find the tiles of a house, the wall of a minor temple, for all space was occupied.

Far down the way under giant trees the road narrows to a pointed opening in a tower. We are coming to the Gate of Victory in the city's eastern wall.

Not strikingly different from the southern gate, it yet has a deep interest all its own. It is — barring distance — directly in front of the central approach to the great Terrace. It is through this eastern gate that all great entries were made, and from here ambassadors and visiting princes proceeded without deviation to the presence of the king, whose palace of reception was the centre of the Terrace. Behind him were the bulwarks of the palace.

Softly we swayed through the gateway, noting the pointed arch overhead, the beautifully finished rooms for the guard inside, and then we emerged on the side of the moat to find a marvel — the Bridge of Giants which spans the moat. With that rare considerateness which marked the instinct of my Effie she neither swerved nor slowed until she had trod the whole length of the absorbing viaduct, then turning with deliberation she stopped with face toward the bewildering sight to let me make its wonders mine forever.

Had I been a Cham ambassador in the tenth century coming before the great enemy king on a mission of delicate and precarious intent, my heart would have failed at this entrance to the powerful Khmer city. The bridge rears to the visitor a mammoth fan of *Naga's* heads, one on the right hand, one on the left, which seems at this point a menace and not a graceful welcome.

Lest *Naga* falter, the polycephalous serpent is upheld by a gigantic figure, powerful and many-headed. From his hands the long, serpent body trails across the laps of great figures, all clasping it in their arms, until the great gate through the wall is reached. One line of the powerful stone figures, that on the left, wears the *mukuta* on the head below which the great face smiles with a certain calm benignity. These are the demi-gods, the *Devas*. The other line of men is forbidding, implacable, a row of giants fit for fairy tales. These are the demons, the *Asuras*.

I look to where the serpent and the double file of heroic figures end in the Gate. High over its opening stares the implacable mask of Civa, terrifying in the beauty of its carving, in its mystery, and in its prodigious size. My knees grew weak as though I, too, would risk torture and death were I to enter the city of the warrior king.

Many a faint-hearted leader must once have turned back at such a menace, such assurance of power, of implacable vindictiveness.

While lost in excited thought, I was slowly wafted over the Bridge of Giants, through the great arch, and on into the healing balm of forest perfume and forest scenes, all on the homeward way. Effie was tired and so was I.

But when the public square was reached again, of her own accord she stepped softly over the greensward to the central approach of the long terrace and stopping before the group of three supporting elephants she waved her flexile trunk before the end of theirs. She was pointing me out a beauty. I beheld in each curling stone trunk a languid bunch of lotus blooms, heavy with their own beauty and with the weight of water from which they had just been lifted. And thus she showed me her race as a race of poets.

She raised high her trunk, and backed away from the presence of avatars revered.

Chapter IX

THE BAYON

Such is the first review of Angkor Thom, the royal city, a walled square crossed with a road from the centre of the south wall to the centre of the north wall, a similar road from east to west, both interrupted by the great Bayon which occupies a point in the exact centre of the city.

The Bayon is the grandest and the oldest of the monuments within the royal city's walls. From the back of my elephant as we passed it on the day of general survey, I determined to attack it. An inspiring motto is to do what you are afraid to do. I was afraid of the Bayon.

On analyzing that fear I learned that it was the temple's most important god of whom I stood in awe, the terrible Civa. To declare the cruelty and majesty and power of the Trimurti the Bayon was built, but of the three Civa most declares himself.

It is all very well to say that the central thought of the Brahmanic religion is one god, one Universal Spirit, but when one takes a step farther, a thousand deities arise to perplex maturest counsel. To begin with there is Brahm, which typifies the universal spirit. From this proceeds the triple expression of that spirit, Brahma the creator, Vishnu the preserver, Civa the destroyer. Lest a tripping tongue use the word trinity, set them down as the Trimurti.

All this seems simple enough — a great head with three expressions of spirit power. But one flounders in the mass of attributes given to the members of the Trimurti. Brahma, for whom the religion is named, slips modestly into the background. He even resigns his province of creator, and Civa takes it, Civa, the acquisitive, who dresses himself with a thousand other attributes, most of them singularly lacking in charm.

He creates, but for the pure joy of destroying. He is nature in all her creative forms, but as the great destroyer he kills what he creates. Altogether, an unpleasant combination. He makes man, but he tortures him with frightful ingenuity. His voice shrieks in the storm as he gleefully drowns babies in the flood or pierces a mother's heart with the lightning proceeding from his vicious eyes. He burns man with the sun, poisons him with serpents, rends him with wild beasts. Then he replaces the battered dead with more men that he may have more to torture. He inspires enemies to wage war that he may glory in bloodshed, he kills grain that crops may fail and men may know famine.

At least this is what priests have made of him. His attributes are born of the jealous fears of priests, and the more thoroughly afraid of him the people become, the more implacable is he represented.

It is easy to see the reason for creating a god so horrible. Angkor's king was a man most powerful, rich beyond any on earth, beautiful in princely symmetry, wise and fearless. He was both worshipful and worshipped. His power was supreme. According to Khmer belief the king was half a god and might even bear the name of a god.

With sinister envy the high priests noted all of this, and feared for their own power. Then they invented a conception of Civa which would cause even the brilliant warrior king to feel there is a power higher than his, a force he would do well to placate lest he agonize and die.

With king and people well subdued by fear of Civa, the priests

Chapter IX: The Bayon

The Figure is That of Vishnuloka the King — He is seated on a throne above his generals to whom he is giving orders for one of the great Khmer conflicts.

could easily extort money and slaves with which to build the greatest temple in which to celebrate the terrible god. This temple would ever serve as visible reminder to the king and all his people of the power of Civa and the virtue of his priests who might soothe for them the deity in his worst hours of dire rage.

With what magnificent, insolent assurance they chose their site for the temple of fear, the exact centre of the royal city with all roads from the city's gates leading to it, and the royal residence close by!

It was in the ninth century that the Bayon was built, about four centuries earlier than Angkor Vat.* This was told me by one of the bonzes who was worshipping before a great Buddha who meditates just across the road from the Bayon. The yellow bonzes intrigued me. The priests I had known were not dressed like the flowers of the nasturtium. With their placid faces, their smooth, bare throats, these were like young living Buddhas. Their amber silks fluttered as they walked on like big yellow butterflies, and I followed them entranced.

Their barefoot tread was noiseless, they spoke never a word, but the pair of them stepped nimbly over tumbled stones and proceeded straight to the terrible Bayon. They gave courage, with their swinging shoulders and half smiling faces, and led me on until I forgot the fifty awesome towers with their watchful faces. Not that the bonzes knew I followed or relied on them any more than a pair of yellow butterflies know when a child is led on.

Up the steps to the first terrace. Here the sun shone on rows of square columns making long lines before long walls of carved scenes. And here the carvings stopped me wide-eyed, open-mouthed. Not like those of my first love, Angkor Vat; no, those are far more gracious and lovely, of more sophisticated art, but these hold one by their quality of directness. They do not lure by elegant suggestions of aristocracy among men and exclusiveness among gods, but by direct simplicity. They have

---

* Ed. Note: From this point forward, the author reports incorrect dates for many temples, especially the Bayon, Prah Khan and others of King Jayavarman VII, who reigned circa 1181-1215 CE. The confusion arose because scholars—noting the condition of Angkor Wat, built by King Suryavarman II in the early 12th century —assumed that more devestated temples were older. In fact, later construction techniques were inferior leading to accelerated disintegration and this miscalculation.

Chapter IX: The Bayon 131

The Cruciform Terrace, Angkor Vat — Lit by torches of bamboo leaves and incense with the scarce seen Khmer temple in the background, this was the stage of the dancers.

homely human things to tell and they tell them without affectation.

There are thousands of feet of these chiselled pictures on the walls of the Bayon, and all form a wonderfully illuminating book on the life of the ancient Khmers. Real books which once existed, exist no more. Archeologists, historians, excavators know the Khmers wrote books, for the Chinese records tell of them, but in the tropics nature obliterates all perishable works of man. The halls of the Bayon hold the records in chiselled pictures.

Crude but strong, these pictures tell us of the life among the common people. The fact of such life being recorded on a temple accents the importance to the church of the lower classes. Angkor Thom's ancient population is estimated at a million. A large half of those, at least, must have been slaves and artisans, to judge by the stupendous constructions, and another large body the soldiery. Both these classes are lavishly depicted in this temple of a warlike and artistic race.

Does not everyone spring with delight upon the representation of a cockfight? Fancy the smiles of the ages which reward the ghost of the little dark artist whose love of sport led him to chisel this childish panel on the wall of Civa's temple. Civa is clean forgot when peering to see if the cocks wear metal spurs.

Above are galleries full of soldiers, rowed by a line of oarsmen, each working his spatulate blade with precision, while fish in the sea flee from the dangerous ship only to meet death in the jaws of a crocodile.

Pure decoration among the Khmers reached a delicious realm of balance and fertile invention. Pure pictorial art is crude but equally fertile. If one gallop tourist-like the scenes pass the eye like a cinema, picture after picture; but students who love these strange ruins dissect them as a botanist a flower and make illuminating deductions as to the accessories of life. They sort out from minute scenes each detail and give them to us in assorted groups.

Thus we learn the forms of a past civilization and glow with delight at drawing parallels, and at finding the lost Khmer not a savage but a soul

The Head of the Serpent is Like *Naga's*, Polycephalous, and the Giant
Who Holds It Is Also Many Headed

kin of the Greeks and Romans. There is pottery, for instance, with shapes as full of beauty as a Pompeian vase. There are barques and barges in which lovely ladies float upon the shaded rivers, and one wonders if Cleopatra floated in greater elegance. Boats are shown in mobile lines of *Naga* with the heads lifted up at the prow. Or they are canopied with embroidered awnings and cushions. It is discovered through the carvings that chariots and harnessings were of bronze ornamented with carvings and jewels, that exquisite litters, chaises a porteurs, were constructed for the portage of high caste ladies, that the king's howdah was the acme of ornamentation. A book might be written on headdresses alone, for men and women, so varied and so elaborate is this form of significant decoration.

At first blush the costume of the ancient race seems sketchy, a skirt at most, a twist of rope, or a floating scarf-end. But the witchery of the student has taught us many piquant things about the costume, and what appears to be a twist or a stiff tab is the elegant silk *sampot*, or sarong, heavy with gold thread and ingeniously draped.

Far down the gallery the yellow bonzes are eluding me. While I tarry with the ancient Khmers they seek Civa's holy-of-holies. I run down the long way and see them round an angle. At the next opening in the wall I turn within to find the fluttering yellow. But all is grey sandstone passages and narrow rooms.

In one view of it the Bayon is a pyramid of three grades. I have been idling in the gallery of the first grade, with its many porches and towers, its grand entrance facing east, its courtyard with two small "libraries," and now mount to the second gallery. The plan of Angkor Vat teaches one the general plan, but the Bayon was built first; its architects were learning. The simplicity of the Vat was only attained after other plans had proved less splendid. The Bayon lacks that simplicity. Perhaps the wish was to mystify, to confuse. Fear grows in an atmosphere of mystery and confusion.

Contracted chambers make one wonder for what ceremony they were made, dark corridors bring thoughts of the fright which must have seized the guilty who came to the temple for absolution or penance. The levels are not all the same, the foot stumbles, and one longs for light.

It is found in the courtyard or cloisters, the space left between the buildings of one gallery and the surbase of that which rises to the next higher.

Ruin is everywhere, and the great stones are thrown down as though in rage. They probably were. This great monument was built by slaves at terrible cost to their class. Thousands were maimed in the building, thousands more were killed in raising the great stones, and the quarries of stone twenty miles away also took their toll.

Slaves sweated and ached before relentless masters, and not all of them were mere hewers of stone. The chisellers were among them. Notwithstanding the enormous birth rate of the lower classes more slaves were needed, and these were supplied by the captives of the increasing wars of this warrior nation. Among them were many who could guide a chisel to sketch the endless bas-reliefs of the Bayon. The cruelty of slave drivers is proverbial. Suffering was the portion of Angkor's builders, and in the season of fevers their depleted strength allowed them to die by hundreds.

Fancy them one day liberated albeit by a foe. What then but a mad riot of destruction could satisfy their lust of revenge? When Angkor fell to the conquering enemy, the men who had built it were the first to destroy it. The towers they and their forbears had bled to build, it was their angry joy to tear down.

One thinks of all phases of destruction up on the high terrace from which rises the central mass in magnificent ruin. In the centre of that mass is the holy-of-holies, the impregnable chamber wherein the spirit of Civa meditates, not the terrible destroying Civa, but his other self which is the highest type of aesthete* and sits for æons in contemplation in the calm centre of infinite peace.

It is a stupendous and appealing thought, that of the Khmer architects, to build a tiny central chamber as God's abode, a place so

---

* An English term for; 1. One who cultivates an unusually high sensitivity to beauty, as in art or nature. 2. One whose pursuit and admiration of beauty is regarded as excessive or affected.

small that he must be alone, and then to surround it with squares, ever descending, ever enlarging, until a space has been enclosed that would hold enough of priests, of guards, of worshippers. The basilica of the Christian seems with its vast chamber to offer no sacred refuge to the Great Spirit visiting his people.

It is here on this upper gallery that one sees again the towers of the giant faces. Zhou Daguan, in telling of the wonders of the great, rich city to which he was sent as ambassador from China in 1295, declares the Bayon had a tower of gold. I, after a quiet hour alone in company with these strange uplifted heads, am ready to believe yet more wonderful things. As shadows of the jungle fall upon them at the sunset time of shifting values, one can well believe them sentient. The great faces take on expressions which pass wave-like as anger passes, or as a smile flits. As twilight threatens they grow grave and sinister, the towers even seem to sway nearer one another in understanding and conference.

What manner of thoughts do the great lips utter when night has really come and the great huddling crowd is left alone? It is the natives who say they hear the whisperings but can never catch a word.

It is all too overpowering. I have studied the plan of the central mass, the third plane, the holy-of-holies in its intricate stronghold, and am not inspired to enter its terrifying confusion. Rather would I follow the yellow bonzes, who with bare feet are lightly springing toward the stair which leads to wide open spaces below.

I hear voices in a side-chamber of the entrance, and look within. Into the shadow of the room Blake is throwing the bull's-eye light of his electric torch and is saying disappointedly to the journalists from Nice, "I've looked everywhere for something off-colour in these carvings and I can't find a thing. Those Khmers must have been totally without a sense of humour."

I fled. And thus I came upon the silent, pleasant bonzes worshipping before a statue of Vishnu. Yet they are Buddhists. I like it, and take it that the pure in heart find God in everything.

Standing in a gallery of the Bayon's first story the vista reaches through the columned way across the green to an enormous Buddha. Looking the opposite way the same thing is seen. Puzzling they are, these Buddhas placed in line with the gallery of the Brahmanic temple, until one remembers that two religions flourished together in the great days of this nation. Both came from the westward, but Buddhism's greatest development came latest and the days of its greatest influence were the days when decadence was already nibbling at the strength of the Khmer.

Brahmanism suited the all-conquering people of Cambodia. Situated as they were on a peninsula, with the war-like Chams to east of them in Annam and the resolute Thais to westward in the land of Siam, they must conquer or die. It is unsupposable that a country so famous for fabulous wealth should be let alone by envious neighbours. So there were always wars of resistance and wars for conquest.

The life of Gautama Buddha on earth was as pacific as that of the Nazarene, and the religion he left was the same. When the Khmers elevated it above Brahmanism they put to sleep their war-like instincts.

My yellow bonzes looked to me more interesting than ever. I followed them down the homeward road wondering at the strange changes of Angkor, The native boy-children now go to the bonzeries like young acolytes, for education. They make them passive, sweet tempered, content. What have our people done for youth that is better than this?

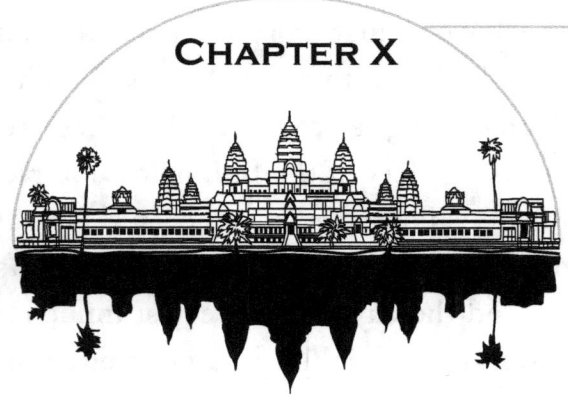

Chapter X

ANIMALS

Sometimes it seems as though Angkor ruined were more powerful to thrill, more subtle to charm than Angkor in its brilliant perfection could have been. A million human beings swarmed the royal city, soldiers with their insistent presence, slave workers as numerous as ants, priests, acolytes and guards at the holy temples. All was movement, colour and noise.

Now all is silence, except for nature's symphonic sounds; all is solitude, except for the peasants and the saffron bonzes; all buildings once gilded and brightly painted are low in colour tones, the brown and grey of stone. The dreamer could ill dream, in those days of gorgeous accomplishment, but now everything conduces to fantastic reverie. With colour subordinate by time, the noblest lines become more apparent and a great insistence is noticeable on the part of all the decorative animals that the Khmers so freely mingled with their architecture. They all take prominent part in the general scheme, a part as important as these same animals take today in the forests and waters among which Angkor is set. The artists who carved them in sculpture or low relief took the native animals as models nor went farther afield for a foreign fauna.

A long list of them, a score of forms, rises in the mind at the word animal. But the figure that absorbs attention in this varied fauna of the sculptor is the splendid conception of *Naga*.

His attributes, his history, are matters to dig out of inscriptions, but his visible form carved in imperishable stone is the first detail that moves a mind staggered by its first view of the terrible beauty of the Vat.

Across the water, across the park, rise the inspired towers. But here at hand, at the edge of the shady greensward, rises the shape of grace and power, *Naga* is raising his fan-like group of seven hooded heads.

Has one ever before seen anything approaching it in architecture? To the European it is an entirely new motif. Quickly the mind flashes for a comparison. It is like a fan. What a flippant simile for a sculpture that is clutching the spirit! It is like a hand upright with curving fingertips. No, that will not do, for the far trailing body destroys the thought.

It is *Naga*. It is like nothing else. The form is the result of many centuries of legend and belief, the tangible evidence of past religion and story. It is not the fantastic creation of artist or architect, but is the symbol of a demi-god. A creature of pure decoration would never have the power to thrill as has the ever-recurring *Naga* encountered through all the Angkor ruins.

The Vat shows him superb, triumphant, lending his upright heads to welcome all who approach, and the length of his supple body to border the causeway. For hundreds of yards he extends, the way broken by approaches from the park and at each approach the heads rising with their thrilling grace.

Naga is the Great Ancestor. He is the father of the race of Khambu, which is the race of Khmers. This is the reason of his presence in all the great temples of Angkor.

Khmer history is as fantastic and elusive as the will-o'-the-wisp. Tradition and folk lore help a little and inscriptions translated by savants help a little more, but the student should always let fancy and fact be woven together that a design may be made acceptable. *Naga* was a deity who chose to envelop himself in the form of a polycephalous serpent of prodigious size. Legend tells of his roaming about the forests on the edge of the Tonlé Sap, and legend gives him attributes of great strength and charm.

After the heat of the tropic day he lay lazily on the shore of the lake, content to listen to the note of the cicada, the evensong of birds, and to watch the shimmering gold of the water. Suddenly a greater beauty than these appeared, a beauty which stirred the god to ecstasy. A daughter of Indra came out from between the palms, and stopped hesitant before a flock of white egrets standing in the water weeds of the shallows. She was exceeding lovely in the glorifying light of the setting sun, and the god felt that he had found his mate. From this marriage sprang the Khmer race. Thus *Naga*, the serpent-deity, is the father of the people who in recognition of this fact gave prominent place to his glorified reproduction at Angkor. Knowing this, could anyone call him a snake?

Again legend tells yet another story. It deals with Khambu — from whom Cambodia derives its name. This person of myth and record is thought to have lived long before the Christian era, a sort of cave man who selected his home in the land of lake and forest and was there assisted to civilization by a race of serpent-deities. In this tale it was he, the caveman, who married the daughter of *Naga*, thus founding the race of Khmers. Take whichever story you like, *Naga* must ever be recognized as the important figure.

Not only is his ensemble sculptured with splendid strength, but the chisel has lingered long in dressing him with exquisite detail. Each of his heads — of which he always has an odd number — is dressed with plumy crests of intricate carving, all uniting to form a halo around the group. In addition the sculptor places on front and back the mystic disc of puissance delicately carved. The long body is never too long for the enthusiastic chisel to decorate with a fine design such as might be on

Chapter X: Animals 141

North Gate, Angkor Thom — The gate is a massive edifice, a marvel of strange grandeur. Above the narrow passage is the mammoth Bramanic head.

the back of a living serpent. And this beauteous, triumphant creature — can there be those who reject him as a snake!

The glorification of local animals is no rare thing among the races of the world. The Hebrews had their calf, the Assyrians their bull, the Egyptians their cat. Always the worshipful animal is indigenous, taken from the fauna of the country. May it not be that the caiman, who extends thirty feet when he stretches himself in the heat after slumber, might have inspired the myth of the *Naga*? The caiman lived happily in the Tonlé Sap until the odious presence of farming man drove him into upper reaches of the Mekong. With thirty feet of snake to start with, and with artists and religionists to alter him, he might well have developed into the polycephalous sculptured myth.

After *Naga* comes the lion, Song, the insolent, impossible lion who challenges the visitor. Walk along the forest ways, lift a face from absorbed reading of a guidebook, and encounter an unsuspected Khmer lion. You are thrilled and terrorized at once. His very dignity is a menace. He stands on a stone platform at the Vat, or guards the royal stair at the Terrace of Honour; or, alas, he lies sadly among fallen stones and leaves; but never he loses his puissance. He is the expression of an idea, the visible evidence of noble attributes, and this is the secret of his never dying power.

He has been much *stylisé* by the sculptors, but even that extreme conventionalizing has not robbed him of his character. He transcends trifles. He is ever a challenge to the trespasser, a guardian of treasure, a creature of power, of insolence, of imperiousness. I, being of habitually humble mind, oft feel apologetic to him in our encounters around the ruins, particularly on the terraces, where from a height he seems to challenge and accuse me.

He never sits on loose haunches like the slithering lions at the zoo, but has his quarters subdued and ready for activity, while the straightened forelegs and upright head present a formidable front. He wears an ornamental frill about his face, and "feathers" on paws and legs,

Chapter X: Animals 143

**Bramanic Face, Bayon — The stones without mortar strain apart
and alter the expressions on the great masks.**

which leads to the suspicion that he is not all strength but is tempered by a saving vanity.

The fact that he is found in prominent place on the most magnificent buildings of the Khmer ruins leads to the conclusion that he was granted god-like attributes, after a happy fashion of those old days in Cambodia. In the bas-reliefs of the Vat he draws chariots like the lion of the Greeks.

We are uniting Angkor's sculptures with the jungle through its fauna. Where in all the Cambodian forests is found the lion? He does not exist. From whence, then, came the model for this glorious beast?

The answer is that the tiger, the native tiger, was the inspiration for this splendid sculpture. And of tigers there are plenty throughout Cambodia, Siam, Laos and all the peninsula. Both lion and tiger are cats, and if the face of the former is decorated with a mane which adds grandeur to the head, the tiger may wear one confectioned from the flora of the forest in which he roams. Without doubt the sculpture is a native tiger altered and conventionalized that he might the better decorate the work of the architect and that he might show himself as the feline apotheosis, a creature of noble character, relieved of the craftiness and stealth necessary to him who hunts by night for life's sustenance.

To see him at his best, surrounded by the mystery that becomes him, gaze long at him on the Terrace, where he stands dominant above the *Tevada* caryatides, or on the king's stair where he diminishes in size as the steps mount, that the forced perspective may increase his distance and detachment.

These two, the serpent and the lion, are given first place as sacred animals, but almost equally important in decoration is the elephant, Aryvat. In his way he too was a god, when as Ganesa he is depicted as a man with an elephant's head. But it is not the god that allures us. It is the vigorous, natural, almost human elephant of the sculptures that gives us a feeling of joy. He is best seen on the face of the heroic Elephant Terrace, that section whereon the king and courtiers sat to review the magnificent parades that undulated up from the Gate of Victory to the very feet of the monarch.

The elephants here, those that decorate the Terrace, are life size, and are neither idealized nor conventionalized nor deified. They are instead portrayed in life-like realism. The hunt in the jungle is brought vividly before our eyes, and here the elephant plays an almost human part in seizing and slaying those wild creatures classed as game.

The elegance of the royal progress is indicated by the elephants dressed with palanquins which seem to undulate along the way with languid step, quite different in deportment from those which carry hunters. And the wonder is that the large scale of this low relief carries such conviction, that its power is almost overwhelming.

If a work of art is judged by its power to evoke emotion, the Khmer sculptured elephant must be given high place.

It is evident that in life he was lord, and that a place of importance should be given him. Thus certain parts of a structure are made to rely on him for support. With a consummate skill which must have been born of love for him he is made to appear as the support of certain smaller erections such as gate towers. His body is concealed under the mass which rises elegantly above him, but forelegs and head and trunk are viewed full face. It is as though he lent his giant strength to hold upright the mounting towers. With admirable direction the heads of three elephants abreast have the three trunks extending straight to the ground, tricking the eye into counting them as supporting columns.

Garuda is the eagle of the Khmer sculptures, who pays high for his honours as a sacred bird, for he is made to depart from bird-like attributes and take a part most strenuous, albeit important. He is made to stand in rows like caryatides and support the terrace coping with outstretched wings. And he is used as a mount by the gods of the bas-reliefs in the gallery of the Vat.

A few days in the jungle show the nearness of the daring and timorous monkey. He seems as curious about mankind as mankind is about him. A reciprocal curiosity exists in lively force. No wonder the Khmers used him as myth and as decoration. Hanuman, the king of the monkeys, fills pages of the Hindu books. Likewise he and his numberless attendants fill many square yards of the reliefs on the Vat. It was inevitable that in their love for the woodland animals the artists should include these astonishing neighbours.

As for the rest of the fauna they are not given god-like attributes, so are free to be depicted as nature made them, and the result is that little rabbits, turtles and birds appear as happily as in a millefleurs tapestry. As water abounds in Cambodia fishes are frequently portrayed, but always in water — perhaps to denote it. And the pranksome alligator is not forgot as he playfully seizes a small man in his jaws.

Chapter XI

THE TERRACE OF HONOUR

No one had spoken of the Terrace of Honour. Everyone had talked of the Vat, and of the Bayon. So it came as a transcendent surprise. It is not recondite like a complicated temple; one need not have read the ten great religions of the world to understand it. It is humanly magnificent, an extent of pure beauty. And it is comfortably free from unguessable significance.

Briefly, it is a platform over a thousand feet long and about fifteen feet high, forming the eastern front of the Phimean-Akas. Its face is covered with sculptures in high relief, topped with a *Naga*-parapet, and it is broken with five grand stairways of entry, three of them in a central group.

Behind it lies the great palace enclosure of the Phimeanakas for which it would seem to have served as a royal observation gallery.

At first the great scheme is not appreciated. Nothing counts but the bewilderingly rich beauty of the Terrace carvings which stretch far down the forest way, like an ever-changing panorama.

To arrive at this prodigality of beauty one passes by the heavy, overpowering Bayon full of dire menace. There the heart sinks with melancholy. Then all at once the open public square. It is an unbelievable place. No effort has been made to erect a dominating pyramid, a shadowing edifice, but all is sunlight and shadow, green lawns, pools and forest trees as straight as masts with foliage high in air. The Terrace traces through the greenery its long line of magnificent carving, and what can one do but stare and ejaculate like a babbling fool, then subside into silence and ecstasy which last through the hours spent in inspecting this wonderland. Amidst all the beauty one is ever conscious of the trees, the gracious fragrant trees of unbelievable height which grow atop the Terrace and make one wonder if the Khmers had not thus intended, for, deplore as one does the dilapidation wrought by nature, it is impossible that the Terrace could have been as lovely denuded as it now is with its decoration of living green. It may have been hard then, as architecture can be hard in the blazing tropic sun, with the intercepting wall of the Phimeanakas rising behind it. But now all is softened by the shadows, illumined by the greenery of vine and shrub and tree.

To be orderly one begins at the beginning which in this case means the grand stair of entry in the exact centre of the Terrace. Startled eyes have, of course, already made wild excursions among powerfully beautiful carvings, but they are called to order and to follow a system. This stair presents itself as an entry in three grades, each rising above the other and receding as they rise. On the facing is a row of superb chimeras, gods of the Brahmanic tales, acting as caryatides. *Garudas* they are technically called, huge fabulous birds standing erect, bodies flattened against the wall, their powerful arms upraised to carry the *Naga*-parapet above them, the balustrade which borders all the Terrace. Also the wings of these great birds are extended upward as though with their quills they would assist in the giant task of support.

At each corner of the entrance platform rises a *Naga* head, and on each grade of the stairs sits the challenging lion, one on either hand. A

Chapter XI: The Terrace of Honour 149

The Gate of Victory, Angkor Thom — We emerged to find a marvel, the Bridge of Giants which spans the moat.

clean heart and a high courage must have belonged to him who sought audience with the king through this impressive stairway.

Now it but mounts to a welcoming forest, to delicious shade and marvellous prospect. When I came upon it Priscilla in purest white was seated at the top on a mat spread by her Hindu, and a brilliant bit of colour, restless and flashing through the trees, told of the Boston maid. Both had slaves, the maid a trio of new arrivals; Priscilla's was borrowed from the Diva, who preferred the Terrace of the Bungalow to that of Angkor Thom and iced drinks to the bitter thirst of noon.

Instead of mounting the stair I study awhile the magnificent monsters who support the Terrace. *Garuda* is the mount of Vishnu who appears on the strange beast in important moments, as seen on the bas-reliefs. A horse would seem more comfortable though possibly less distinctive. The *Garuda*, being fundamentally a bird, has the advantage of wings which make possible the aerial flights so necessary to gods, so envied of men.

Here on the Terrace he is given the head of a vulture and also the head of a tiger, the sculptor alternating the two forms; and here, too, does the *Naga* appear, but in an inconspicuous way, more like a decorative space filler than the dominating serpent of the balustrades. But the line of *Garudas* on the Terrace is powerful as an architectural necessity, that of sustaining the cornice, and forms a decoration of such nobility and interest as to deserve a place among the world's best examples of decorative sculpture. To the Greeks the palm for the use of the human figure in architecture, to the Khmers the palm for the *Garuda* and the *Naga*. Magnificent god-animals, pure inventions, yet having qualities that give them reality, that make you turn to them again and again, always with gratification.

Walking slowly along below the Terrace front, one arrives at an angle of exquisite beauty. Here is finished the muscular puissance of the fabulous, gigantic bird of Vishnu, and the spell cast is that of celestial women. A lovelier contrast could not have been discovered.

Chapter XI: The Terrace of Honour 151

Devas or Demi-gods Holding the Sacred Snake *Naga*

They call the *Tevadas* the sacred wives of the god-kings. I like best to think of them as terrestrial maidens whose sole province is to enliven a too serious world. They are placed side by side in happy repetition along the Terrace wall. With arms and wings upraised they support the cornice, yet one could easily imagine that at any moment they might all take flight like a flock of swans and vivify the sky over the forest. It is their faces which prompt this thought, faces smiling and serene yet with eyes downcast and such a look of mental reservations as precedes an incalculable act.

The loveliest of the maidens is she who occupies the angle of a perron, she who has no duties as a caryatid but who instead holds between her palms the bud of a lotus and adores it with a smile that makes one wonder what the flower typifies to her. All the figures are kneeling in a fashion only possible to the knees of Asia and all are dressed with the richness of princesses. Each dainty head is covered with a cap of pearls and gems rising into a coronet, and the half-nude forms wear necklace, girdle, bracelets, all of fine jeweller's work.

It is perhaps by chance that these charming maidens are guarded by a monster lion who sits on top the Terrace just above them. Those who are restoring the Angkor ruins did well to replace him in his ancient post.

Next is a parade of elephants that lures one on in this enchanted place. The sculptors of the Terrace here turn to life and not mythology for their inspiration, and have made a frieze of the regal beasts. Forms of caryatides are finished and the king's elephants file through the forest in stone as once they did in flesh.

But to him who sees them with a stranger's eyes they are thrilling, staggering. With the grass around their feet, with the heavy forest above them, they become real, they move, they take on vitality. They are no smaller than the beasts one rides and sees lumbering down the road. But most of all is the unusualness of the great procession — totally unlike other decorations, not conventionalized at all, but a picture of life.

The nobles of the Khmers go out to hunt. They go into the great

Chapter XI: The Terrace of Honour   153

The Bayon Occupies a Point in the Exact Center of the City, Angkor Thom

jungle that has ever occupied the land about Angkor, the jungle that keeps up a silent fight with mankind for the possession of territory. The trees are close above them, lianas lasso them, yet the splendid march continues. The magnificence and daring of this hunt make all others seem paltry. The man with a gun after fluttering birds and cowering rabbits seems contemptible beside the chase where men, nearly nude, pit courage and cunning against man-destroying animals in the wild.

One thinks of a hunt as conducted by mankind. A closer look shows this to be the hunt of the elephants. Each big animal is forceful with life, each is eager to surprise and overpower. For centuries his kind have lived intelligent lives in the forests of Cambodia and in the hills of the Chams, but ever and always annoyed by hunting beasts whose hunger led them to prey on whatever animal was feebler or less cunning than themselves. It was but just that such should receive a lesson. The elephants were obviously the ones to kill the marauders of the jungle — not for food as beasts of prey kill, but for the sake of peace. Thus they go to the hunt not as beasts of burden, as mounts for men, but as jubilant fighters.

This is all shown by the way the great animals are taking on themselves the business of seizing and killing the creatures of the jungle, doing it themselves, not leaving it to man, and doing it with a verve and skill which is born of urgent desire. Puny man sits atop the elephant, sure of his invincibility, but with paternal tolerance the great hunter who knows his jungle seizes his quarry independent of guiding.

In one case he strangles that most vindictive of big game, the charging rhinoceros. The nonchalance with which he holds the dangerous horned enemy, speaks of the courage of the true hero, he who makes light of his feats, for while he is in combat or in triumph carrying on his own hunt, he is porting on his back an encumbering howdah and a self-willed little prince.

One of the elephants of this big herd carries a horned deer, limp and overcome. It was killed by the arrow of an archer, for an elephant would scorn to attack a deer. That noble pastime is the prerogative of mankind.

One of the Fifty Odd Towers of the Bayon Which was Built in the Ninth Century [Ed. Note: Actually built in the late 12th century.]

In the line of hunters one takes notice of the harness, strong and simple and sometimes suggesting a means of mounting for the agile helpers, easily a necessity in the forest where steps and platform are lacking. The bell invariably hangs from under the throat. It is probably a softly tinkling bell with a sound of plop-plop, like the bamboo bell of my elephant at the Bungalow. The beautifully wrought bronze bells found in the royal city would make too loud a tone in the forest. The howdah is one of utility, and lacks the ornaments and awnings that make gorgeous the seats of princes and princesses on parade. It is small and light and carries but one rider, he who assumes in it the favourite position of a prince, seated with one knee sharply flexed, the other straightened with the foot resting on the elephant's back. An individual accompanies him who has the happiness to serve the chief on the exciting sport.

And thus the great procession of hunters, elephants and men files by, or seems to, with their feet in the grass and the forest over them. They reach at last a perron, where stairs of entry mount again to the top of the Terrace of Honour.

Here the heavy relief stops, and its naturalism is discarded for conventionalizing. The elephant is still the motif, but here he is used as decoration of architectural purpose. Imagination leads us to suppose that three elephants stand on either side the wide stone steps, holding up the terrace with their powerful broad backs. But all that comes into view is the row of three great heads with trunks let down to the ground. It is as though they had just faced about and stood immobile awaiting orders. But there is more than that — the elephants of the Terrace bas-relief are strenuous and unbound. These are elegant, formal, without reproach. Each wears on his head the elaborate high crown of ceremony, a magnificent decoration for a magnificent beast, lifting him into greater spirituality. As if to increase this effect each trunk holds in its up-curled tip a drooping sheaf of languid lotus-blooms, an act that only an artist's heart would prompt.

Search for a reason why this stair should be so ornamented with

Bas-relief, the Bayon — The thousands of square feet of their chiseled pictures are all that remains to tell us of the everyday life of the people.

majesty and beauty, and you remember that the great Khmer king was found through this entrance, that it was here ambassadors from other kings mounted to have audience, and that even the king himself might pass this way.

More than that, this elephant perron is the point that commands the centre of the public square of Angkor Thom, and looks directly down the long, straight avenue running to the city wall. At the end of the avenue stands the Gate called Victory with its narrow opening, its guard-chambers, its high tower and the four terrifying faces of mammoth size which threaten or which welcome according to the inner thoughts of him who passes.

Here too, through that gate, is the stupendous Bridge of Giants stretching over the moat, one of Angkor's most staggering, most daring sculptures. Here sit the fifty-four *Devas* on one side with smiling faces capped with the mukuta — cap of the gods. And on the other side fifty-four *Asuras* with bitter faces and more elaborate headdress, men of both sides holding in their laps the length of the giant *Naga*, who raises his fan of heads towards the approaching stranger.

But it is terraces which are immediately before, not bridges, so we return our attention to the centre of Angkor Thom and, passing the whole line of elephants, reach the northern limit and arrive at a sight bewildering.

It is called the Terrace of the Leper King. The official guide said it and believed it. But I set down the name as a superstition, a legend. The Cambodian of today intrigues me but I do not always accept his tales about the ruins. They may not be Cambodian at all, but merely the fantastic deductions of some recent French resident. And if they be in truth Cambodian then they are but a superstition. It is only those who read the ancient inscriptions in Sanskrit and in Khmer who strike the truth, the real truth about the ruins. But there is rarely such a one about the place. I myself do not know Sanskrit, nor yet Khmer, though I preserve as a souvenir the writing of a little boy of ten who was seated beside the Terrace.

Bas-relief, the Bayon — A cock-fight on the shore of the moat at Angkor Thom.

He was keen to know what strange matter might be held within the fabric of a wrist-bag. He frankly bribed, with a round, green fruit carved apparently of polished jade except that its savour — he instructed me to sniff it — was that of orange-blossoms. The mouth smiled but the eyes were anxious until the bribe was accepted.

First out of the bag was a box of sweets given as fair exchange for the unnameable fruit. Eyes as well as mouth smiled then. Next a penknife. The bare, brown body heaved with a deep-chested sigh of delight. Next a fountain pen. To puzzle him it was placed within his fingers, a long black stick, impenetrable, bewitching mystery of strange visitors. Mystery is the wrong word. Dexterous brown fingers cunningly unscrewed the top, exposed the pen, and eyes signalled nervously for paper. Marvellous brown infant, he took the check-blank proffered, and quickly wrote all the length of the paper a writing so symmetric, so cabalistic, that it is saved as a precious relic of the ruins, for even so did the young clerics of the Khmers write on the parchment provided to their hand many centuries ago. Possibly their pens, however, were not Watermans.

The terrace called of the Leprous King – horrid name – is really the abode of *houris**, a sort of celestial palace where the most beautiful of women abound. You can prosaically view it as a high square terrace a few meters north of the Terrace of Honour. It is faced with brown old stones carved in rows of seated figures. Having thus quickly compassed its size and intent you can avoid heat and fatigue by motoring away down the road to the Bungalow where creature comforts wait, and handsome sloths like the Diva.

But if you linger a bit, and if the time of day is late when shadows are soft and a breeze blows the leaves, you will hear a laughing call from all the seated ladies, and you will turn back and make discoveries that will beautify many a later hour of reverie or reading.

From fallen leaves and tumbled stones rises a wall of six and, in places, seven tiers of carving, engaged figures nearly in the round. Among them are men and *Nagas*, but almost all are women, the royal ladies of

---

* From the Persian *houri*. A feminine noun meaning; 1. A voluptuous, alluring woman. 2. One of the beautiful virgins of the Koranic paradise.

the palaces. Floods of summer and winds of winter throughout many centuries have worn the stones. Trees growing on top have dislodged them, and man has been disregardful or filled with hate and vengeance. So here as everywhere ruin is apparent. It adds to the bewilderment. We are amid things hard to interpret in their perfection, but baffling in the uncertainty of decay. But these princesses have called and we are charmed. We must contemplate their beauties, and learn from their abraded faces the riddle of their temperaments.

Each line of figures arranges itself in groups. The centre of each is a giant, a god, or some fabled being who is outside the necessity of being beautiful. Rather is he fat and ugly, but not without a humorous benignity. He wears jewels and thus gives signs of riches, and by his size evidences power and high position. Pampered he certainly must be, surrounded as he is by piquantly lovely ladies far advanced in the arts of coquetry. Yes, they even have coquetry of dress, although at first glance one thinks them nude. When the smooth skin is the brown of certain bronzes, less of stuffs are needed. Jewels take their place in the sweltering tropic heat. These ladies wear theirs in rich profusion, for they are the daughters and mates of kings and princes. There are collars of gems which cover the chest, there are armlets and bracelets which make heavy the languid arm, there are girdles above the draped *sampot*, and there are those wonders the headdresses. Jewelers in those days worked long and late to confection these astounding things.

But all seems hurt by time. One wants to get nearer the souls of these women of the past, to divine what words the happy lips would speak if they were living. And so one passes, ever looking for less damaged carving that should show none of the alterations of time.

All at once at the end of the Terrace a way opens an unexpected way. It leads within. If the ladies on the Terrace face called the stranger, then those within call more insistently.

A passage leads within, then turns sharply to the right. One stands within a narrow slip less than three feet wide, between walls which are low at the entrance but rise to twenty feet perhaps, and in this recess one walks parallel to the outer wall, but hidden, completely hidden as though in a well, with only the sky above.

It is here that the sculptures are found in their old perfection, almost untouched by the passing of centuries. Explanations of this exist, but after all is it not better to let it rest a mystery why the ancient builders carved a beauteous front, then placed its duplicate a few feet before it and filled the space between the two carved walls with earth, thus burying one of them? It was only a few years ago that a hole in the ground revealed a smiling lady and excavators eagerly unearthed the entire lovely scene unhurt.

Left alone in this slip of a passage one is near the soul of things Khmer. Nowhere else is one so close shut in with them while the blue of heaven shines overhead. Laughing girls are all around you, girls with smooth brows, eyes serene, and humour obvious. Even the chief who sits among them is sympathetic here, as though the Khmer loved to see his women happy.

The floor is strewn with leaves fallen from the tall trees above and among them is discovered the revered *Naga* raising his many heads to ornament the centre of the lowest tier of carving. It is as though he were just emerging from the ground, from his cool, dark home underneath.

This brief passage is one in which to linger in happy amazement, but something always impels one to go on, to penetrate to the last figure this unbelievable place in which intimacy with the lost race of great Khmers seems at last attained. But the quick turn to the left reveals not more carvings but instead a flight of narrow steps that take one directly into the open, the top of the Terrace which had for approximate measurement a hundred and twenty feet by eighty-five, though this is altered by disintegration of the walls. It is more a belvedere than a terrace, and forms no part of the long structure with the elephants and *Garudas*, yet it produces a most profound impression. It may have been ornamented with gorgeous silken canopies in its days of glory, but now it is made lovely by the forest which sinks its roots deep down within it. It is as though the carved stone belvedere were a mammoth jardinière and the trees were the plants thus elegantly potted.

But trees are forgot when the eye falls upon a stone figure, a solitary bit of sculpture seated with happy composure looking over the scene. It is as though he had been left there, one dreaming Khmer while all his race fled to oblivion. He is called the Leper King.

The name makes one try to fit romance to the place. A leper must be isolated. It is true that this terrace, however magnificent, is far separated from the long Terrace of Honour. A leper needs a retreat. What more beguiling asylum could he find than that most secret, almost subterranean, passage reached by the narrow stair of communication? And if human companionship is in great part denied the invalid, here is its lovely counterpart carved in verisimilitude. If fate were relentless these sculptures were kind, and the sweetness of their beaming faces never failed.

But the statue of the Leper King gives no sculptured sign of malady. The figure bewilders by its strangeness. It is different from other Khmer sculpture, and smacks strong of India. It seems an exotic, a *rara avis** brought from another country, or chiselled in some later era. These are emotion provoked thoughts. When the critical eye begins to take notes a realization comes that this figure is one of the rare works in which the sculptor forsook the rigid rules of Khmer art and dropped the severe conventionalizing demanded. In this figure the artist threw his cap over the windmill and declared he would make man as he saw him. But he didn't know how. His art had not taught him. What he produced was a failure when compared with the drawing of the human figure by the great naturalist artists of other high civilizations. His teachers had given him conventions which were his invaluable tools, and inasmuch as he failed to use them he lost in style and in strength.

Nevertheless the figure attracts. It is seated, and in the Oriental position, one thigh slanting upward to a bended knee, the other lying along the ground, the knee flexed. The shoulders and limbs are too round, no muscles indicated, making the whole too "sweet." Notwithstanding

---

* A Latin expression for a rare or unique person or thing.

the Hindu appearance the body is shorter than that of Indian sculptures and the waist less fine. The entire absence of drapery is unique in all the carvings of Angkor save for some insignificant figures in Inferno among the bas-reliefs of the Vat.

Enthusiasts of Khmer sculpture prove their case that no other exceeds it in variety of facial expression. The head of the Leper King is more than beautiful, it makes one want to solve its riddle. That the sculpture is a riddle, even to explorers, is shown by even so ardent an archeologist as Jean Commaille, who repudiates the idea of the statue belonging to the belvedere and declares that a long time ago before the French occupation the natives placed it there.

The head is made almost effeminate by the hair-dressing, the long locks being arranged in neat curls such as little girls wore in mid-Victorian days. On the crown is the base of a headdress which makes one suddenly realize the lack of jewels on this figure when all the figures of the terrace face are made gorgeous with them. The mouth is perhaps the most unusual feature of the carefree face. It is strangely enough a little open, lips parted as in a smile. On the upper lip is the fine line of the moustache, the charmingly conventionalized line seen on other sculptured figures and which never fails to give a look of pleasant distinction to the face. If the Cambodian lips are too full, the fine, wavy line of the moustache alters the sensuality into delicacy. Like all statuary at Angkor the figure is carved of the fine-grained stone called *grès* by the French, a sort of limestone.

With many questions unanswered, but with a strong desire for research, and a regret that all romantic legends may not be swallowed whole, one leaves the seated figure, leaves him to look out over the public square where perhaps the moonlight may play tricks with shadows and recall old festivals. But that is the tiger's hunting hour and one may not safely go there to see.

Chapter XII

PHIMEANAKAS

The French word for palace is ever on the limited tongue of the brown young men in uniform who run the motor cars and serve as guides. They give out such false information of the many buildings in and around the city of Angkor Thom as takes much study to controvert. Most appealing is their suggestion that this and that ruin is the palace of the Queen Mother, so pretty does it sound in French — *le palais de la Reine Mère*.

But, alas, who can find a queen-mother in the old race, one queen-mother par excellence who would have to herself a structure of the enormous measurements of Prah Khan or Banteai Kedei? The king having Solomon's fashion in wives it is more than evident that all women were housed en masse. Those who study the ruins year after year flout the idea of innumerable palaces still existent and hesitate to assign more than one or two edifices to royal occupation. The royal palace best known in Angkor Thom is the Phimeanakas, the structure which has the Terrace of Honour running along its entire eastern front. It was built in the tenth century A.D., which makes it a possible residence for Harshavarman and for the strange-named kings during the classic period of Khmer art and down to the time of the overthrow of the Khmers.

In speaking of the Phimeanakas as a building one misleads. It is rather an enclosure, a large space about six hundred and seventy-five yards deep and two hundred and eighty wide. Around this space was built an enclosing wall pierced by two gates on both north and south, as well as by the grand gate of entrance in the centre of the Terrace on the east. A second enclosing wall was built inside this. Within the vast space thus protected were erected all the buildings made necessary by custom for royal living, which means for the accommodation of all the royal wives and children and for the enormous number of dancing girls and attendants who amused the king during the days and nights when he abstained from his favourite pursuit of war.

If one has visited the royal palace of the present Cambodian king at Phnom Penh and has studied its plan rather than its sad pinchbeck, he can readily imagine how many buildings must have been contained within the walls.

It is to a Chinese Ambassador that we owe all the truly human accounts of life in and about the Phimeanakas. The Chinese character of today is full of friendly curiosity. It was the same in 1295 A.D. when Zhou Daguan came to Angkor as Ambassador from his ruler Kublai Khan.

It was a long way to come by junk and sampan, down the coast and up the river, with no propelling power but wind and muscle. The ambassador meanwhile went through the same mental processes as we ourselves, the gradual separation of the mind from all accustomed things and the delighted acceptance of the new. Zhou Daguan revelled in the strangeness of all he saw. The fame of Angkor had spread through Asia; to its rulers was ascribed invincibility in war, and wealth beyond that of any known king. He was ready to be astounded — even more, he was determined to be, as is sometimes shown in his flights from literalness.

Being a gentleman of cultivation writing was his aristocratic

The Towers of the Four Faces on the Third Story of the Bayon

resource. He decided to set down on paper what he saw about him in the bewildering land of Cambodia and especially what occurred at Angkor, He wrote a diary. It is on the writings of this Chinese gentleman, added to stone inscriptions, that we depend for pictures of the life in and around the royal city.

The days he described were the late days of the twelve hundreds. Although the fall of the Khmers followed in the years immediately succeeding, the social conditions existing then were the same as in the four or five centuries precedent. Customs change slowly in Asia. Family life in 800 was unaltered in 1200, and is still the same today. On that one bases many deductions about the palace of the Phimeanakas, the home of the king's somewhat swollen family.

At Phnom Penh the modern palace seems fantastic, a sort of Coney Island or Earl's Court, and with the sun beating down on paved courts and reflecting on stucco buildings it seems a place to see quickly and to escape with a feeling of a tourist's duty done. Even the little sanctuary of the Sacred Sword appears as a showman's trick-box.

But did one know at the time of visiting it that the Cambodian ruler of today arranges his palace after the manner of his forbears at Angkor, the royal enclosure would receive closer study. It is in effect the key to the lost romance of the Phimeanakas.

But Zhou Daguan has left his diary, and from that we will pull out plums with eager thumbs, forgetting that some of them are over-seasoned.

Most of all is he stirred by riches, the evident riches that flash in the sun, that glow in the light of candles and torches. He adores the golden decorations, he is ecstatic over the masses of jewels heaped on the supple yet languid beauties of the court, he tells with enthusiasm of architecture and sculpture enriched with gold, a tower of gold, gold lions to guard steps of approach, and here it may be that he failed to examine if the gold were solid or applied in leaf, lest he fail to impress his readers as he was impressed.

A Tower of the Bayon — A bonze seated beside the face of Çiva.

It was evidently before the Phimeanakas that he was received in audience by the king. Strangely enough he omits the name of the ruler, before whom he is presented, mentioning him merely as "the new prince who is the nephew of the old," but other records give his name as Jaya-Varmediparamecvara. To know it is far from pronouncing it, however.

Reconstructing the picture from the ruins, we see the Sino-Mongol Ambassador approaching the Terrace of Honour on a suave, bright morning arrayed in the superb raiment which has ever been associated with the ceremonial life of his country. He mounts the steps of the stone elephants, passes between upraised *Nagas* and insolent lions, and approaches a window of gold. There behind a dazzling curtain rests the great Khmer king. When the right moment arrives, agile maidens, jewelled, perfumed and flower-decked, draw aside the curtain, and the king is revealed within the gold frame of the window. Thus his subjects have brief audience. And thus the Chinese Ambassador first saw him.

The gold window charms us. To a gold throne we are accustomed, but this is new to the mind. It preserves the mystery that should hedge a king. It keeps him from disillusioning contact, it preserves him in time of danger, to be recessed in a harbouring edifice. The building which held the window is now but a mass of tumbled stone in the centre of the long Terrace, but a remembering of other windows still standing leads one to think of it as a large and spacious square with deep embrasure constructed with the elegance of the windows throughout Angkor. To this were added those dazzling parts which made of it "a window of gold."

It is probable that the Ambassador gained most of his impressions of the Phimeanakas from its outer ramparts, for he says, hungrily wishing for more, that "I have heard that within the palace are many marvellous sections, but the defences are very severe and it is impossible to penetrate them," But he also speaks with the assurance of one who has seen of long verandas, and covered corridors, irregular without great symmetry, which sustains the belief that just within the outer wall must

Dancing Figures on a Square Column of the Bayon

have existed council rooms, audience halls and their dependences wherein the king discussed affairs of state with his own ministers and those of foreign lands. It is probable that the Chinese visitor reached no farther, for again and again he longs to see with his own eyes, experience with his own five senses, the innumerable palace departments which he hears are as marvellous as inaccessible. And being denied he uses his imagination, especially in regard to the great crowds of women who flowed in and out of the palace, and more especially those who stayed within.

Quoting from the wide-eyed journalist, he states that a favoured lady — mother of a king's preceptor — had accorded to her "a part of the Royal palace where, on a raised dais, sparkled the jewelled beds; and a palanquin of gold, rendered charming by banners and fly-brushes all with gold handles."

He learned that the sovereign had five wives, quaintly apportioned thus, one special, and four others for the four cardinal points of the compass. "As for concubines and girls of the palace I have heard the number given as from three to five thousand, but they rarely cross the palace threshold." These were divided into several classes, the most ordinary of which performed services necessary to the maintenance of the palace, and these were married and passed freely in and out, being often seen on the roads.

Thus the palace of Phimeanakas became truly a city of women and girls, not entirely Occidental in its conventions. The number given by the great Chinese visitor was probably in excess of the truth, yet the king who reigned in Cambodia when the French formed the Protectorate about 1907, enclosed eight hundred in the palace.

Many of these, of course, royalty never saw. A very large number of them belonged to the department of amusement, music and the dance. Here were trained those supple knees into flexings more than painful to the European knees, which anatomists say are made on a different plan from theirs. The first figures one sees in Angkor decorations are the dancers. There is rarely a decorative design complete without them.

Chapter XII: Phimeanakas

The Vat Shows Him Superb, Triumphant, Lending His Upright Heads to Welcome All Who Approach

To make them acceptable in temples they are dressed in religious legend and called sacred, *Apsaras* mad with glee, or *Tevadas* in the ecstasy of rhythm. In a country where the dance is a pastime of the gods it might well be considered a necessity and luxury of kings. An inscription on stone tells of the King Yasovarman teaching the dance to princesses and himself giving them the measure. The daughters of the great of the earth danced in his presence.

All over the ruins of Angkor are found bas-reliefs showing the maidens who danced before the king, and who entertained him with music and with the mere fact of youth's joyousness. These illuminating scenes of the bas-reliefs are like illustrations to the text of Zhou Daguan, Herein we see the king — so often called the prince — seated in the convention accorded to the monarch, the right knee up, the other down, the finely drawn body slightly leaning to one side, and his size as much larger in scale as would indicate importance. Thus are the greater gods represented.

To continue the chiselled picture, the king has called to his presence his favourites among the queens and princesses and they are grouped about him in beauty and elegance, while above they are canopied by draperies of exceeding richness. Music, repartee, story-telling, occupy them, flowers and perfumes scent the air, jewels flash, slender fingers play. fully caress, the pleasant faces brighten with laughter — the great art-loving warrior king is at ease.

How the girls of the palace can be found in such numbers is described by Zhou Daguan: "Any family which contains a beautiful daughter never fails to take her to the palace; daughters of high officials are offered as royal concubines, and the presenting of such irresistible gifts by their parents is an act of courtesy destined to provoke some favour from the king."

The diversions, the dances, the playfulness offered by all these girls made delectable the king's days of peace. But besides this they made gay and interesting his sorties without the palace. If he were carried in a gorgeous *chaise-à-porteur* for some near destination, they tripped beside him in a gay troupe with fans, banners and the fly-brush which has strong necessity to recommend its presence in no matter how regal a presence. If he were mounted on an elephant, an illusive maid was perched there like a butterfly, in grand parades they followed him in dazzling palanquins which flashed with metal and semi-precious gems.

The Chinese diarist after his enthusiasm for the women of the Khmer king, turns his attentions to affairs of government. A quotation on this subject is picturesque. "Twice each day the king holds audience for the affairs of government. There is no prepared list. Those of the functionaries or of the people who wish to see him seat themselves upon the ground to wait. After a time distant music is heard within the palace while outside the conches are blown as a welcome to the king. An instant after, two girls of the palace lift the curtain with their slender fingers and the king, holding the Sacred Sword, appears at the window of gold. Ministers as well as the people clasp their hands and strike the earth with their brows; when the sound of the conch has ceased they may lift the head. Following the good pleasure of the king they approach, also to seat themselves. In the place where they sit is a lion-skin which is regarded as a royal object; when the affairs are terminated the prince returns, the two daughters of the palace drop the curtain, all the world comes to its feet." Thus Zhou Daguan pictures for us the scene enacted on the Terrace before the principal entrance of the Phimean-Akas.

The king need go no further than this central terrace during times of peace, for here he met his people in his judicial capacity, and here he reviewed armies and parades. Here also he watched the contests of strength and skill which represented the sports of those days. Before him lay the long public square stretching north and south while ahead lay the straight avenue leading to the eastern wall of the city, to the Gate of Victory holding aloft huge faces of the Brahmanic deity, the guarded gate through which no enemy might pass. Up this long avenue filed the troops returning from war, or assembling for new conflicts.

On the square were wrestlers struggling with as much skill as wrestlers employed in the Colosseum. The build of the Cambodian fits him for such work. Runners showed their speed, with the terminus of the course directly opposite the seat of the king. Small sports loved by the common people were conducted among little groups of folk which constituted the side-shows. I wonder if the king enjoyed as much as I the cockfights depicted on the bas-reliefs with such human frankness. They appeal to every visitor among the ruins. Of course one is ashamed to be amused at trifles among serious archeological pursuits — but one is, nevertheless.

It was when the king himself went out on parade that the scene was brilliant beyond telling. Zhou Daguan tells us that the new prince, meaning the ruler in 1295, was covered with iron so that arrows of the enemy could not harm him. But I like best to think of him as seated on his elephant in the nonchalant grace and elegant undress of the Khmer half-god, on his head the *mukuta* rich with pearls, on his breast the jeweled harness, and around his body the jeweled girdle above the *sampot*. Thus arrayed he shone above the crowd on the royal elephant, which was itself a creature to admire, dressed with sparkling head-piece, harness and bands around the trunk and legs.

Banners floated in the air held by scores of youths and maidens, the music of the march made light the eager feet and mounted to the fragrant flowering trees above. A chorus of voices, the sweet, unstrained voices of the south, rose and fell in rich phrasing. Sections of the army headed by great generals, marched in the procession, and numerous servitors of both temple and palace joined the throng. The king was on his way to worship at the Bayon. Great as was his power it must acknowledge a greater, that of Civa.

Out of the Phimeanakas pours a troop of palace girls dressed in jewels and cloth of gold, flowers woven into their tresses, lotus buds waved aloft by slender hands. Some carry lighted torches which perfume the air as they burn, others carry sacred objects in gold and silver, vases of perfume, flagons of oil which are to be poured out before the gods of the temple.

Men of high estate ride on elephants. Other dignitaries are carried in chariots — the graceful bronze-wheeled chariots of the bas-reliefs, and these are the great men of war. Wives of the kings, princesses of the palace, are elegantly sequestered in palanquins borne by slaves and worked with shining gold and flashing gems. Sunshades in white and in gold, make gay the nobles, those significant Eastern parasols.

And at the end of the whole sense-exciting procession rides the god-king himself, holding in his strong right hand the Sacred Sword.

All this and more is recounted by Zhou Daguan in his valuable diary. The procession moves on the Bayon where cunning high priests receive in the name of Civa the riches presented by a propitiating king.

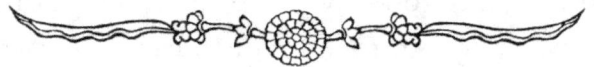

The Chinese historian hesitated at the outer court of the Phimeanakas because "the defences were severe," but now the most insolent and prying of tourists may wander at will into the most secret recesses, for their exclusiveness exists no longer. Passing within the open door back of the king's post on the Terrace we seem to be thrust into an amazing park not quite a jungle but filled with trees through which extends a wide walk with smaller paths to right and left. Such is the enticement of the wooded way that one forgets ruins in examination of the smoothed doorway of a tarantula nest, or in finding wild-grown the flowers of our conservatories. Suddenly the characteristic stones appear, fragments of carvings, an unexplained platform, and finally a ruined temple of two stories and a sanctuary.

Off to the right a path coaxes. It ends in a large basin like a dry reservoir of a small town. Its borders are of stone which is so carved on the inner surface as to make one abandon the theory of the reservoir and wonder if the place were not a sunken garden of ornate walls, a spicy garden of the East wherein young maidens played in the evening freshness or in the illusionizing moonlight.

With so niggardly a remnant of a palace, how can one reconstruct the edifice and review the life led therein except by remembering the modern palace at Phnom Penh and by reading snatches from *T. T. K.*?* The name Phimeanakas signifies palace-aërial. That is a clue when added to the excerpt, "In the palace is a tower of gold on the summit of which sleeps the king."

It remains but to find its place among the fallen stones, and that the savants are doing. "The king lived in a pavilion of two stories," is another statement, and both give colour to the belief that the king was never allowed to touch his foot to the ground. Not so remarkable when one remembers the fashion in footwear then prevailing. To press the soil with the naked foot was good for the people, "but a distinctive sign of gods and kings was never to touch foot to earth." Even in going about the many buildings of the palace enclosure the king must be carried in a litter lest the sacred foot meet indignity.

All about the enclosure were little buildings which housed the enormous personnel of the palace. If the hundreds of women who served had homes without, in the byways of the city, there were shelters needed for the hundreds more who never left the gates except in attendance on the king.

There was a school for training the many agile dancers in steps and poses. And there was a suitable sheltered platform on which dances were given. Also were there shelters for musicians and the masters who taught them to sing and to play the stringed instruments and the winds.

For all these classes and many more there were little shops which harboured stores of silken stuffs for *sampots*, gauzes for veils and nets for protection against mosquitoes and little things that crawl in the night. Others kept carpets and matting, the latter to serve, as it does still, as a cool bed on hot nights.

---

*Initials of "Tcheou-Ta-Kouan", who is referred to as "Zhou Daguan" in our updated text.

Other shops kept perfumes, rich, intoxicating scents to pour on glossy shoulders, or spicy odours for the hair. Among them was the sandalwood we love today, and the origan* which Parisian makers offer now as a latest novelty.

Other edifices were for the guard, and some were for the confinement of offenders against palace laws, a place for men and one for women. There were baths, for bathing is as necessary to the Cambodian as food; there were kitchens, dining halls, and a stronghold for treasures.

The explanation of the loss of all these buildings is sought as one roams about the present park enclosed by the encircling outer wall of the Phimeanakas. It is found in the remembrance that dwellings and their dependences were constructed of wood, and that wood can last but a short time in the passing of centuries. All of nature is against it. The floods descend and the damp rots the wood. Ants and borers attack and disintegrate it.

The magnificent solidity of the masonry in and about Angkor deceives one into thinking that everything was built after the manner of temples. But a glance at the native houses of today shows a scheme of domestic building which was in use centuries ago. Stone was not used in their construction except as a base in which to secure upright poles. These stones are found now in the Phimeanakas, with holes to contain the uprights.

Thus one can reconstruct the great palace of the king, a great walled city within a still greater walled town, having its grand audience chambers, its sumptuous residence for the monarch, its pavilions for amusements, its department of justice, its shops, its shelters for the troupes of dancers, singers, musicians. Among all these ran innumerable paths or lanes, and included were the pleasure gardens and shaded park-like tracts wherein living models for *Tevadas* walked arm in arm. One could almost pity the king that he might not walk with them and still keep the law about the feet of gods and kings.

And so, dreaming on the past, I pass out of the eastern portal and

*prop. n. A botanical term meaning a genus of aromatic labiate plants.

down the steps of the elephants, becoming all at once a miserable worm of a tourist stepping into a Ford to be buzzed home to luncheon. Perhaps the humility was due to the presence in the car of the odious Blake and the egoistic Nice journalists who were for driving it off to leave me while I was straining to catch it.

Chapter XIII

THE VILLAGE OF SIEM REAP

Long association with a people begets love for them. I am loving the Khmers. That they vanished six centuries ago is unimportant, for do I not see them daily, the common people, softly chattering, softly walking as they pass the terrace of the Bungalow almost like shades?

A few inhabit a village across the moat and make lovely the twilight hour with lights from the home-fire which stream deep into the waters and bring thoughts of *le feu sacré* which was of old carried in beauteous portable altars to the Sanctuary. These happy people live in another group somewhere behind the Bungalow, and there sell bananas for my elephant's regaling.

But down the long way they come in silent scores from the big village of Siem Reap. It does not interest at first, this village, not until the ruins are familiar and particularly those bas-reliefs which picture daily living. Then it appeals as a possible clue as to what became of the Khmers.

The vivid Artist, like a limp hibiscus-bloom, languished in the motor-car when we drove into the village and would not leave the automobile for the best of Siem Reap's diversions, not even to view the Cathedral built of stones from the stair of Bak-Keng. She was thirsty, not merely thirsty but *dying*. 'Twere a pity the world should lose so much of loveliness. What would the lady take to drink? Cocoanuts, the nectar lying within green cocoanuts!

All the world is full of cocoanuts at Siem Reap. Every bamboo home has towering bunches hanging over it. Every roadside group of babes plays under the shade of cocoa palms. The wilting hibiscus lady should be restored at once.

Languages come easy to me. I addressed three women standing near the motor-car in perfect English and plain pantomime. They all laughed frankly until the babies astride their hips nearly lost their hold, and waited expectantly for more of the same amusement.

It is angering to be ridiculous. The driver was persuaded to go on, and to stop at a shop, a shop of the ancient kind, a small platform on which sat the proprietor among her wares, all on the same level. It was delightful, for it recalled the bas-reliefs, the one in which a shop is pictured.

True to the analogy between those times and these, the vendor was a woman. Zhou Daguan, the great diarist, spoke with admiration of the women vendors of the Khmers. Small trade, he said, was in their hands, and he strongly recommended the pecuniary advantage of taking such women to wife.

The thirsty Artist looked hastily over the goods of this small wooden market, hard brown yarns of exaggerated size, peanuts more diminutive than is just, bananas yellowly delicious but dry. No juiceful cocoanuts.

Again the linguist used her pantomime. The vendor was old and laughed not; she merely scorned.

"But where?" insisted the Artist, waving a red-draped arm to include the entire village. The vendor took it for a foreign curse and sat benumbed.

The French are trying their best at Siem Reap to maintain together the traditions of Europe and those of Cambodia. Because French shops are built in a close row, and of masonry, they have so built them here. But because the Cambodian has always had them without a front and has conducted family life just back of his line of wares, he occupies them thus.

A block of buildings, a line of open shops, extends on one side of a barren square of green. It might be the haunt of green cocoanut vendors.

The hunt began in the first shop. No cocoanuts in sight. They might be in the larder, but one scarce likes to penetrate the larder of a stranger.

We hesitated dispirited — for we loved our flamboyant Artist and hated to see her athirst — and a ring of conspirators formed about us. They were but village girls — yet they seemed like village boys. Two marked differences only, they wore the *sampot* draped in an ugly bloomer-y way, while that of the boys hung straight.

It was their animus that was boyish, as well as their looks. They came up bravely as a boy will, unaffected, un-shy, They stared, no, not that, rather scoured with intelligent searching; but as they smiled the while, the process glowed with friendliness.

Meanwhile one stared at them. At the physiognomy Asiatic, to determine which strain prevailed, Annamite or Malay, Chinese or Indian. And at the hair, worn short like a man's and dressed upward from the brow *en brosse*. Bare arms and shoulders suggested a Venus done brown in the oven of the sun. Bare feet and ankles elastically repulsed the earth in stepping. They laughed, then showed lowered lids and quiet enigmatic smiles like ladies on the Terrace of the Leper King.

One of the girls wore earrings. Among the treasures found by the diggers around Angkor Vat were ornaments such as these, a sort of filagree studded button with nail-like shaft. They were of gold, but of such peculiar alloy that it glows a pale bright red like new copper. Then the effect of beauty was spoiled by the horrid hole in the ear lobe through which the earring's shaft is thrust. And yet, pursuing traces of traditions, the great ears of all the great Brahmanic gods have ear lobes slit and weighted with a jewel.

Besides the warm vitality of the girls which illuminated all the shop, what was there of interest? One glorious, glowing pile of silverware. But not the ordinary silverware of commerce, the forms and ornament of the manufactory, but subtle, satiny, strangely moulded, such silver as might appear in dreams to a lover of Angkor. Its loveliness almost paralyzed me who stood before it worshipping.

Nam-Dinh — she whom I had oft accosted as she passed the Bungalow — must have seen me lost in the lust of possible possession, for she made toward me a hasty step. She seized my wrist — her touch astonished me, it differed from a touch accustomed as her race differed from mine. She adroitly clasped upon my arm a vine-like bracelet sparkling with rough, yellow crystals. Then she cooed soft monosyllables of approval, sweet Cambodian words without the hissing sound of aspirates.

She set her fine, square shoulders firmly and having bestowed royally she looked on my stammering embarrassment as a princess might have done, cool, detached.

Just then the Artist called me. She and the Beguiler were giving their souls to fabrics, wild, colourful fabrics dyed with the temperament of the tropics, printed with the art history of the centuries.

They stood in a sea of colour. They had wanted cottons. The cottons, stiff with newness, were tossed mountain high behind them, purple, orange, green, all shot with contrasts. It was as though a sunset were upon them. Then they had asked for silks, and silks had been unwound from little bales until they formed a sea on which were repeated all the colours of the cotton mountains, but richer.

And in the midst of this post-impressionist landscape stood the pair, Artist and Beguiler, wound in *sampots* of deep red and yellow printing. The Artist announced lamely that they were looking for the nasturtium silks of yellow bonzes. An excuse was due to the vendor who seemed far from appreciative of the invincible charm of the white man.

The audience grew. It does in Indochina, or any sort of China, if one stays too long in one spot. More laughing girls appeared, un-shy yet

On the Way Across the Gardens to the Central Temple of Angkor — *Naga* forms the balustrade; building to right and left are called libraries.

modest. Blake passed, Blake from the Bungalow, but as he passed, not stayed, he was forgiven.

And then within the hot shade of the shop appeared a native figure, unusual even in Cambodia, the village fool. Even the group of silver vessels ceased calling, also the pile of coloured textiles, when his proud, foolish presence claimed imperatively attention. He was tall as a skeleton is tall; he was as light of skin as a Chinese. And he was dressed to the last detail like the nobles carved on the Bayon a thousand years ago. But with this difference, that all his classic costume was made of village rejectimenta, bits of rolled paper wound with lengths of string, tags of red calico and scraps of tin, feathers from fowls and tin-foil from packets of sweets. Nothing was left out, not the headdress nor the earrings, not the necklace nor the girdle, not the bracelets nor the anklets. Except for the loin cloth these were on a naked body, but he was impressively clothed in the mantle of his own vanity. It made one ruminate as he posed, full of scorn, for all to admire. He smoked like a prince the half-smoked cigarettes of the gutter, but he looked with pretended wonder on coins offered him and dropped them jauntily on the ground. Yet one might see he was nearly starving.

No one seemed to see him except ourselves. The silver called again and I left him. It was impossible not to adore a little group of silver boxes gathered into their encircling silver basket. It was the ideal trophy to take home from a strangely artistic people, a work intricate yet perfect. One box was round, and one was square, one long, and one was shaped like a wild duckling afloat on a pond. The whole set might thrill one's visitors if they were offered from one box a cigarette, from another a sweet; or the whole collection might happily house the cosmetics of a dressing table.

Was she deaf, or insolent, or angry, the woman of the shop, when I tried to signify that I would buy her set of silver trifles? Not a syllable from her red-stained lips, not a glance from her eyes. Then the Beguiler, who knows by instinct, explained that this was her private and personal

Naga, Angkor Vat — Each of his heads-of which he always has an odd number-is dressed with plumy crests of intricate carving, all uniting to form a halo round the group.

betel-nut outfit, and that it was the apple of her eye. It dashed me, but I still think it unfair that, although all shops have them, I may not.

However, there was a silver chalice, so precious that it stood behind glass. That, after all, was preferable, and that I would have. Its lines were such as one finds in museums which harbour Cretan bowls, suave, erudite. Its decorations were carved with talented hand, its hollow was hand-hammered into dappled satin.

The case was locked. A small boy, brown and succulent, got it opened for me. My hands trembled with ecstasy of contact. What price would be accepted for the piece?

The pantomime was understood. But the chalice was not for sale. It was part of the merchant's family equipment, and was kept in the shop because family life was conducted there. If sold, where could another be found? Where, indeed!

The boy with the key was called by the group of soft-chattering girls ever pattering about in the background. Returning to me he pointedly spoke some shibboleth of strange syllables. He said it again, and the third time he pointed to the gift which so embarrassed me, the bracelet of Nam-Dinh.

Illumination! He was saying in Cambodian French, "Thirty-five piastres."

It was the chalice I wanted, not this trinket! But the natives of Cambodia say they must pay a yearly headtax of two-thirds of that — and it is agreeable to know that Nam-Dinh's royally-carried head is paid for this year.

Meanwhile our lovely inconsequent Artist revived her ancient thirst. In a whirlwind of colour she threw herself into the motor-car, and for ten hot minutes in the burning sun we laboured to make the chauffeur understand that we were on a quest for cocoanuts, green ones, large as kegs, full of gallons of velvet liquid slipping coolly around the inner surface of a matchless bowl. At least he understood cocoanuts.

We drove from shop to shop of the improved part of the village,

Lion, Phnom Bak-Keng — His dignity is a menace, you are thrilled and terrorized at once.

what one might call the French quarter, as absent French have built it. Each merchant scorned us with a stare.

The car drove along the river, the little Siem Reap that takes a summer excursion as a lake over numberless square miles of woodland, riceland and homeland. In the winter it observes conventions and stays at home, within its banks, and welcomes bathers. They are unlike bathers in the mad Atlantic or madder Pacific, they neither leap nor shriek, but steal softly into the water dressed as for a stroll. They make no preparation, but walk in off the road with admirable nonchalance. And once in the water they rub arms and body and *sampot* all the same, then stand half immersed as quiet as the water-buffalo bathing before the farms of the Tonlé Sap. Bathing is a quiet function such as is known to the delicate frog who slips in and out the water without pother.

When maidens bathe, a fresh *sampot* and shoulder scarf are picked up on coming out of water and folded around the figure until the wet ones can be removed. And that is all there is of a maiden's toilet in Siem Reap.

Big water-wheels are placed beside the river bank. In turning, little cups of water are emptied from the rim into a trough overhead which reaches across the road and discharges in the field or garden. Light and effective, worked by the pressure of the river's flow, they have been in use for centuries. Looking at them one can believe in garden irrigation from the big reserves of water built in ancient Angkor.

Bullock carts meet us along the road. They are always active, extending a road or carting stones. Among other works of the constructive Khmers were miles and miles of fine roads through the country, some of which are being recovered from the jungle, though at heavy cost. The old roads were all raised above the level of the land they traversed, which made construction a still greater task. But this is the country of floods, and for several months each year is under water. The homes of the common people have always been built on slim piles to keep them dry, but each would be isolated in the season of rains

Lion on the Cruciform Terrace, Angkor Vat — He never sits on loose haunches but is ready for action.

were the roads of communication not raised. And the bullock carts working on the roads today are line for line the same as those graved on the ancient bas-reliefs.

It is but a few years ago that all visitors to Angkor found these carts the only vehicle to carry them from the boat they left on the Tonlé Sap through the forest to the Bungalow at Angkor. If one dreads the glassy green flame of a tiger's eye in that drive taken at night in a motor-car, what fears might assail when only a lumbering bullock was matched against the fleet foot of the jungle's king! Some day there'll be a motor-car itinerary all the way from Saigon to Angkor. But that will be a detriment. Where then will be the gentle intermezzo which prepares one for Angkor; and where the thoughtful interlude after seeing it?

Meanwhile the thirst of the desert is upon us all, the Artist suffers not alone. At the Bungalow, in the afternoon shade of the blue-tiled terrace, with the joyous Vat in the clouded distance, mute dark boys are serving cooling drinks, many of them, all one can swallow. The Diva is sipping the sweet syrup and *eau de seltz* that make her fat, Priscilla spicily takes lime juice with gin in a tall, thin glass — while we go on our parched hunt for a fruit that hangs over our heads in tons.

We are crossing a bridge; we plunge into the populous part of Siem Reap, a part untouched by France. No masonry is here, but all is as sketchy as bamboo can make an architecture. The houses are mere shells, like the open lean-to of the Adirondack mountains, but picturesquely raised on toothpicks. Such frankness of living, such opportunities of exchanging opinion. Not even a gate for barrier. And the floor of the house is made convenient rest for temporary callers who dangle their legs over its edge.

We stopped before a house — it might as well have been any other, so undistinguished was its brown informality. Our driver disappeared. From the ground sprang innumerable babes. Some were astride their mother's hips, some ran alone. Some wore a forelock like a tiny patch of fur above the brow. These were the boys, and they would wear this ornament on their shaved heads until reaching the age of ten or so when they would be taken before a certain statue of Buddha in great Angkor Vat to have it cut, with show of ceremony.

It was like the gathering of a babes' club. They came and came, until they numbered nearly thirty, and all were beautifully brown and nude, and all stared intelligently. They clambered up to the floor of the open house and gravely seated themselves. They leaned against the corner piles and waited. They sat down on the ground and thought. Their faces were round, their brown eyes straight, their pettable shoulders were fat and firm and edible.

They cried not, neither did they smile, nor utter a single note. They simply stared, thirty pair of Cambodian eyes searching out the soul of the savage foreigner.

A rustle sounded, as of wide leaves agitated. A cocoanut palm, beautiful as a dream-tree, was thrashing its foliage far up against the sky. A bare, brown leg came from out the clustered green, and then another. They applied themselves to the elegant smoothness of the tall, grey trunk and began a long descent, bringing the slight body of a boy.

Then the impossible happened, the boy's father approached us, carrying tons of green cocoanuts!

The green tops were hacked off, three white chalices of pure nectar were exposed, and three thirsting mouths were applied.

No use describing this revel of sense. Those who drink in the heat of the jungle know its ecstasy. No words could convey it to the inexperienced. We drank to our Artist but for whose thirst we had missed this joy.

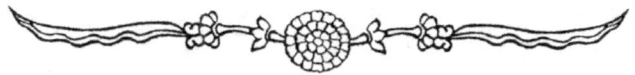

The mellow hour after dinner on the terrace of the Bungalow, the hour when the towers of Angkor are upheld like five dark lotus buds against the last pale light of day. Coffee and cordial glasses of Cointreau are filling little tables. The Artist and the Beguiler are displaying their purchases from the shops of Siem Reap, the *sampots* of the pattern shown on old stones.

The bracelet on my arm becomes worth boasting as a trophy — but people are all turning to look at something on the far side of the terrace. Blake is there orating briefly, and his harsh, jerky syllables are not unlike the cry of the lizards transfixed by the light on the wall above him. He has something on a little table before him that all are crowding to see.

"It is neat, isn't it? And made by hand too. You should see the pretty native girl who gave it to me." He was swaggering insufferably.

Someone moved away thus clearing my view and I nearly swooned with rage. Behold the celestial chalice of silver that was refused to me at Siem Reap!

Chapter XIV

SMALLER TEMPLES

Evidences of two religions showed themselves at the Bungalow. It was afternoon, after the siesta, the hour when heat was little abated, but when Europe - trained muscles required habitual activity. At the back of the house on the veranda of a Cambodian cottage lay a sleeping Buddha. At least he looked the recumbent stone idol, he the big porter, whose deep staccato voice gave courage to every boatload of strangers transferred in midstream at Siem Reap.

In front of the Bungalow passed a Romanist priest. But not as a lazy mind pictures a priest. This one was perched on top an elephant, and wore a pert, white helmet such as Priscilla and the colourful Artist set above their piquant faces. And over his black, Chinese mandarin coat flowed his Jovian blond beard.

I looked at the quiet, brown Buddha and felt that his choice, the religion of repose, was the better part. But the priest on the elephant awakened envy. I would follow the Romanist, not Sakya-Muni, and summoning a slave I demanded that Effie be saddled with a howdah and led to the Eiffel Tower from which it was convenient to climb onto her mountainous back.

The hill of Bak-Keng is just a pleasant stroll from the Bungalow, but the sleeping Buddha on the porch of the cottage had shown me the pleasure of inactivity, so I swayed over the distance on top the softly stepping elephant.

We turned up an inconspicuous path into the forest — all paths at Angkor are inconspicuous; it is only by experience one knows them to be important. This one soon became wider and faced an astonishing approach which mounted in its beautiful destruction to the very top of the hill of Bak-Keng, This was the approach of other days by means of which the devoted Khmer mounted to the Brahmanic temple above.

Just as the Italians robbed the Roman Forum of stones and constructed of them modern buildings, so the inhabitants of Cambodia removed the blocks of limonite and sandstone of which the long, wide stair was built and carried them away to use in building the citadel at Siem Reap. All that is left of the stair is a few slabs to mark the steps, and two guardian lions now fallen to earth, which rest on the first platform.

The steeps are assailable by nimble feet. But even one who confesses to loving an elephant cannot think of his feet as nimble. Effie, after allowing sufficient time for her passenger to seize the plan of the lost stairway, returned with deliberation to a path so narrow that she must have been ignorant of her size to attempt to follow it.

She brushed from before her the branches that overhung, the young trees which crowded, a quiet, determined mass which stopped not when lianas caught a shrieking passenger and tore garments and skin with their wicked thorns.

The zig-zag path mounts over two hundred feet to the plateau at the top, not an Alpine height, but 'tis enough. From there one sees three satisfying sights, a troop of monkeys, the ancient temple, and the view. The monkeys first, because they do not last. Like timorous, curious folk they huddle, and pause to stare, then scatter and leap into trees with a "*sauve qui peut.**" Jumping from limb to limb and from tree to tree they

---

* A French expression loosely translated as "Run for your life!" or "Save yourself!"

never come near the ground but scuttle downhill at a tremendous pace, high in air. A pity, for they are such smart, grey monkeys, furry and well turned out. And one would like much to feed them peanuts or talk over the descent of man.

The elephant recalls a straying mind. She faces about toward the temple. It is a testimony to the love of symmetry and balance which evolved its style. The confusion of the Bayon is gone; in pure simplicity of rectangles its beauty is achieved. It is a pyramid mounting in terraces, five of them, and long ago these were crowned with a tower enclosing a sanctuary.

On the four sides, noble flights of stairs mount the heights, on each grade of which stood carved lions. Added to this, each terrace was once ornamented with tiny towers, twelve on each, so spaced as to flank the stairways and to stand on the corners of the edifice. Fancy the charm of sixty little towers pricking upward from the sloping sides of the terraced pyramid and carrying the eye ever heavenward.

They say a gold image of Buddha was originally set within the Sanctuary, an image of solid gold. I can well believe it, for it was only a week ago that one of the bonzes found such a figure in the ruins, a few inches high, "*en or massif*",* recounts the manager at the Bungalow. And now it has safe haven in a French museum.

Signs of the bonzes are frequent on the hill. They have built their many little structures that seem meaningless in the presence of the Khmer remains. They have altered in minor matters the original intent. But one forgives them much because they drape themselves in nasturtium shades of ample silk and wear ever the face of pleasant calm.

One can no longer evade the wide view. It has been waiting all this time. It has seemed too tremendous a thing to face.

Below Bak-Keng lies all the world of mystery, the world of the Khmer, more mysterious than ever under its cover of impenetrable verdure. The jungle has blotted it out. An ocean of trees waves below at the bottom of which lie the wrecks, the ruined temples and palaces.

---
* A French phrase meaning "in solid gold."

Nothing but tree-tops is visible, not a tower of the Bayon, not even a line of the great raised roads that united all parts of the kingdom. One great monument alone outreaches the trees, the central group of Angkor Vat. Its towers alone stand above the verdure thrust upward in five cones, dominating the forest and indicating its master. One can fancy the entire jungle reaching to the horizon as the park for this sole building.

Here is realized the power of the tropic wild growth. We look down upon a royal city, upon temples outside it of great extent, and far away to places where other known edifices stand, over a district where a million souls were housed. Yet the jungle obliterates all.

Looking from the hill of Bak-Keng it is easy to fancy that no matter where one chose to fly down and alight, perhaps there too would be found remnants as large and as fine as those of Angkor, lost centuries ago and never rediscovered.

The elephant pads slowly down the zig-zag path and descending, the trees gradually blot out the view. We arrive at the Baphuon. It is full of sadness. It has been maltreated, and so little of orderly beauty remains that many slight it. But to the real lover of the ruins it is a book of history, for it contains bas-reliefs by means of which is reconstructed the life of the ancient civilization. Were it not for the inspired patience of the chisellers at Angkor Vat, the Bayon and the Baphuon, a fascinating romance would be lost.

Not only have the forest and the conqueror had their way with the great temple, but some later destroyers worked with unforgivable motive and assiduity to tear things apart and reconstruct. The result is ruin and confusion. One is conscious only of a tumbled entry, a long, raised path leading between two depressions, with at last a ruined pyramid of terraces.

The original plan has been traced out, but destruction is what one sadly sees. A magnificent entrance once stood within an outer, encircling wall, impressive with antechambers, extending far to right and to left where it widened into other groups of square chambers. Passing through

Chapter XIV: Smaller Temples 199

Terrace of Honor Upheld by Caryatid *Garudas* and Topped with *Naga* Railings and Lions

the centre of this, one stood on a low viaduct that continued straight to the second enceinte. On either hand and below the viaduct extended a long rectangular pond, a basin, filled with water. In the court enclosed by the second enceinte were two small independent buildings of the class called "libraries." Some day we shall be given a better name, but as yet the secret of these perfect separate structures is undiscovered.

The temple for which all these features prepared the worshipper stood in this court, a perfect square, a pyramid of terraces with a central tower. Alas, the tower is gone, the terraces are grown with trees. Still one clambers in ruined galleries and finds among the carvings those piquant scenes that keep one ever fascinated. Carving must have been on a plane with writing in those days, so lavishly was it extended over yards and yards of wall.

Scenes from the Ramayana are the subject, all tales of Brahmanic gods, yet from these are plucked many a valuable bit of information about common life. It is safe to believe that the gods were depicted as using the arms of war, and the utensils of living, such as were known to the artist. The bow used by Kama with which he kills Bali is undoubtedly the same as that used by the archers of the Khmers. Ravana rides in a wheeled car that copies that of Khmer nobles, and torches illumine a scene that are like torches unearthed in the ruins.

The Baphuon was said by Zhou Daguan to mount with a tower of copper. The Chinese are ever flowery in description of things that move them. The temple tower is not known by any material evidence to have been covered with metal, but its height and magnificence were great enough to thrill the ambassador into poetic exaggeration.

The Baphuon stands to the south of the Phimeanakas and its great Terrace. But a short distance to the north of these is all that remains of the Monastery of Tep Pranam.

A colossal figure of Buddha is all that the eye of the casual observes, for whatever was built of a Buddhist Monastery has disappeared except the tablet that tells of its erection in 1005 A.D. by Suryavarman. Buddha

Chapter XIV: Smaller Temples

The *Tevadas* Are Dressed with the Richness of Princesses — They Are Called the Sacred Wives.

sits on an expanded lotus on top a rectangular pedestal, declaring the value of Meditation. But he looks lonely, deserted, uninspiring. Once he was sheltered and adored; now he is lost in the forest and is without a following, all that is left of a purely Buddhist structure in the district where nearly all temples were Brahmanic even though Buddha was adored within them. The monastery buildings, having been built of wood, are quite obliterated and but for the power of this serious figure the place would never be visited even though it lies directly on the route most frequently travelled.

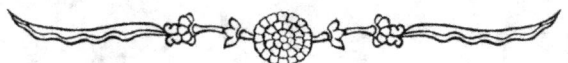

In the public square, on its eastern side, are suggestions of beauty which one is ever passing by, structures half ruined, towers half hid. Unless one is born with a questioning mind backed by contrariety, the group gets left out of the experience at Angkor. Why do the uninformed guides flout certain things and push one into others like a surly nurse? In this case I will be insistent and stop the Ford and leave the native to his cigarettes. I have heard piquant tales of these ruins and I must see them closer.

They face the Terrace of Honour, that is, they form a group running parallel to it, but a dignified distance away. Between the two lies the pond with a raised road running through it. It is not of the slightest importance, yet even the profoundest student will turn from the great Khmer ruins to gaze fascinated at the white herons (or false herons) stepping through this water on wiry legs.

The dainty birds are as unafraid as ducks in a pond, an attribute most winning, even to the man with a gun. The pool reflects the forest edge which recommences after the open space of the public square. And just within the trees stands the little group of unexplained buildings. As they themselves reveal nothing but an empty chamber they are apportioned

Chapter XIV: Smaller Temples

The Elephant Terrace, Angkor Thom.

various functions by the curious traveller or the deductive scientist. One has ascribed to some of them the role of homes for ambassadors. Another authority repudiates that on the ground that residences were usually built of wood, even the king's palace, and that a lesser man than the monarch would not be better lodged than he. All of which seemed foolish, for if the king had wanted masonry his architect would have supplied a palace of stone. The most comfortable dwelling must have been of wood or the king would not have chosen it.

Another calls some of the structures of which there were about a dozen, the shops necessary to the palace. That is a picturesque thought, and fancy at once dresses them with silks and gauzes, with gold caskets and silver bells, with perfumes and oils, and surrounds them with rich nobles who arrive in palanquins for a morning's shopping. But that fancy too is unsupported by those who make a life-study of Angkor.

No, these buildings are all for ceremonies of a very special kind, almost surely religious, although the governing system of Angkor Thom, its judgments and sentences might easily have monopolized a group of edifices such as these. Those which are of tower build are now called by the natives the towers of the rope-dancers, and from the same source comes a fiction about a rope of buffalo hide which stretched from one tower to the other whereon a man might show acrobatic ability.

A tower at Angkor is always a stimulator of thought, of wonderment, for among all the towers built not one contains an interior, every one of them is blind, no windows; not one holds a staircase, nor platforms on which to mount. Yet strangely enough the towers are built in storeys, ever receding storeys, until the summit is reached. But these storeys are not much more than great cornices, heavy projections with which a roof is sometimes edged, as they have no height, but are raised one after another with little space between.

Even so the great towers of Angkor Vat are built, in steps, as it were, gradually decreasing and forming the tall, tall cone which at twilight looks like the lotus-bud. That such towers had no use save ornament is

Chapter XIV: Smaller Temples 205

Procession of Elephants Hunting with Archers on Their Backs

incomprehensible to us. Fancy the joy of looking out from the top of the Vat's tallest tower over the whole of the Angkor group, including the city of Angkor Thom, the artificial lakes, way off to the Grand Lac or Tonlé Sap. Or fancy a vibrant bell hung high in the tower and booming out beyond civilization, out over the jungle.

None of these things are possible in a shaft of solid masonry with but a little core of space in its centre. But the Khmer idea was not without its grandeur. The tower was the sign of the Sanctuary; it sheltered the greatest god, his image or his symbol. Where it was reared a holy spot was indicated. To cover this holy spot was its definite province.

Yet it is always with regret that one looks on a tower that cannot be climbed, especially such friendly towers as those that reflect in the sweet pools of the white herons.

The most inviting paths lure, with glimpses of carved ruins beyond. A fallen lintel chiselled with deep volutes and dancing *Apsaras* promises tantalizingly lovely things if one will but penetrate the forest shade. One does, of course. And then one falls upon the lovely confusion which is Prah Pithu. All about are the charms of wonderland, a city lost by the prankish power of the woods. It is as though the ruin had been wrought in a spirit of fun rather than of vengeance, or through decay. A troop of children would find here an inspiring material for "playing house." Five small temples have here crumbled down to friendly heights. The path leads on, it skirts them, and gives a chance to discover their construction which is easier to read than when one first encountered Khmer design.

Someone has said that within the precincts of Prah Pithu stand two stone elephants. That is the reason for persistent exploring of a group which has lost all form. The elephants lure one on as elephants ever do whether stony or in the flesh.

At last a platform is reached, an important stone platform, and before it a cleared way through the trees which shows an open space beyond. And this spot is the object of our unguided quest.

The platform descends by steps at its farther end, to a grassy slope leading downward, where stand the sculptures, two elephants side by side, a little diminuated, a reflective pair. As seen against the sunny air of the space before them they seem patiently awaiting an arrival, as once they waited. But never again can the old scene of beauty be repeated when the cleared space of sedgy grass was a flower-edged pool on which floated the golden boats. Then the elephants guarded the approach from the water to the temples of Prah Pithu and welcomed the lovely worshippers who parted the curtains of the shallop* and lightly stepped ashore.

The elephants show to the hasty visitor a damaged front. The graceful trunks are gone though one can easily trace the floral mass on which their ends rested. It is a pretty thought of the old artists that elephants are flower-lovers — which is a very different thing from the ruminant flower-eater. The figures stand on low flat pedestals, as though on duty, not as though elevated for adoration, and they wear the floral collar and the light harness of the attendant's convenience. They may not be finely modelled works of art, they are far from the anatomic school of Barye, but they impart sensations, and what can any sculpture do more than that?

Back along the path to the public square one goes with the conviction that the entire Angkor Thom is but one great mass of ancient structures, and that one might penetrate the forest at any point and come upon wonders unexplored. If the city held a million souls within its walls it must be so. There were streets upon streets, lanes upon lanes, and all were filled with buildings. Does the explorer's list of nine hundred and ten include them all?

Could not I myself plunge straight into the twilight of trees and underbrush and find a gem that is still unknown to modern man? Someday I mean to try. But it will be at a season when snakes and spiders are underground, and when tigers have not yet returned

---

* In this usage, it implies a broad boat used in shallow waters, primarily as a pleasure barge.

after their flight into the mountains, having been driven by the floods to higher land.

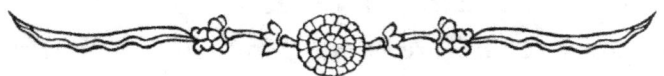

Some ancient Khmer must have gone to Babylon. There he must have been overcome with the beauty of its hanging gardens and he must have returned to reproduce them. I saw one in all its beauty, on the road which curves around Prah Khan. It is not named a garden, however, but is known as the temple of Ta-Keo. But I saw it at its present best.

It is a square pyramid formed of three terraces which mount high, then much higher, until the plateau of ruins at the top is reached. Over the whole pile grows a gracious wealth of greenery, thrusting upward, trailing downward, climbing willful, creeping timid, until the whole is like a splendid garden. All was an entrancing mingling of shaded green of leaf and grey of stone — all except the top grade which was a blaze of colour. The Boston maid and our Artist were flaunting frocks of apricot red and yellow, Priscilla swayed in pale iris blue, and even the men who dallied with them were in blazer stripes of blazing value, as all called and waved handkerchiefs of savage taste.

An eye that sees thus a sacred temple profanes it not. Mine came back from joyous riot to trace out in orderly fashion the plan of the ancient builder.

A moat denoted the importance of the monument, this time a square one, not an oblong. One simple bridge or causeway crossed it, and this was on the eastern face where was also the only gate through the enclosing wall or enceinte. The inner enceinte is furnished with three *gopuras*, those symmetric groups of chambers whose uses may be supposed but not entirely decided. The top grade, reached by flights of stairs, contained five towers, one at each corner, with one of considerable height in the centre, this one harbouring the Sanctuary.

One of the smaller towers holds a figure significant but amusing, that of Civa with his Çakti, or wife, sitting on his knee. Those who show levity at this must be disciplined by learning that each of the three greatest gods of Brahmanism, has a second self called his wife in whom are vested qualities useful to the god but which he does not care to carry himself. This wife is often male in appearance, and she is said to be more active than reflective.

Chapter XV

THE BUNGALOW

I sing the Bungalow.

To those who have not yet been to Angkor — all the world will go there soon — the magnificent ruins represent the whole interest. To those who are already there, the greatest building of the group is the Bungalow. No archeologist, no artist, even, is superior to its charms.

After a few days' stay therein you give it a wholehearted affection, though at first one may be unappreciative and take it for granted. It is low and affectionate in aspect. It sits on a pleasant green by the roadside and is shaded by mammoth trees which yet leave it open to moonlight and the stunning southern stars.

A tiled veranda serves as corridor, each bedroom opens on a court like a tennis lawn, and each room has its own big bathroom with floods of water. Night's rest becomes a joy. Nine o'clock is the welcomed time for beginning it. Yes, nine o'clock, for the tropic sun must be eluded by rising at six-thirty, breakfasting at seven and starting off before eight for the morning's supernal delights among the ruins.

They know how to arrange for sleep at the Bungalow. Air is

Chapter XV: The Bungalow 211

The Elephants at the Corners of the Terrace — They wear elaborate crowns of ceremony and hold in their trunks a drooping sheaf of lotus-blooms.

furnished by big windows thrown wide, at opposite ends of the room. Besides this the door is of the classic pattern made familiar by barrooms whereby feet and legs are the clue found by the observing outsider as to who lives behind.

No, it is not immodest, not after the third or fourth day. Modesty seems to be an affair of climate when analyzed. After lights are out, all sorts of figures may be seen emerging from the doors of barroom pattern, and flitting across the grassy courts and down the blue-tiled veranda-ways. And they are not dressed in modesty's garments long and thick. Heat affects the memory as it relates to clothing, and one forgets to put it on.

And so one goes to bed with a view of lawn below the door and of stars above it, nor cares one whit. Only, the boy who does the boots makes too early a clack on the tiles with his sandals at dawn.

So I thought one night when his footsteps waked me before the light. Something unusual about it made me listen sharply. He did not move on. He stayed just the other side of that scant swing-door — a most trifling barrier against a night marauder. He continued to stay. The only sound was the occasional change of posture of the feet on the tiles. Dawn came with my imagination working torment. And dawn showed me the outline of spare, thin legs just the other side of the door. I lay still in the bed but shivered in the dawn breeze.

The bed of the Bungalow is an ethereal Temple to Sleep, built of whitest linen on its flat mattress, and of gauzy net in its high upper structure. When one goes to bed the long, net curtains do not flow in a bridal-veil showering to the ground, but are tucked in hard and tight between mattress and spring, all around the square. Thus one is completely caged in a tight white box: thus is access to one's highly valued body made difficult to such small night-prowlers as darting lizards and little snakes and the charming world of night-flyers - bats and beetles.

You grow to think this the loveliest sort of couch. So it is, in the tropics. But when you are about to be attacked by a native who has long been standing outside your door, it becomes a trap.

This book is not one of mad adventure, in it no life is lost nor greatly endangered. As the coming day gave me boldness, I struggled out of the lapped and tucked-in curtains, slipped across the room and peeped distantly through the crack of the door. A diminutive native horse turned away in astonishment and alarm, clacking over the tiles!

How friendly then it all seemed. The great coldness between men and beasts that exists in other countries was not here. That tiny, lonely horse standing close to my bedroom door had come as to a friend. I even like lizards in my room now that I understand — though I pray I may never set my bare foot on one in turning out of bed.

The terrace outside the dining-room is another gem of the Bungalow. It is here that the most resourceful hotel host meets his guests, on arriving or at lesser times.

He met each one to-day with smiles covering dilemmas.

"Just received a telephone from the Messageries that twenty guests are arriving on the boat this evening."

"But the house is full!" protested all.

"Yes, the house is full," he agreed, shrugging and rubbing palms together in out-worn stage-business for hotelmen. But he smiled a cherry-red, friendly smile from a trusting heart. "We shall arrange."

And he did. He actually persuaded forty tired tourists to re-arrange their effects and alter their beds, to double up and squeeze up and make place for the coming twenty. The nicer proprieties took to the jungle - a healthful shock to them - in the process of doubling up, when by splitting rooms in two with curtains, brother and sister, mother and son, had temples of sleep in the same large cubicle.

No one liked it much. The solace was a saintly feeling of self-sacrifice and brotherly love. This was most noticeable on the part of the Diva who consented to let her maid sleep with another maid and who overcrowded her own lofty apartment by letting her husband share a corner of it on a cot. The two reporters from Nice, however, spat venom at being cast into one chamber.

The twenty were delayed — "Le bateau est dans la boue." A tragic cherry-red smile beamed through the announcement. But at this time of year, late January, it always sticks in the mud at some part of the journey.

Therefore when they arrived at nine we were all fortified by an exceptionally good dinner of Parisian dainties, and warmer than ever was the saintly feeling of self-sacrifice, of brotherly love.

The strangers came. They passed tired but spirited through the chairs and tables of the big, square terrace which smelled spicily of fresh coffee, cordials, expensive vintage smokes, and on to the grassy squares onto which gave the bedrooms.

"Impossible!"

"I cannot sleep two in a room!"

"I must be alone."

"Unbearable!"

"Some of the people already here can doubtless give up a room."

"The bureau in Saigon assured me there were plenty of rooms. So I'll not submit to this."

The crowd came trooping back for dinner in this mood, making these remarks.

We, the seniors, slunk off to bed knowing that no gratitude lay behind those hostile looks. But Monsieur of the Direction smiled and placated and fulfilled as ever, and the next morning the clouds had packed away.

The morning had been spent clambering over the terraces of Prah Khan, that pitiful ruin which nearest approaches the great Vat in size. It

Chapter XV: The Bungalow 215

The Terrace of the Leper-king — Each line of figures arranged itself in groups, the center of each being a giant, a god or some fabled being.

is probable that had we known the feats of strength necessary for viewing this tumbled mass, we would have prepared for it by three months or more of physical training. Prah Khan is not revealed to the lazy nor yet to him of atrophied leg.

It abounds in chambers of such green calm as haunts the caves of ocean, but these mystic retreats can only be visited by the athlete. And the company at the Bungalow were not athletes.

After the exercise of the morning, luncheon was, during its first half, a determined effort to stop the clawings of an internal devil. Hunger is a most demanding passion, and a weakening fatigue is not a sweetener of tempers. And Cambodian waiters, alas, speak only their own agglutinate tongue, and become panicky if addressed in another.

But the two journalists from Nice were the only ones who raged, flounced, snorted, and primitively misbehaved, before the feeding.

After déjeuner, the terrace — and the contrast of peace after storm. What oil is to troubled waters, so is a glass of wine and a cup of coffee to troubled man. A dozen persons sat about with faces that smiled even in repose. Voices were low and sweet and the matter they expressed was like angels' converse. And all because the passion of a vicious, hungry fatigue was satisfied at the Bungalow.

The heat descended and wrapped us round, until the rattan furniture seemed like hot cushions piled about the body; the blue-tiled floor was as a plate-warmer under the feet. The lizards of the wall neither clucked nor darted. Obviously the time of the siesta had arrived.

Sleep nips two or even three hours out of the day at the Bungalow. The morning is for the serious ecstasy of studying the ruins. But late afternoon is for some innocuous pleasure. Sleep is the preparation for this delectable hour of strolling, of taking tea on the terrace, of reading or of studying the bands of natives that are ever slipping softly along the road with bare and silent feet.

The fatigue of crawling over Prah Khan made a motor ride seem alluring. A motor ride in the jungle. Anomalous. Mowgli would shriek

The Terrace of the Leper-King Smiles Among the Jungle Trees Above His Terrace of Court — The inner wall with the best preserved carvings. It is a mystery why the ancient builders carved the beautiful wall and then placed a duplicate wall a few feet before it, filling in the intervening space with earth.

maledictions should he spy our machine.

Presently the Ford — another shock — drove up and waited. The decorative young Bostonian who illuminated nature with her frocks got in beside the Artist, the Beguiling Guide in front. The engine buzzed, the driver was as stone. Of course. We had forgotten to tell him.

"Néak Pean," called the ready Bostonian splash of red, and the driver repeated it after his fashion which little resembled ours.

Guides are faithful helps in the heavy morning tours. Resented, of course, for half the spell of the ruins flies away at the pointing of a finger, at the drone of a voice. The Cambodian guide cannot be said to drone, however, rather he blurts wildly a mispronounced syllable of what he understands as French. No English of course. He knows of only two languages, that of Cambodia and that of the country's "Protector," France.

Some of these little dark men of Cambodia who serve at the Bungalow had their part in the Great War. France used even this far country to replenish her depleted man power. And thus these quiet people were plucked from their banana groves and rice fields and set in the trenches to "go over the top." The "chamber maid" who makes the beds wears naught but a sarong or *sampot* on his sable person, and is tied to the soil. But he was a skilful aviator in France! Back to the *sampot* after all was done. After the wild flights over the terrible fields of blood and destruction, the return to the sheltered peace of the jungle village, the casting off of "horizon blue" and the freeing of the body.

Here comes a query. Should one look upon an aviator of the Great War as a member of a savage tribe because he is now found in the jungle half naked, living in a bamboo hut, softly, quietly tropic in his inertia?

After the European "bath of blood" how well he understands the bas-reliefs of the Vat. Long hours in contemplation of the battles chiselled there must now mean more than myths; they are vitalized and touch his own life with smashing conviction. We travelers — sometimes mere tourists — walk the long galleries guide-book in hand, trying to

The Statue of the Leper-king Smiles Among the Jungle Trees Above His Terrace of Court Beauties

identify the tales of the Ramayana, the struggles between the *Devas* and the *Asuras*, conflicts of Khmers and Chams, and the muddled tempest of the battle of Hanuman's ape-men. These are the strange plums we pluck from this unknown feast of art and archaeology, if we apply ourselves to the task.

But he, my quiet bedroom boy, is our superior as he ponders, walking the marvellous ways of stone. About him is the mystery of a phantasmagoria, for these Brahmanic tales are mixed with his being, are a part of his aura.

We, the invincible Europeans, we look with a puzzled superiority on these fairy tales. But he, the Cambodian soldier returned from the Great War, draws deadly parallels of the conflicts.

The native who drives for us Henry Ford's great gift to all the peoples of the earth, was dressed in a hot linen suit, heavy leather boots and hat which would produce sweat on the brow in Iceland. European influence is written all over him. He has also a pride that brooks no orders, and an overbearing insolence to the drivers of bullock carts on the road. But he was dull and indifferent. Perhaps he hated us that hot afternoon.

The hour was late. The sun was low enough for the tree-shadows to cover all the way. The greatest heat was gone and the soft air caressed as we flew through the scented jungle and passed under the gate of Angkor Thom. From the flowered roadside came a piercing note continued on one key longer than is good for the eardrum. A cicada. One would have said it was the disconcerting bore of the steam whistle which attaches to the peanut stand of New York's Greek vendors. No poetry blooms around this sort of cicada.

Past the Bayon with its Brahmanic towers, past the Terraces of Honour, the Phimean-Akas, out the farther gate of the city of a million souls, and around the turn of the drive which skirts the temple of Prah Khan, whose ground plan almost equals that of the Vat in size. All these things are friends to those who know them, but even friends are passed by when other matters call. And we were bent on seeing Néak Pean, the tiny temple in the clutch of one giant wild-fig tree.

"I like its name," said the splash of soft orange-red from Boston.

"The guides never take us there, it has an aristocratic aloofness which makes it choice," explained the Beguiler.

Spoiled children of civilization.

The motor stopped. We might have stopped anywhere along the way and found as distinctive a place. The wondrous trees grew sky-high above us, dropping perfume, the birds called among them, but we were buried in the jungle with no sign of the glory of man. A little path perhaps. Yes, the sulky gentleman in linen suit and peaked cap was indicating one, a mere thread on the carpet of the forest.

We followed it alone, leaving the white-suited man lighting a cigarette, with a sneer, an unmistakable sneer, on his brown face. Which sneer was certainly possible to read without the help of Pali, Sanskrit, or modern Cambodian. He did not approve of our Anglo-Saxon ways.

A path is sure to lead through a thousand delights at Angkor. This one did. Treetops canopied the way, as high above as heaven's blue, such soul-moving trees that one could believe them sentient. And they are all new to us, as though one were wandering in a world of fancy. One kind is a flame of red flower, another is sharp and naked as a dead pine, another has a straight, tall bole mounting to impossible heights, with a marvellous power of stirring emotion. And these gracious trees shed perfume and drop small tropic blossoms, pink and pulpy, that invite the feet to tread the flowery way. Another tree hangs out fluttering bows of pink and creamy ribbons against a background dark and glossy, all of it a trick of leaves.

And in these treetops are two creatures of intensest charm and fascination, orchids and monkeys. Which you prefer is a mere matter of opinion like roses and onions. As for me I choose both. It is their freedom that gives them charm. An orchid in a florist's window represents mere money; a monkey in a zoo is pathetic. But orchids flaunting colour down the path to the jungle's heart are adorable, and a band of gibbons playing up aloft are nearly adorable. The orchids call you by their startling beauty, the monkeys by their panicky fears and daring curiosity.

No ruins met the eye, as we wandered on. The light lessened and the forest twilight breathed poetry. Farther on was an opening, the remains of one of the innumerable sheets of water with which the Khmers beautified their buildings. Across its bogginess stretched the path. We paused. Should we cross and continue in the forest beyond with twilight falling in its rapid tropic haste?

We looked around on the loneliness and quiet of it all. In the brush which sheltered us was a native hut. To look at it was to shiver. It was empty, deserted. Built of bamboo, three feet above the forest floor, its face was open, its roof and walls all rents and holes. A bunk in one corner was heaped with leaves as though a wild animal nested there. A native hut of the poorer class, long deserted. Yes, but why deserted? Had a ravening tiger come in the hours of hunting, the hours like this of darkening twilight, and pounced upon his prey so lightly protected? Such things happen, they say. When hunger impels, a child is snatched while at play.

We stood looking at the trail ahead. The breezeless heat gave a sense of something impending.

"Shall we go on?" Our Artist spoke, poised as though for flying ahead over the marsh path.

Caution hesitated.

Then all four gazed down the darkening way transfixed.

"A straying calf," whispered the Beguiler.

"Sh-sh-sh!" caution counselled.

A hundred feet away, down the slope where brush and marsh-grass meet, a tawny shape was slowly undulating, half revealed.

All four stood transfixed and watched its sinuous progress as it passed through the sedge and thus slowly out of sight.

Boston half opened a parasol for a charge, the Beguiler took out a penknife, all four of us wheeled and softly accomplished the few steps back, past the deserted hut with its sinister atmosphere, and once in the shelter of the big trees flew fast as nymphs and fauns in classic woods.

Yes, it was a tiger!

But this is not a book of wild adventure.

There were miles of forest drive in the deeper twilight, and dark had come when we reached the lights, the flambeaux and hearth-fires of the native village on the shore of the great moat, lights which streaked red across the water.

Then the blessed Bungalow. How gratefully we greeted its smiling manager, how suavely we admitted having had a bonne promenade, how prayerfully we shut ourselves in the safe embrace of our bedrooms, how appreciatively we consumed at dinner the rare viands and wines of Felix Potin with a lively gratitude for the privilege of eating a dinner instead of being one.

But of our encounter we dared not speak. The envious would have called our wonderful tiger a rabbit in the grass.

The hateable reporters from Nice would have scoffed.

As for Néak Pean, we were not on its path at all. That was perhaps the little joke of the sneering chauffeur.

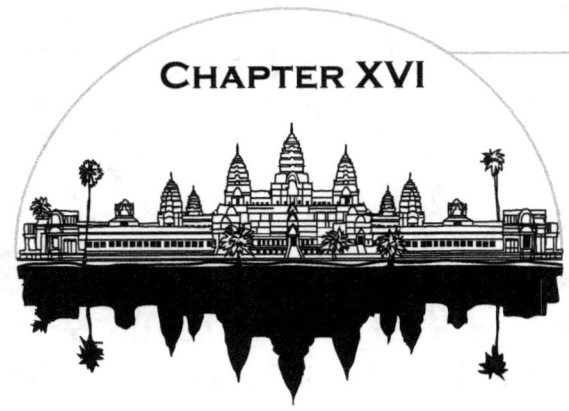

CHAPTER XVI

BANTEAI KEDEI, TA PROHM

Two large temples stand near together outside the limits of Angkor Thom, Banteai Kedei and Ta Prohm. It is easy to see why they are outside. Like Prah Khan and Angkor Vat they enclose such large territory that no walled town could find space for them. They are indeed walled cities in themselves.

The native guide tells me that Banteai Kedei is the Palace of the Queen Mother, he says it in the blurred French by which the Cambodian conveys his thoughts to the Occidental. That it is misinformation I am sure, but I hug to my heart the romantic lie and carry it within the gates.

The outer enceinte hems, as in other cases, a huge rectangular oblong, walled, and was once surrounded with a wide, wide moat. The space within is a forest, a park, with one broad, defined path which leads through shaded loveliness to the beautiful plan of the temple miscalled a Queen's residence. Here one passes the remains of an entrance *gopura*, slips over a raised path, sidles through a rectangular building of four courts and many chambers and attains at last the temple itself arranged in galleries of one level, not mounting as in Angkor Vat.

If the foot stray far to right or to left of the temple, and if one be wise in noticing signs, a second wide moat will be discovered surrounding the temple except at the approaches on the east and on the west where it is broken by raised ways to the sanctuary.

But I, thinking on "*la Reine-Mère,*" began to dress the small chambers of the edifice with life. They appear to be unending, some of them so severely small that I appointed them to ladies' maids or bachelors. Wherever one enters there are more and more to be seen and one longs for a positive knowledge of their original intent.

A score of little courtyards give light to all the place, and make necessary frequent doors in the open. These doorways are all bewitchingly decorated with carvings of the highest order, not the lace-like low relief, but in panels of verdure which curves high from its background.

One hesitates to pass within the door when held by such charm. The volutes on the panel at the side form a series of designs each reaching a point which fits within the hollow of the design above it. Thus mounting, the repeated design covers the panel. But the charm of the conception lies in the tiny feminine figure set just below each point, a fairy goddess of jewel-dressed head, of folded knees and clasping hands, who entices, who enthralls, and who suggests her own imminent flight to the land of fable. This is the place where one most wants to be alone — with the little head that is so playfully thrust outward — and with a chisel and a hammer and without honour.

The French do well to impose dire punishments and fines on one who takes from the ruins even one tiniest fragment. The warning signs tell of purses demanded as fines, and of long months in prison, which warning is intended to force honesty upon the five hundred workers among the ruins, and the native population who at times stumble upon priceless relics which are sent to French museums in Indochina and in Paris. If Khmer curios are exposed in places other than these, it is because someone has not been found out. But France will soon alter this condition and will allow museums of other countries to buy from this treasury of a little known art so long held close.

In the ruin and confusion of Banteai Kedei the carvings take one's interest. They are piquant, exquisite, not too frequent. Compared to others of the very old structures they seem meant, not to instruct the religious, nor to affright the timid, but to make adorable a human habitation. And so I persist in the guide's apportioning of this temple to the Queen Mother as her residence.

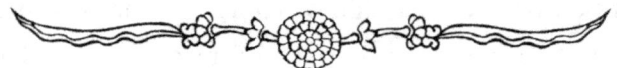

Ta Prohm makes with Banteai Kedei and Prah Khan the third of a group of three which are tied together with similarities in construction and detail, and which were all built at the same epoch, outside the city, about the year one thousand. Experts call this the early classic period, extending this marvellous time to the beginning of the fourteenth century or a bit earlier. Its latest and completest monument was Angkor Vat, built when experiments had ceased, built as the result of accumulated wisdom in art and in mechanics.

These three earlier temples show decorative designs repeated in the Vat which are yet more inspired than they, dancers who were fresher then perhaps, not having danced through so many centuries, and gods which are more powerful even though less graceful. Here is a place in which one may draw a parallel between Khmer art and Khmer habits of life. For five centuries the same carved figures were employed on building after building; for an even greater length of time the native Cambodian has copied his fathers in the minutia of daily living. The habitat of the common people is the same today as it has been for centuries, a small affair of the convenient bamboo with thatched roof. The bullock cart that rolls along the road on its work of restoring ruins or lost roads, is

Chapter XVI: Banteai Kedei, Ta Prohm

Phnom Bak-Keng — Here among the ruins the gray apes live in splendid isolation.

the same vehicle as that depicted on the ancient bas-reliefs. This content with things as they are is characteristic. If it does not make for modern industrialism in Asia, so much the better for that part of the world.

Ta Prohm has set itself in the usual great area confined with the long wall of the enceinte broken by central gates at each of the four points of the compass. We have grown to disregard this wall and its dry moat unless announced by a towered gate. The space it encloses is to us but a space to be traversed before reaching the object of our eager walk — the temple.

In the outer wall of Ta Prohm are four gates, each made imposing by a tower. It is the same tower of four giant faces which distinguishes the Bayon from all other temples of Angkor and which marks the gates of the city wall.

The same fog of mystery which clouds all the past of the Khmers, folds round these towers. They are like nothing else in all this orderly architecture, and seem to have abandoned all previous architectural traditions. The tower mounting by receding grades had gradually evolved and was the tower of one generation of constructors after another. All over Angkor one sees it repeated in brick and in stone where its symmetry is both logical and adorable. Such towers date earlier than the eccentric shaft of four faces and were also erected after. The wondrous towers of Angkor Vat are evolved from these.

But the four-faced tower is evolved from nothing in architecture. It is rather the peculiar invention of priests. In the story of religion is found the genesis of the terrible tower which upheld the face of Civa.

War, luxury, and religion should be put down as the deities worshipped by the Khmers, but religion was divisible. It included from the earliest times both Buddhism and Brahmanism. And the latter was yet again divisible, notably into the separate cults of Civa, the creator-destroyer, and Vishnu, the preserver. The happiest sort of harmony existed among them, and all gods were worshipped in one temple with a lack of sectarian prejudice that would be of advantage to modern churches.

Chapter XVI: Banteai Kedei, Ta Prohm

The Baphuon — Later destroyers worked to tear things apart and reconstruct. The result is ruin and confusion.

In temples built to the Brahman Trimurti, Buddha's image is found, and figures of Sakya-Muni are known which bear a Brahmanic symbol. Likewise Civa's emblems decorated Vishnu's temple and vice versa.

But in the tenth century when the Khmers were in the high years of success, came a fresh wave of Brahmanism which seized on all the people high and low. And its variety was the cult of Civa. No longer might other gods be combined with him, for he was a jealous god and would allow no other. The newly revived faith, the neo-Brahmanism, swept the country. The line of distinction between Civa and Vishnu which had hitherto been faint and wavering when existing at all, was now blackly defined with Vishnu on the obscurer side of it. Civaism became the fashion, then the obsession. The king embraced it and it was made the official religion of Angkor Thom.

To give fit habitat to the newly preferred god, the Bayon was built, built on the central spot of the royal city. To make it unlike all other temples, to overshadow them with a magnificence which should be special and unique was the demand made on the architects by the priests.

Thus came the four-faced tower, an architectural monstrosity flouting all laws of proportion and many traditions. But it fulfilled the desire of the priests. It made the Bayon, Civa's temple, unique, and it expressed the supernatural power of the god. None can look without emotion on the giant faces, calm, eternal, powerful yet sinister.

The same towers were set at the five gates of the royal city to overpower strangers and to remind its indwellers. No temple other than the Bayon bore them, but over the eastern door of the outer enceinte of Ta Prohm one was erected.

Then their building stopped. The swelling tide of Civaism lowered, and architects returned to their proper precepts.

Could one but see Ta Prohm with one glance of understanding its plan would give delight. The temple is a square — in concentric galleries of course, but the enceinte which holds it is in outline a Maltese cross

Chapter XVI: Banteai Kedei, Ta Prohm 231

Pré Rup — One of the minor temples.

with corners filled in part. A moat follows all the angles of this wall which is broken only by two entrances, one east, one west.

What one really sees is not at all the same, but perhaps it is no less beautiful, no less mysterious, no less worshipful. Almost at once one strays between ruined walls into an apartment or a court. Its walls might denote either, and it is roofless. Doorways open out from this anterior hall, but time has also made breaches in the walls, so that all hard lines are curved in lovely abandon. Among them nests the flora of the tropics, ferns and orchids, and above are draped leafy lianas. The place has an atmosphere, as though often used, but by spirits of the wood. As if to verify the thought the trees which are rooted within these walls are the strangest ever seen. Their trunks are covered with a pale and glossy bark like that of yellow birches, but from them flow strange wings like jibs on yachts — yet more like long, trailing skirts of giant women, heavy silken skirts extending far over the brown-leafed floor. It is as though the trees were forest ladies who had tried to flee but who were petrified in flight and turned into trees like Daphne pursued.

The magic is wrought by the eccentric wild fig, the same which holds in its clasp the miniature temple of Néak Péan. Not content with beauty alone, it mounts the walls to disrupt them, and grotesquely sends out a big glossy root like a *Naga* which runs around two sides of this enclosure at the wall's base and, scarce diminished in size, is thrust through to travel still longer.

Ta Prohm's state of ruin is a state of beauty which is investigated with high delight and left with regret. But one can always come again. And one always does.

Unexplained as yet is the vast reserved space, the *acrama*, in which this temple and all others are set. Here the park is two thirds of a mile in one of its dimensions. The park of its neighbour, Banteai Kedei, is but little smaller, that of Prah Khan is even larger. This feature of architecture in the tenth and eleventh centuries was continued in the twelfth or thirteenth by the constructors of the last great temple, Angkor Vat.

Chapter XVI: Banteai Kedei, Ta Prohm

Prah Pithu — A city lost by the prankish power of the woods.

It would seem unnecessary to oblige those who would worship, to traverse such weary length of path. If it were now, and in white countries, no one would go to church at all. Were the space intended as a garden or a shady bosquet*, all the harder would it be to proceed to the altar of the gods and the droning of ritualists.

Records of the Khmers are few and hard to untangle. One looks to such an expert as George Groslier to solve riddles and make the deductions which only a savant can make and the laity respect.

He it is who fills this great surrounding space of the temples with human habitations.

The idea startles at first, so unusual it is to consider a temple as other than a meeting place of God and man, a place set apart for that alone. But a reading of the lists of temple guardians and servitors makes it plain. They were numbered by the thousand. A stele at Ta Prohm mentions figures so large that they must have included persons in the immediate vicinity who served but did not remain. Thus are mentioned: "18 principal officiants, 2,740 officiants. 2,232 assistants, among them 615 women dancers. A total of 12,640 persons which comprise those who have the right of lodgings. 66,625 men and women who perform services of the gods. A total of 79,365 with the Birmans, the Chams, etc."

Other inscriptions tell of hospitals within the temple precincts — most astonishing revelation to the impudently ignorant Occidental who sees the great Rockefeller Institute as the first hospital in Asia. These hospitals had their medical corps, assistants and nurses — women among them. One of their services was to care for the ill and the old who came to say prayers and offer oblations. We have never heard of such provision at Lourdes.

From the sparse inscriptions graven on the ancient stones in Sanskrit and in Khmer is learned the prodigious list of offerings demanded daily by the gods — or at least by the high-priests. It includes tons of rice, pounds of butter, quarts of rare oils. A corps of workers had to dispose

---

* n. A small grove; at thicket. From Italian *boschetto*.

of these, not in store houses but under the pedestals of divinities and among minor temples throughout the district.

The list of persons attending the great temples piquantly includes dancers, sacred dancers. These, too, must have lodgment, must be fed and when very young must be trained. Soldiers also were necessary as guards, for the wealth of a temple in gold and gems was beyond the telling. Each statue was hung with jewels, the space below its pedestal filled with gold long since ravaged.

In his frequent investigations, poring over shovelfuls of earth, stalking tirelessly over the enclosure which the Khmers called acrama and we lamely call park, Groslier has discovered tiles of the sort which roofed the domicile of the Khmers, and other detritus once belonging to daily human living. He has thus built on a sure foundation his theory that the great space was filled with houses for the accommodation of all the classes mentioned. Nothing could seem more reasonable.

Traces of such building are seen only by the student, but one can easily imagine them. The fragility of the materials of which they were built, wood, with clay tiles or even thatch for roofs, is sufficient reason for their disappearance.

With this idea in mind one can people the space between the outer enceinte and the temple as we stroll toward the central sanctuary of all the great temples of Angkor. Thus disposing of the park, one becomes interested in other unanswered wanderings. There are, for instance, the almost numberless small chambers formed at entrance *gopuras*, at corners, and in the crossing of galleries. That strikes one at Angkor Vat, which is in such unspoiled order that one comprehends at once the builder's harmony.

For what use were the corners and crossings formed into little rooms? Again Groslier has deduced a romance. These are the chambers of those who desired to immure themselves in the temple precincts, to lead the life of the temple, the ascetic life or the *dolce far niente**. Each chamber, each group of chambers was shut with double doors operated

---

* An archaic Italian expression that literally means "sweet do nothing." A person who doesn't need to work or do anything useful.

from within. Privacy was complete. Each long gallery open only to space, and high above the ground, offered a delicious promenade for the reflective. That I have proved for myself.

As one approaches nearer the sanctuary the little chambers grow more frequent in proportion to the galleries' length, and the innermost gallery contains far more than the outer, until the number in the Vat swells to sixty or more.

Some treasure must have lodged in these secluded nests, some human treasure that needed the best protection man could give. It was undoubtedly the living treasure of the gods, the sacred dancers of the temple. Khmer gods, with rare discrimination, demanded human offerings — but alive. Noble families brought to the gods their loveliest daughters. These gave their youth to the service. They were to eschew love and marriage, motherhood and all worldly joys to attend on temple ceremony.

In a golden palanquin hung with gorgeous curtains the lovely freight was brought, accompanied by the parents who dedicated her to the great gods of the Trimurti. She was prepared for the ceremony by a toilette most meticulous, bathings, perfumings, careful dressing of the silky black hair which escaped in two long tresses to fall full length over the shoulders. The heavy silk *sampot* was expertly draped and tied, then the heavy jewels were fastened on in a wealth of coloured light, the coronet headdress, earrings, necklaces and girdle; bands of gems clasped arms and ankles. Through this gorgeous array shone the warm personality of the maid herself as she stepped from her curtained palanquin and proceeded through the temple's galleries escorted by high priests, even to the very Sanctuary itself where Vishnu or Civa was asked to find her worthy in his sight.

But who holds such rare goods holds them in peril unless securely housed. In the inner recesses of the great temple they hid their loveliness and only flashed it before the eyes of high priests, kings and nobles during high ceremonies.

Lest the weight of religion oppress, think on the life that was led within the temples. Ancient annals make it read like life at a spa in summer. The pictures of the bas-reliefs and the inscriptions as well, if read aright reveal a life so various, a part of it so secular, that even experts are timid about decided opinions. Judged by Christian churches, a Cambodian temple is an anomaly, but one arrives nowhere by comparisons between East and West.

Although thousands of persons lodged within the temples, living in great part in structures which by reason of the materials of which they were built have long since vanished, yet the most punctilious of religious ceremonies were ever in progress in the close concentric galleries.

It is also known that the great wall of enclosing was built around the palace of a king or a noble, forming the same park, and that this also was filled with habitations, while near the centre, as in the Phimean-Akas, was reared a temple. Therefore, one need not wonder at the varying opinions of the experts. The endeavour to call all Khmer ruins temples, and the wish to make them all palaces, results in fine material for controversy. One like myself who enjoys skimming the cream of romance, rejoices in the evidence that shows fairly little difference between the two.

Life, abundant, vigorous, pleasurable was carried on within the encircling enceinte of both palace and temple. In the former every opportunity was given for worship; in the latter a secular life was not robbed of its indulgences.

Visitors of wealth within the temple were given suitable lodgings and the best of food, and had liberty to circulate at will. Religion was administered among the guests in the park in a form far from oppressive. Inscriptions on the stones at Angkor and elsewhere are stimulating to our imaginations.

"In this charming place, ornamented with habitations of ascetics, full of troupes of penitents, is heard the murmur sweet and heavy of the sacred readers, where the fires are lighted and where the altar is smothered in flowers.

"In the acramas rises constantly the sound of sacred texts recited by masters and disciples, enounced with force by a joyous crowd, the highest word covered by the harmony of musical instruments.

"The multitude of banners floating in the air, the harmonious music which mounts even to heaven, the melodious chants which accompany the stringed instruments, the animation of the dancers, all render the place comparable to the paradise of Indra."

Access to such a monastery was not denied to any one, not even to the common people who in Cambodia were very common — and that women of quality were admitted freely is but one more testimony to the fact of their high valuation among the Khmers. Even today the Cambodian woman is allowed no heavy labour, but is always spared hard tasks by father or husband. Provided these same visitors contributed with lavish hand the rich offerings acceptable to high priests for their altars, the visitor might even penetrate to certain sanctuaries.

On the other hand restrictions were prescribed which now make delicious reading. A visitor might not drive his chariot within sacred limits, nor close his parasols, those lofty decorative parasols of rank, nor might he feed his dogs nor cocks. A long code discovered at Lolei awards specific punishments, including heavy fines, and for those who were penniless a hundred strokes with a bamboo.

As one takes the shady path covering the long distance between the outer enceinte and the temple, one can animate it with all classes of persons, with visitors high and low, with servitors, and doctors, and priests, musicians, and the agile dancers, and can see as their accompaniment the rolling bullock carts bringing in and carrying out the wealth of offerings in the way of food. Thinking thus on all these things the path becomes too short, and Ta Prohm is hard to leave.

Chapter XVII

WATER

As the hart longs for the water-brook so longs each human being at Angkor for volumes of water, not only once but several times each day. Bathing becomes an obsession.

So it is easy to see why the Khmer built reservoirs and other hydraulic constructions. Today they are all inoperative, but their remains are evidence of the Khmer's love of water. If the vestal virgins who stand in the river's brink at Siem Reap are descendants of the early race, then their eternal bathing might be counted an inheritance. But it is the sun, the tropic sun, that is sufficient reason to make amphibious even the brief sojourner.

But bathing does not alone account for the water storage, nor does pure decorative beauty of reflecting pools, nor any other one reason, for water is so lavishly and variously disposed at Angkor.

Because Angkor Vat is ever before us, gloriously greeting the morning, poetically closing the evening, we take it as the first example of Khmer hydraulics. Ever before us lies the moat in beautiful expanse.

Its dimensions are always an astonishment to those who are

accustomed to the meager moats encircling certain castles in England and in France, two hundred meters wide and nearly three miles around. Such a body of water must have served some other purpose than that of moat.

Angkor Vat is only one of many. The royal city itself, Angkor Thom, is encircled with a moat; though only half as wide as that of the great temple it is far longer, about eight miles. Think of the labour of digging this great ditch to its original depth of fifteen to eighteen feet, and of supporting its banks with blocks of stone. But no one in authority cared a whit about labour in the good old days of the "varmans" for it was all done by slaves and they did not count, being for the most part the captured soldiery and populace of enemy countries.

Outside the royal city the great temples have their moats. Prah Khan is encircled with the same wide water that makes beautiful the entry to Angkor Vat. Ta Prohm misses the water following the outer enceinte but places the moat nearer, following all the interesting angles of the inner enceinte. Ta-Keo again is surrounded by a moat on its outermost circumference. So the Khmer had miles and miles of water wider and deeper than the nearer rivers.

And this is by no means all. Within the great temple enclosures were often dug great basins or ponds. These added so much to the beauty of architecture that they are readily thought to be purely ornamental. Two of these are placed directly before the principal entrance of Angkor Vat, one on either side the great stone concourse. The masonry that held them is now gone, but two sheets of water stay to mirror the towers of the celestially beautiful temple. That they are now called elephant pools means nothing more than that the native guides seek to give a name to all features for the appeasing of tourist curiosity.

Two unwalled pools that also add to the beauty of remains are those on the public square opposite the Terrace of Honour.

Before the Bayon two great basins were dug on either side of the way leading to the eastern entrance, which must have reflected the great temple with tremendous effect. Nearby, the Baphuon was provided with two long bodies of water lying before it on either side of the great approach in which were mirrored the splendid columns of the causeway extending more than two hundred yards. Curiously enough no pools were round, always rectangular.

Small pools conserved water within the enclosures of other temples, but Banteai Kedei was magnificently provided. Close to the temple lay a wide moat with a broad paved walk on either side of it, but a further supply of water was placed conveniently near in a vast basin called Sra Srang — a whispering name like wind blowing in the reeds which now border it. It is a veritable lake and even now holds water though in niggard quantity. Its size — for those who like figures — is eight hundred meters by four hundred.

But all these are the small reservoirs, the convenient pools, mere landscape decorations of garden size compared to the great sheets of water spread magnificently in Khmer country. There is the great parallelogram which thrusts its length east of Prah Khan to the eastward, and there are the two huge lakes called barays by the Cambodians, Baray of the East and Baray of the West.

The little temple of Néak Pean stands in the centre of the first of these, and steps going into it seem to argue its use for pleasure and for pleasurable worship — a place where one might take religion as a dissipation rather than a self-flagellation. One thinks of flower-boats and music, of maidens and of youths.

But the great barays were built with intent so magnificently serious that they cause thoughts of the sweating slaves who built them and of the mighty engineers of a mighty king. One of them lies to the east of the capital, Angkor Thom. Its measure is roughly five and a half miles in length, one and a third in width. And it was dug by the hand of man. One aches to think of the slaves even though so long dead. Digging is hot work in Cambodia. How can one think of the people of the tropics as lazy!

The Western Baray lies southwest of the city, west of Angkor Vat, and its dimensions are a little less than those of the Eastern Baray. The former is beautified by the lovely temple of Mébon, a pyramid of receding terraces on which are placed many detached edifices, the most effective being the five towers which crown the top. Could any conception be lovelier, a vast expanse of sky-tinted water as setting for a perfectly ordered temple. Spirituality went hand in hand with the gratification of the senses in old Cambodia, and its followers were not forced to be ascetics.

The other great lake was not without its temple, also named Mébon — of the Western Baray. Here is a variation from usual temple plans, for this one on a tiny circular island contained a square of water in its centre, and in the middle of that was erected a tiny edifice, the whole enclosed in a rectangular wall of enceinte.

But all this water, for what was it conserved in these reservoirs whose construction represented an amount of labour incalculable? Experts give reasons varying according to their prejudices. One can dispose of the smaller pools and lakes as places for bathing and boating, even as waterways for little circulation. Moats around the temples would give water for the large family of visitors, attendants, guards and priests; and must have served as well to water gardens, though it is true that during the season of rains there is more of water in Angkor than man would choose to have.

But the barays are set down as municipal in character. It is suggested that they were used as great storage reservoirs for fish, live fish. Thousands of tons of fish are taken from the Tonlé Sap and the Grand Lac by the native population during the season of lowered water. A mean advantage is taken of the fish when the lessening of the element in which they live crowds them together by thousands in streams grown shallow. They are then easily caught in the voracious seine. It is thought that the Khmers, thus securing them, transferred them to the great barays where they could take up their usual fish life, preserving happiness and health until

Chapter XVII: Water

Ta Kéo, on the Outskirts of Angkor Thom

such time as the Khmers chose to catch and eat them. They were kept for consumption until the days of inundation, the season of rain, when the Mekong forced its waters into the Tonlé Sap and all the land was deluged. At that time the fish took their liberty in the opaque flood and were hard to catch.

Another expert, thinking over and investigating the Western Baray, tries to dress with fact his theory that the great sheet of water was an inland harbour to bring boats almost to the wall of the royal city. Were it associated with a stream for but a little way it would connect with the water at Siem Reap and boats could thus pass out to the Tonlé Sap, the Grand Lac, and to the great world.

However it may be, stored water was a necessity of the close population of Angkor and splendid projects were executed to provide it whether for decoration, for irrigation, for fish preserving or for navigation.

Chapter XVIII

PRAH KHAN, NÉAK PEAN

There is the same preface to all temple visits at Angkor. The active day begins soon after the night ends. The stars are glowing large as though they had come nearer to court closer human communion. It seems a perversion of taste that one should prefer a netted bed to such an invitation. Still with the mind undecided as to which is the better part to choose, one is later waked to the cool freshness of a sunny day by a strange call, a whipping of the air, almost a whistle, yet louder. It is as insistent as an alarm, as fascinating as the call of a whippoorwill or cuckoo — which never sound like birds at all.

It is the call of the gibbons, the thrilling call of the little monkeys up aloft in the great trees which overshadow the Bungalow. They have obviously taken over the task of waking the foreigners who sojourn among them, for the cry is far too loud to be regarded as breakfast talk among themselves. High in the golden freshness of trees at sunrise the calling gibbons are hidden, but their wail brings back old Chinese poems of lonely longing, when men had gone adventuring and wives waited years for their return; when maidens of the courtyard knew the tender melancholy of love. Old poets all found sadness in the call. To me it is a whip, a whip under the lashes of which I am forced to arise gaily and buckle on my armour — of the filmiest — and trot out across the grassy courts to the terrace, there to drink inspiration from the most stirring edifice in the world, Angkor Vat. In the early morning it floats, water below it, clouds sustaining it.

The moment of the motor-car arrives, the air is full of noise and smells to make the moment horrid. Eager to secure for themselves the best, the two journalists from Nice and the priest of the Santa Claus beard and white cork helmet seize the first motor as a vulture seizes prey. The next car becomes a corbeille de fleurs, the poppy from Boston on the front, the back filled with Priscilla, as a lily, the Diva, as a full-blown rose, with some gay young men as foliage.

All the cars dash away into the distance as the minor Brahmanic gods dash through space in old legends. The rejected Ford is champing the bit and pawing the earth, but we want to lose the rest of the visitors and see things alone.

This is what happens every day of ruin-roving, and thus we start for Prah Khan, the Beguiler, the Romancer, and the artist. But there seems to be no word for "go slowly" that is known to the chauffeur and to us, so we are shot northward like a comet over the long, straight road of fragrance, through the southern gate of Angkor Thom, straight north to the centre of the city, which is the Bayon, where we curve around three of its sides and then through the public square and on, on outside the distant city wall; and then, after all this fierce flight, the car stops at a place without distinction. But it is Prah Khan, the edifice of such wide extent as almost to attain the dimensions of Angkor Vat.

Five hundred men work every day at the task of making the Angkor ruins accessible and of restoring fallen stones to their original places.

It is a statement which must be repeated often to oneself in severe reprimand especially if one is inclined to weep over untouched destruction at Prah Khan. A thousand men a thousand days could scarce

Chapter XVIII: Prah Khan, Néak Pean 247

Prah Khan, that Pitiful Ruin which Nearest Approaches the Great Vat in Size

rebuild its superb construction. And if they did, would the place be half as marvellous as now? Then it would be frank architecture, grand of plan, exquisite in ornament, but bare, without atmosphere. Now it is an entrancing mystery deep in the jungle, soft and alluring in the twilight made by heavy verdure, accessible only to the ardent lover of past days who is gifted with agility — and a pair of rubber soles.

Prah Khan is one of the places one cannot afford to miss, for it dates back to the ninth century, the time when Khmer art reached the high level, the time when the great temple of the Bayon was built. In it one sees the same decorative maidens and madly dancing Terpsichores* that delight one in Angkor Vat, which was built three or four hundred years later, but at Prah Khan they are done with greater freshness.

A little path penetrates the forest. We take it as the chauffeur lights his cigarette — reminder of the cunning commerce of the B.A.T.** Without noting, we have passed through the wall of the enceinte, so unimpressive has this feature become. Yet it is to consider, this wall, for it encloses a rectangle nearly half a mile from east to west, and but eighty yards less than that from north to south.

Outside of this wall once lay a wide full moat, after the fashion of Khmer buildings. Inside lay the park and in the centre of that, but leaving the greatest space towards the east, was set the temple.

The Vat of Angkor has given familiarity with this plan, otherwise one might not be able to follow it in the ruin which is Prah Khan.

The long path is as ever a delight where the darlings of New England garden-beds grow wild and no tree is like unto those which are familiar. It proceeds through a park. But an enchanted one. The temple must have been asleep a thousand years to attain such far detachment from the world. Its entrance, set close on the forest floor, has two square columns heavily framing a door within and sustaining a splendid pediment. Trees close in and make a deep twilight, moss and ferns cluster in the damp, and dead leaves brown the earth. All announces desertion and destruction; overturned stones tell of overthrown kings,

---

* In Greek mythology Terpsichore was the Muse of dancing and choral singing.
** The British-American Tobacco Co., in Asia.

Chapter XVIII: Prah Khan, Néak Pean 249

A Fallen Stone of Graphic Eloquence — *Apsaras* dancing about chariots, *Naga* head and serpentine motif.

exquisite carvings which decorate them tell of the high development of art destroyed by a higher development of warfare.

This is the central entrance to the group of three that leads within the second enceinte of Prah Khan. To right and to left stretch the walls, but this is the *gopura* — there is no English word equivalent for the Khmer architectural convention, a cross of chambers, each arm a room.

Within this enceinte is a smaller park. Within this, again, is the temple, in three concentric squares, the sanctuary in the centre. In this plan are variations from the plan of Angkor Vat. While that has but one enclosing wall, this has two. While that has its galleries raised in grades, each higher than the next, the galleries of Prah Khan are all on one level. With the plan well in mind one dares to enter the great ruin.

But useless is an ordered brain to one who threads the rocky mazes of this sad temple. No methodic way is possible. At first one holds to order and marks a certain mass as the *gopura* of the first gallery, another as the passage to the sanctuary. But straight progress is stopped by a fallen column or a pedestal overturned. A window becomes an easier exit than a blocked door. In a gallery one must achieve the height of the wall to make an exit or turn back, and that one never does. The explorer's passion drives one on.

But what does it matter if the plan of the builders is lost from one's consciousness? It is entirely lost in the building itself and only an archeologist can divine it. Ever more and more fascinating grows the ruin as it takes on the disorder of a cave. That is it, it is like a cave, but one found on a planet other than our own.

The chambers are filled with a green light such as fills the caves of ocean, a light which is almost palpable. A small, square room is mysterious with its efflorescence, the carvings beside its one square window are veiled with it, a fallen pedestal is plated with the same green light grown tangible in the form of moss. It would scarce be surprising to see wide-eyed fishes floating in and out of the shaded window. In such a chamber the gods of Brahm seem dead, or fled with the vanished

The Four Faced Tower of Civa Overgrown by the Jungle

Khmers. Perhaps it is here that tigers and cougars make nocturnal visits. Through openings made irregular with heaped and leaning stones other shadowy green chambers show their mystery, and give hints of floating ghost-shapes, men, maids and gods.

Through a far passage joy returns on a sun-ray.

A bright splotch of colour leaps the barriers. The Boston maid steps smiling within the green room of lugubrious fascination and one no longer thinks of floating fishes but of mermaids.

The carvings on Prah Khan show the hand of the vandal, probably a fanatic, for he has used hammer and chisel to obliterate all symbols which might denote which god was worshipped here. A row of pedestals exists of the sort used to carry civaïque symbols, and on this is based the theory that Civa was worshipped here in the early years. The chisel and hammer which took away the lines of carved deities who formerly sat comfortably within an ogival frame of carving, may have belonged to a Buddhist. For it must never be forgot that both Brahm and Sakya-Muni were worshipped by the Cambodians. Both cults flourished at the same time, both even used the same temples. But it is true that the sack of Angkor came at the time when the pacific cult of Buddha influenced the nation in favour of peaceful meditation.

As for chisel and hammer I have often longed to replace my conscience with these tools of the acquisitive. Tiny carved figures just of pocket size have an impish way of insinuating that a leap from the leafy volutes in which they rest could easily be made. A tempted poet has even written a long poem of his temptation, to show how noble was his resistance when left alone with a hundred such about him. So I am not alone in thievish impulse.

Carvings at Prah Khan are cut deep. That is a proof of their age. Note at Angkor Vat the lacelike flatness that overlays the stone. Experts prefer the little dancing bayadere of old Prah Khan to the same figure carved on later temples. But an astonishment to us is that the same figures are repeated for four or five hundred years. Novelty seemed not

Chapter XVIII: Prah Khan, Néak Pean

Ta Prom's State of Ruin is a State of Beauty.

to appeal to the decorator then as it does now.

When the thighs ache from climbing over walls, and the heart thumps in fear of perilous falls, there are delicious spots in which to stay still. They may have been courtyards where high priests gathered and guardians slept, but now they are walled bowers over which the trees extend to heaven's blue. The soft air moves the sprays of orchid blooms that bless the boughs which feed them, and the sun sends cheer to chase away the melancholy of hidden chambers of the interior. Far up among the branches the leaves are noisily agitated. We look up, Priscilla shrieks prettily, the young men laugh. We are the objects of a contemptible curiosity. We are being observed with sneering minuteness. The tall, tall trees are alive with grey apes! Detestable things are caged monkeys in city parks, but these are distinguished creatures, our hosts for the moment, as Prah Khan is their home and we are but visitors. They are Kipling's Banderlogs.

More climbing takes us among columns in double rows, the square ones of the porches, and discovers a row of splendid shafts in the round. The path runs along a wall and we know that on its further side is a pillared veranda giving on a court in which is placed a gallery still smaller.

But we have had enough of blind wandering. It all seems a wondrous mass of beauty tossed together in superb confusion. Perhaps on the confusion depends much of its charm by reason of the contrasts produced. In a chamber which has replaced its proper roof with shading trees are overturned blocks of stone suggesting the work of vengeful giants, yet the desolation is nullified by a slanting lintel carved with so exquisite an art that one smiles in sudden ecstasy. It is pure decoration but the space is filled with rich invention, with perfection in balance, blending floral forms with Brahmanic symbols to form a harmony. Such is the work of even the early years of the classic period of Khmer art.

Thus one finds contrasts in the sadly ruined temple which make one loth to leave. But the territory outside the city of Angkor Thom has many temples, and they irresistibly call to be examined.

Ta Prom - A Pilaster — The great buildings, built without mortar, can ill withstand the encroaching jungle.

The biggest should come first by all the laws of sight-seeing. The most important is the phrase that governs. But a spirit of contrariety sends me scuttling off to Néak Pean — the last word being pronounced "Ponn," and the whole name signifies curved *Nagas*.

Néak Pean is one of the temples that makes one dream of the olden days of luxury and beauty. It was worthwhile to live then and to be a woman among a race which has ever adored its women. It is to the overpowering temples of Civa that men and armies repaired; but it was at the tiny temple of Néak Pean that eager princesses laid their lovely offerings of wrought gold and pungent perfumes.

Fancy it as it was in the old days. To begin with there was the artificial lake, a wide extent of water in the shallows of which floated the flowering lotus. In its exact centre — the surveyors of Angkor were expert — stood the exquisite miniature temple of one small chamber, the sanctuary, a temple as finely ornate and as well-proportioned as an alabaster vase. With art delicious this wonder was made to appear like a vision in the land of faerie. It floated upon a full-opened flower of the lotus, the petal tips curling back to touch the water. On the corolla of the flower, curved around the temple's base, were two *Nagas* whose tails were twisted together at the back and who raised their fan of heads on either side of the steps in front which mounted to the sanctuary. Thus they guarded the gem and gave gracious welcome to whosoever directed her light barque to draw close to this lovely haven.

On this circular pedestal of poetic imagination rested a square temple with four carved doors, one open, occupying all the facade except for the square columns which flank it. Above rose the tower with pointed over-door groups of carvings, symbolic, graceful, inspiring. Each closed door bore the figure of the humane god Vishnu standing at full height, but lest he impress too strongly his grandeur in this dainty spot, the space about him is filled with minor carvings which vary on each door. They did well to place Vishnu on so lovely a temple, not Civa the destroyer. Had I to choose among the Trimurti the god for a soul's gentle protection, that god would be Vishnu the preserver.

Within this lovely casket was a seated stone figure. The door was ever open, suppliants might at any time lay before Buddha their offerings and their prayers. Over his feet they poured perfumes and rare oils; over his shoulders they draped fine gauze from the far kingdom of China, and within his open palm they laid the sacred lotus.

The chamber was too small to admit them and they stood without in a bending group, swaying toward the *Naga* heads for support or salaaming gracious salutations to the god of peaceful meditation. The golden boat floating beside the approach again received them under its rich canopy and nested them among its cushions. Rowers moved the shallop so slowly that the *Naga*-prow seemed to progress of its own volition. And so, the gods appeased, the spirits rose, and soft music spread over the waters in which the rich notes of male voices blended, and life went happily in the lovely twilight hour.

Néak Pean is not now this bewitching place. It is only the book in which one can read of romance and the religion that invariably accompanied every act of man in the kingdom of the ancient Khmer. But one must know its former estate to love it. It is not a temple for the hasty tourist. Moreover it is out of the usual route. One must insist to get there at all, for the chauffeur-guides are by way of flouting it.

A longish walk precedes it. That walk is through the artificial lake. The first disillusion. The lovely sheet of blue and green on which floated swans and lilies and the golden boats of princesses is dry and brown with sedge-grass. Only the archeologist can discover signs of masonry and ornament along its edge.

Dry of foot one reaches the tiny temple. Here one may easily trace the encircling *Nagas*, the rare round pedestal which so interests the student, and the front doors of the cell-like chamber which contains the seated Buddha. Over the doors rise the great carved pediments, almost ogival with their bordering scroll, The square columns are also visible in part, and in the ruins is discovered an elephant betrayed by two forefeet and a head, which are thrust from the corner in a way to suggest that each corner was in appearance stayed by the willing back of the colossal beast.

But the entire temple is held in the clutch of an enveloping growth of tree roots, not roots as we know them but the demon roots of the great wild fig. It is a tree which abounds at Angkor, which seizes upon ruin after ruin and seems directed by a malevolent intelligence. A seed dropped long ago on the single tower of little Néak Pean sprouted and grew during the years before the re-discovery of Angkor. When eager enthusiasts broke through the brush they found the temple nearly covered. The roots had run down over this casket as lava from Aetna runs over a cottage. In their search for the ground they had covered almost entirely the lovely altar to the gods, and, after finding the earth, had spread their size beyond the bonds of probability.

Néak Pean stands hidden, but it stands in greater perfection than if it had not had the enveloping roots of the ficus to hold its stones from falling apart. That is our consolation. But it is a pity. The astounding trick of the forest claims too much attention. One looks at that in cheap wonderment and at first the lovely conception of Néak Pean's architect is forgot.

The tree has left two faces open, and these one can examine, with Vishnu well exposed, surrounded by legendary carvings. The cell may be entered too, but with the vanishing of Khmer princesses vanished also the perfumed oils, the golden caskets, the flowers. Instead is damp and mould, and one gladly leaves the interior to the stone figure within.

Chapter XIX

FOR THE CHARMINGLY UNINFORMED

If Angkor intrigues you, you see it all as fast as possible, hungrily, ignorantly, and then begin to ask a thousand questions. Most of them are asked by the profoundest scientists as well. That is gratifying in a way, for one likes to have something in common with the erudite even though it be ignorance.

But it is not that one is ignorant, it is that the past refuses to give up secrets which are the keystone to theory's arch. Angkor now belongs to the great world of the traveller, the artist and the archeologue, and discoveries are daily made by the patient and the scientific. Questions, then, may he asked with hope of some day getting an answer.

Who were the Khmers, asks the traveller with child-like confidence of the Bungalow's manager, who is efficiency itself as a host and ought to know. He waves a hand, seemingly towards a shelf of pamphlets telling of steamship lines and land routes. He is right! The Khmers were travellers of various sorts. They were the mixture that travellers always are, and they found at their journey's end an indigenous race on which they imposed themselves.

A map will help the story. It will show how easy it was for other races to push out from their own countries into the valley of the Mekong and overrun the rich land of Khambu or ancient Cambodia, a land where life was so easy and resources so great that it was famed as a district in which to pitch the family tent.

India sent her hordes. They came from the south, bringing with them the Buddhism of their locality. They crossed the seas and landed somewhere near the top of the long peninsula which is tipped with Singapore and has Siam above. Then they spread over the country south of the mountains.

They also came from India overland, and these were the Hindus of the North. And they also brought a religion, that of Brahma. These were perhaps a hardier people, a better breed.

But the Khmers were not pure Hindus nor yet Hindus with a strain of indigenous blood. The mysterious Khmer has destroyed all records of his race such as are generally in use in identifying. He has been so progressive in a hygienic way that he has reduced to ashes all the precious skeletons which would tell the story of the race to those who by turning over a human skull can find more than a sigh for poor Yorrick.

As we wondering moderns see it, the race came from nowhere more substantial than the caves of legend, rose to preposterous heights of development, constructed a dreamland of palaces and temples — and then vanished into the legend land from which they came. But for the phenomenon of Angkor and sporadic ruins nearby, the slate of history would have been wiped clean of them.

But the phenomenon of Angkor was left, still exists and amidst its fragrant beauties are left indications which the wise may read. One of the important indications has to do with the Chinese.

It would seem more than probable that the Khmers being a mixed race by reason of immigration were largely mixed with Chinese. This would account for much. This would give strong reason for their love of art, for their creation of an architecture superior to that of India.

The centuries of the Khmers' phenomenal development, from the sixth to the tenth centuries, was it not just the time when the caravans of the Chinese were travelling to the west and south? In the time of the Tang emperors great overland routes were made and followed. No distance discouraged them. Across the wide map of Asia crawled the camel trains of trade. It is stimulating to think of them, bringing silk and gauze, jade and wrought jewels, meeting every sort of obstacle, but still picturesquely crawling. Then there were the daring Chinese junks which floated down the coast.

And into Indochina came the traders with their wares. It was not far to come. The Chinese province of Yunnan lies just north of the peninsula on which Cambodia spreads its rich territory. And coming, they saw the commercial possibilities of the place, its prolific plains of well watered rice, and they stayed and called their fellows. Most determining of all the elements that compose the Khmer is the Chinese. He it is who helped to whiten the skin, to straighten the hair, but most interesting of all, he furnished the quality of mind that was capable of high development.

Not to go beyond our smattering of Asiatic history and legend, let us adopt the theory that the great originator of the race, Khambu, who married the daughter of *Naga*, was a stray from China.

The bas-reliefs show war-like qualities highly developed. War seems to have been the actuating motive of king and populace. The war spirit was dominant even in religious scenes.

But why not? It was not because the Khmer loved battle but because his was the most envied country of the peninsula, and he was ever required to protect it, at the point of his spears and arrows, not forgetting the Sacred Sword, l'Épée Sacrée, as the French Cambodians call it.

Fantastic stories of the country's riches got abroad. From the country of the Chams, which is Annam, and from the country of the

Thais, which is Siam, came visitors who gazed astounded on the luxury at Angkor. The King was arrayed in a splendour undreamed of, the ladies of his court lived in a luxury unfathomable and smiled happily from among their jewels. Temples were the repository of wealth untold, and surpassed in size any others known. And all this indulgence was surrounded by the ever-productive rice fields so well equipped by nature that it is possible the wealth of the population came largely from this source.

Envy ate the heart of the Chams and the Thais, and each in turn went out to war to possess themselves of the Khmers and their fabulous wealth.

Thus was ancient Cambodia drawn into battles unsought. But she won them. In almost all important conflicts the splendid array of the king's army depicted in Angkor Vat met victory. Home they came bringing with them countless captured soldiers and citizens, all of whom were put to work in the rice paddies or to construct the wonderful buildings that charm and inspire us now. They stayed perforce, and staying mixed the blood of the conquerors with still other elements.

When pestilence took off tens of thousands of the over-worked slaves, nothing more natural than that the Khmer king should decide to attack his enemies for some disguising reason, and thus he was enabled to refill the ranks of labourers. Thus the wars continued through the centuries, and the Khmer grew ever richer and made luxury and religion his reasons for living and for developing an art which expresses his vigorous elusive soul.

It is here that the second childishly astute question is asked. Where did the great race vanish after having reached such heights?

A group of half-nude, quiet folk are padding barefoot along the road to the bamboo village across the moat of Angkor Vat. Are they the Khmers? If not, then where are they, the lost ones, the warlike and artistic people whose kings were worshipped as demi-gods?

Remembering legends of demi-gods in the Ramayana the imagination suggests that one day hundreds of years ago they mounted

Chapter XIX: For The Charmingly Uninformed

Reflections in the Pond of the Bonzes

sky chariots and flew away on the clouds to some heavenly country, there to live in everlasting joy. The quiet natives of today's Cambodia half believe some such legend.

It seems far more probable than that the race of Khmers who built the ruins were all killed in battle. Yet one has to believe the scraps of history that tell of the gradual undoing of the race by outside enemies. The vigorous Chams of Annam rose strong in the thirteenth and fourteenth centuries and in terrific warfare defeated the king, alternating their attacks with those of the Thais of Siam. Thus were the Khmers exhausted and thus they fell shortly after the period of the highest development had been reached, the time when Angkor Vat was completed. The envy of the enemy killed them. Yet what became of the residue? Every conqueror leaves alive the race he conquers. Where are they? One flouts indignantly the idea that the present Cambodian, gently inert in mind, quietly content, could be of the blood that fought fierce battles to gain luxury and puissance.

And yet — and yet — there are striking similarities between the details of daily life now and those pictured in the bas-reliefs. Things change slowly in the East. But where is the love of luxury and its appurtenances, the charming indulgence of the sybarite? Where are the golden pleasure boats, the curtained palanquins and the lovely perfumed ladies they bore? Blown away on cloud chariots to the celestial land of the gods. Half the joy of wandering through the enchanted Angkor would be gone if one believed that its heroes and its maidens were the forbears of the chattering peasants holding market on the steps of the moat's causeway.

A race arose from obscurity; it built the most marvellous edifices of Asia; it was subjugated and it disappeared; its gift to the world was smothered under the jungle; the buildings and the people were forgot. That is the tale in brief.

And who found them after six hundred years of neglect and forgetting? Another race to whom art is a necessity to inspired living,

Chapter XIX: For The Charmingly Uninformed 265

One of the Four Pools in the First Gallery of Angkor Vat

the French. One day a Frenchman came across a temple of the Angkor group. It was to him like coming upon an unguessed Paradise. The natives showed him more. Mad with ecstasy he stood before the lonely magnificence of the Vat. He penetrated the jungle to the terrifying ruin of the Bayon, unique in the world. And all the world over which the treetops waved he found to be filled with soul-stirring wonders.

He had wandered up the waterways from French Indochina. He had crossed the border and was in Siam. Then to Siam belonged this treasure unsurpassed! And Siam was letting the jungle devour it, and ultimately there would not be one stone upon another to tell the tale of splendour. France must be the owner of such a field of art.

They manage these things well, the European nations in China. Generally a worn-out missionary gets killed by natives in the coveted country and it is shown that nothing will assuage the grief of a bereaved nation except the annexing of the country in question. No deaths occurred in the acquiring of the slice of southern Siam by the French Protectorate, only a political juggling, an imperative swapping of territory.

In 1907 France gleefully received the Angkor group. Nothing more important has occurred in the world of art for centuries. To France be all gratitude for plucking the ruins out of the jungle's strangling tangle and appreciation for making it possible for the world to visit them.

More questions follow. The mark of interrogation is never inactive in a land so new and yet so old. Answers are found but slowly. The old race left no literature. Yes, they were literate, but the manuscripts they left behind were writ on short-lived stuff which centuries ago was disintegrated by tropic damp and tropic insects.

Of vital importance are the points of compass. Every building faces east except Angkor Vat. The meeting of the lines east-west and north-south marks the sanctuary of the temple, though the part of the building toward the east may occupy the larger space. It is not that entries are made only on the eastern front, but that the principal entry is made there.

Prah Khan — It is an entrancing mystery deep in the soft twilight made by heavy verdure.

But the jungle has made us moderns glad to enter at any point where trees and ruin allow us.

Those who find interest in construction look for the faithful cement that has held the stones of these monuments together through centuries of neglect. There is no cement. That is one of the marvellous facts of Khmer architecture. Throughout all these mammoth and intricate structures, the builder so prepared his stones and nicely fitted them that they have kept their places unaided and even have resisted disintegration. The stones of Angkor are a brown limonite and a hard close-grained sandstone of dark gray.

The bas-reliefs are the only documents, but these unhappily concern themselves little with the records of the people. They pass by historic facts but enumerate long lists of temple offerings which are after all but a recital of comestibles such as grains and flavourings. There are also steles and tablets, slabs of stone engraved with writings both Khmer and Sanskrit.

Slowly these are being deciphered, and as slowly we are pushing further into the mystery that surrounds Angkor. Fascinating pursuit. The pictures on the bas-reliefs, thousands of square yards of them, tell most of the story. From these are sorted out the accessories of living and of fighting, and by arranging them, each with his kind, the old life can be reconstructed with assurance.

Perhaps one is most troubled by the religious legends that are declared on every building. The tales brought with Brahmanism from India are bewildering in their complicated length. One must have been brought up on the books of the Ramayana to be moved by these tales. It is difficult to weep over the theft of a monkey-wife or to regard her as radiant with tender beauty.

But the churning of the Sea of Milk one must not neglect, for does not the "Barattement" figure three or four times importantly?

The two great gods of Brahm which one cannot escape among the ruins are Vishnu and Civa. The latter is most popular, most puissant, most unpleasant, a sort of Moloch who keeps folk faithful by bestowing

Chapter XIX: For The Charmingly Uninformed

There Are Delicious Shady Spots in Which to Stay Still

a rare blessing, but who in general rules through fear. He is as elusive to the European as a fairy who constantly changes his shape. He may be the ascetic, lost in meditation and heavenly vision, or he may be a god with four arms, each hand holding an attribute or emblem. The trident or dorje is one of his emblems and was formerly placed on top of temple towers as a finial — but in metal which has perished.

Vishnu must be recognized at sight. He too is furnished with four arms at least and holding emblems. But he may also appear as an antic acrobat perched on the shoulders of a monstrous bird. That is his mount *Garuda*. Civa rides abroad on a white bull, Nanda.

Beside these is Buddha. The contrast is terrific. Yet peaceful Buddha held his firm place in Angkor throughout the centuries side by side with Brahmanism. Perhaps the Hindu brought him there, but it is suspected that the Chinese interpretation of the cult, the Great Vehicle, was the most valuable to the Khmer. The harmony with which all gods were housed in one temple is a lesson to warring religions. Civaism, jealous and demanding as ambitious priests made it, yet allowed Buddha to be adored in its temples. Vishnuism, the milder form of Brahmanism, included Buddha among its gods as shown in Angkor Vat.

It is not to be didactic — rather it is with apology — that this little digression is made on the religious subjects pictured in Angkor Vat and the Bayon. It may save consulting a public library — and there is no public library at the Bungalow.

With absolute delight one turns to the writings of the Chinese ambassador, Zhou Daguan, He speaks a language picturesque and tells tales of his own astonished curiosity. He stayed in Angkor between 1295 and 1297, and informs us on what was going on at that time. His writings were happily preserved and were translated a few years ago by Paul Pelliot, the great French Sinologue. Would he had had an ancestor who kept a diary in the tenth and eleventh centuries, for that also was a time of great development among the Khmers. From the records of Zhou Daguan are deduced the customs and luxuries of a

Chapter XIX: For The Charmingly Uninformed 271

Néak Pean — The little temple at Néak Pean suffocated by the giant grasp of the tree roots.

scantily recorded race.

After the fourteenth century, oblivion.

Then there are the kings of the land of Khambu — Cambodia. They stand waiting for the visitor at Angkor to accomplish the strange syllables which are multiplied to form their names.

Khambu, the first king, being more or less a myth, is dismissed with the note that he gave name to the country but his date being somewhere before our Christian era we will ignore it as history has done.

Centuries of development pass whose exact history has unhappily perished. We come then to a line of kings of more precise record. In 802 A.D. reigned Jayavarman II, to whom is accredited the building of Prah Khan, the great edifice standing just north of Angkor Thom and which comprised both palace and temple within the spacious limits of its enclosing wall and moat. Primitive were the centuries that went before, but from this on Angkor's people grew in greatness.

Skipping two reigns we alight on the name of Yasovarman who made his mark a deep one in the twenty years beginning in 889 A.D. He it was who achieved the magnificent project of the royal city of Angkor Thom, and weighted its centre with the marvellously strange temple of the Bayon. He built Phnom Bak-Keng and sank the great basin of the Eastern Baray.

Europe was having her years of darkness in the centuries when the Khmers were growing prodigiously in intellect, in wealth, in military power. Charlemagne seems but a ruffian adventurer compared to Yasovarman, Hashavarman followed, responsible for the finish of the Phimean-Akas, All blessings on his shade if 'twas he who set before it the Terrace of Honour.

Jayavarman V, 968 to 1001, erected the Baphuon with its tower, said to be of copper.

Half a dozen kings followed, each one beautifying the land with temples outside the Angkor group, which are hard to reach. The next important king was Suryavarman II, who reigned from 1112 to 1162.

Chapter XIX: For The Charmingly Uninformed 273

The Wild-fig Tree on the Centre Island Completely Enfolds the Little Temple in its Grasp

He concerns us greatly. He helped to build Angkor Vat.

Four more kings reigned, fought, acquired, and maintained Khmer supremacy, until the time when Zhou Daguan began his famous visit in 1295.

After that time the Khmers were ever less and less victorious over the other peoples of the peninsula including the Siamese. Then fell the evil day of their complete rout and the mad destruction of their wondrous works.

After that the people disappeared, and therein lies a mystery which even history cannot clear. And after that the jungle came in. Listen to Mowgli's Song Against People:

> *"I will let loose against you the fleet-footed vines —*
> *I will call in the Jungle to stamp out your lines!*
> *The roofs shall fade before it,*
> *The house-beams shall fall,*
> *And the Karela, the bitter Karela,*
> *Shall cover it all.*
>
> *"I have untied against you the club-footed vines,*
> *I have sent in the Jungle to swamp out your lines.*
> *The trees — the trees are on you!*
> *The house beams shall fall,*
> *The Karela, the bitter Karela,*
> *Shall cover you all!"*

Romance is not hurt by noting that twice during the centuries of oblivion missionaries brought word of Angkor, though the word was unheeded. In 1604 a Portuguese priest, Quiroga de San Antonio, told of two hunters who perceived magnificent ruins in the jungle about 1570. And in 1672 a French missionary, Père Chévreuil, spoke of the place, calling it Onco.

After that, silence until a broken line of French explorers drifted up the Mekong and the Tonlé Sap. The line began in 1858 with Henri Mouhot and was continued by Commandant de Lagrée, Francis Garnier and Delaporte. The latter was the first to make, in 1871, an equipped expedition with large personnel. The first complete plans of the ruins were made by the Lajonquière in 1900.

In 1898 was formed by the French the institution called l'Ecole de l'Éxtrème Orient, a body which was keen to make scientific explorations of the Khmer ruins and to take means to preserve them. But Siam was in control of the district and only by her permission could the French enter Angkor.

Persuasion was used — of a kind known to international politics, and by means of a clause in a Franco-Siamese treaty of 1907, three provinces were returned to Cambodia — and Cambodia was already within the French Protectorate. Alors! the future of Angkor and the Khmer ruins was assured, being in the hands of France.

THE END

Circa 1908.

"When beauty assails, reason has no part."

Helen Churchill Candee
October 5, 1858 - August 23, 1949

APPENDIX I

Life's Décor:
A Biography of Helen Churchill Candee

By Randy Bryan Bigham

Author, journalist, world traveler, Orientalist, socialite, trendsetter, political insider, lifelong advocate for women's rights and — long before the advent of the flapper — a cigarette-smoking, fashion-loving flirt....

Not by any imaginative stretch could Helen Churchill Candee (*née* Hungerford, 1858-1949) be called a conventional Victorian lady. Yet the distinguished Washington, D.C. social leader, known for her beauty and charm, never lost her respectability, her grace or her determined way on the trail she blazed to achieve independence and success.

To strike out on her own as a pioneering interior designer, art critic, consultant, writer and lecturer, may have come easily for one whose adventurous forebears landed at Plymouth on the *Mayflower*. Still, to her contemporaries, Candee defied description.

It was unusual enough for a wealthy woman to apply her good taste and knowledge to advising architects, manufacturers and private clients on decorating. But Helen's pen was potent, too; she reported on rural community betterment, childcare and etiquette for popular women's magazines and even wrote a "how-to" book on female autonomy through wage-earning.

Her early journalistic work almost always touched on women's emancipation. Apropos of the suffrage issue, Helen wrote in 1894 that "change and progression are the watchwords of the times," and the traditional view of women having "no ambition higher than a replete preserve-cupboard" was wrong. She said the modern woman must learn "there is more in life than she has been extracting" and "let her mind apply itself to larger regions of thought."

So what was she about, this globetrotting pretty lady of good family and lofty connections, who liked to expound on bourgeois issues of gender and status? Why wasn't she content in her urban high-life, presiding at the tea table or organizing charity tableaux?

She was certainly unusual. Unlike most men and women of her social position, Candee's wealth and breeding didn't prevent her recognizing the evils of class privilege and discrimination.

"Theoretically, the fundamental social rule of our Republic is the equality of all persons," Candee observed. "Practically, we are unreasoning snobs."

She advised readers to fight "iron-bound prejudices" and cease with "endless insistence on unimportant customs." These, she maintained, accomplished nothing but an "obliteration of individuality."

Today Helen is still hard to peg. A mother of a doting son and daughter, she likewise delighted in her children, finding in them much of the inspiration for her democratic views.

"Children know nothing of principalities or powers," she wrote in 1901, "and would be as ready to make a grab at the mustache of the German Emperor as at their mother's apron strings."

Yet she craved solitude and study as well, escaping to exotic lands for months on end to write, paint and, as she put it, "enjoy nature and avoid humanity." Normally reserved, she could be outspoken and demanding. An intellectual to the core, happily ensconced in the quietude of libraries and museums, she also sought distraction in fellowship, levity and a great deal of romance.

"Without romance," she asked, "what would our lives be?" Admitting that youth was the playground of love, Helen stipulated that "no woman is so old that in her heart she has outgrown the habit of being a girl."

The contradictions in her personality were the contradictions of her era — a time of societal foment and transformation in the role of women, the status of the lower class, and the spread of science and media. The Victorians and Edwardians were struggling with the past to address the future, old attitudes and morals were colliding with the new. Helen Churchill Candee had a front row seat to the duel.

Born in New York City on October 5, 1858 to Henry Hungerford and the former Mary E. Churchill, Helen Churchill Hungerford belonged to one of the oldest families in America. Notable descendents included Elder William Brewster, the spiritual leader of the original Pilgrims who landed at Plymouth Rock on the *Mayflower* in 1620. A white ash chair belonging to Brewster, made in the Plymouth Colony in the turned style of the day, remained in the family for many years; it's now in the Pilgrim Hall Museum. Was it this beautiful specimen of early American furniture that inspired the career of Brewster's antiques-loving descendent?

Helen's father was a prominent merchant as was her grandfather, William Churchill, and her mother was a well-known hostess, both in New York and in Paris, where she lived out her final years.

When Helen was a child, the Hungerfords moved to the country, first to New Haven and then Norwalk, Connecticut, where she was reared and privately schooled, attending one of America's first kindergartens, operated by Rose Porter.

Growing up, Helen was close to her mother, whom she remembered as "an absolute, though kindly, monarch," and in later years the two regarded one another as friends, an unusual perspective for the time.

Helen was musically gifted and showed signs of literary talent at a young age. She was also beautiful, and during her first season attracted a batch of eligible suitors. But she didn't want to marry and instead devoted herself to civic and educational causes and charities.

In her mid-20s, however, Helen Hungerford fell in love with Edward W. Candee, a prosperous Norwalk businessman, and the pair soon wed. Unfortunately Helen's new husband was as dissolute as he was wealthy, and the marriage horrific, Candee severely abusing his wife and their two children, Edith and Harold, and finally abandoning them. Her family's motto "Faithful but unfortunate" held true for her during these years.

Circa 1901.

With her parents' help, Helen managed to acquire a decree of separation from Edward Candee, and to the chagrin of her affluent family and friends, who offered financial assistance, she chose to support herself as a writer, contributing essays to magazines, including the *Ladies' Home Journal* and *Scribner's Monthly*. Much of Helen's early work was geared to practical household hints and advice on etiquette but as her career progressed she wrote on weightier issues such as women's rights, childcare, education, and community government.

Some of Helen Candee's most insightful stories dealt with the delicate art of social interaction at which she was almost too astute. In reading her wise maxims, one catches a glimpse of Helen's gentle yet strategic understanding of humanity. In *Outlook Magazine* she wrote:

> *You can never learn what people really are, unless you have the grace to listen, not with polite patience, but with sympathetic interest, to anything they may tell you. You are at times terribly bored, but that is of slight consequence in view of the fact that your companion is enjoying the conversation, and you are laying the foundation of a friendship which will in time prove its value.*

In an article for the *Ladies Home Journal*, Candee urged readers to hone their skills at empathy. "If we put imagination to work and warm it with love," she wrote, "we can learn much of what others are feeling."

While writing encouraging words for others to read in household magazines, Helen's own household wasn't happy. Separation from her husband didn't offer the peace of mind and freedom she needed, and she eventually sought a divorce, a far from easy decision at a time when a broken marriage was a social disgrace. Divorce wasn't a simple matter legally either, but Helen finally obtained one in 1896 in the Indian Territory of Oklahoma; she actually lived in the town of Guthrie for several years, recording her bucolic adventures for the press back east.

"In March the whole land is abloom with fragrant pink," Candee reported. "This is the promise of June and July peaches. They come in abundance; almost everyone has a few peach trees tucked in around the house."

It was during this time, through her agricultural stories about the region for such prestigious news journals as *Atlantic Monthly* and *Forum*, that Helen rose to national prominence as a journalist and a proponent of the U.S. government's settlement of Oklahoma. Her widely discussed articles are considered by historians to have been crucial to establishing the territory's appeal to Americans, leading to its statehood a decade later.

For Helen, promoting Oklahoma was a mission she was glad to undertake, and she minced no words in her veritable campaign, as an article she wrote for *Atlantic* in 1899 shows:

> *Oklahoma, land of prosperity, sunshine and brotherly love, has a thorn in its side. That cause of pain and irritation is the failure of her sister states — and especially those in the East — to recognize the truth concerning her. They prefer tales of outlawry and border ruffianism to accounts of successful agriculture, and are inclined to shut their ears to all stories save those that thrill the imagination.*

Meantime, Candee's visibility was increasing as a features and fiction writer, columnist and editor for a number of other publications — *Harper's Bazaar, Woman's Home Companion, Literary Era, The Century* and *The Illustrated American*.

For all her progressive views about female independence some of Helen's articles reveal she could be a wily coquette when the need arose.

"If you fling demands at tired men who hold favors you don't get them," she wrote in *Harper's Bazaar* in 1900. "If you 'ask pretty,' tactfully choosing the time that suits the man and never mind yourself, you are more likely to win. And so it comes to this, that you must take your choice of these two things: demand favors and go without them, or win them through tact. And this condition will prevail so long as men are strong and women are charming."

Helen was also prospering as an author. Her first book, *How Women May Earn a Living*, part of Macmillan & Co's four-volume Woman's Home Library series, became an instant best-seller on its release in January 1900, winning rave reviews from the *New York Times* and other highbrow critics for its common sense philosophy. A review in *Book Buyer* noted that it was "descriptive rather than didactic," was "bright and readable," and showed "a keen appreciation of current conditions and future possibilities."

The literary editor of *The Nation* was not convinced Helen was comprehensive enough, but lauded the "candor and intelligence which form the character of the book."

Even so, Candee's message was a revelation at the time and *How Women May Earn a Living* is considered a landmark in feminist literature. Helen wanted to inspire and help women, but she was honest in her assessment that not all would succeed in a career:

Circa 1905.

> *Failure is not always the fault of the occupation chosen, nor of a woman's talents, but comes because she lacks those traits of character that force success.*

How Women May Earn a Living instructed readers on the proper approach they should take to work as well as to which professions they might enter. And there was no doubt as to Candee's view of female liberation — the book was in fact dedicated to "all those women who labor through necessity and not caprice."

Following this critical and popular success came another — a novel called *An Oklahoma Romance*, based on Helen's experiences in the territory. Published in March 1901, the book brought still more national attention to the settlement that was fast emerging as a mecca for farming and oil. How much of the central story line, a rather steamy affair, was fact or fiction is uncertain, but one has the feeling that Oklahoma offered more than a literary adventure for Candee.

What is certain is that critics liked the book. The *New York Times* lauded its "freshness," adding that it was "a bit of contemporaneous history, painted with form and color, and has unusual value and interest."

A review in *Pearson's Magazine* concurred:

> *It is a love story bringing the hero and heroine together under the exciting circumstances of the great "Run" for desirable plots in the new Territory, and gives a striking picture of the destruction wrought by a cyclone. The atmosphere of the book — its local color — is surprisingly well given. Those in search of novelty may be sure to find it in this Western romance.*

Despite the promise Helen showed as a novelist, and the positive reception she won for *An Oklahoma Romance*, she never wrote another book of fiction.

By September 1904, Helen Churchill Candee had moved with her children to Washington, D.C. where she blossomed socially, becoming a favorite with the most powerful diplomatic circles.

"In the touch and go of society," she said, "a light wit and ready tongue are invaluable." She obviously had these traits in abundance, for Candee was soon at the center of cultural life in the nation's capitol. As the *Washington Times* noted:

> *A member of the city's most exclusive smart set, Mrs. Churchill Candee has attained a reputation as a brilliant hostess. At her home some of the world's most prominent persons have visited.*

Helen, who spoke several languages, was a natural with dignitaries from foreign embassies, including the French and the Italian, particularly with the military officials of those countries, and she entertained frequently for them. Her friendship with an Italian Navy commander and his wife led to the marriage of one of her protégés, the daughter of an American admiral, to a high-ranking Italian officer.

Helen's home at 1621 New Hampshire Ave. In April 2007, The Fund for American Studies (TFAS) acquired her historic four-story brick and limestone house to expand their office facilities. TFAS has been educating young leaders on the values of freedom, democracy and free-market economies since 1967.

Helen was originally a Republican but later supported the Democratic and Progressive parties, entertaining lavishly for congressional and senatorial leaders, cabinet members and candidates of every stripe. One of her closest political friends and allies was the great orator, pacifist and suffrage supporter William Jennings Bryan, who served as Secretary of State under President Woodrow Wilson.

In Washington, Candee was soon applying more than her beauty and charm to the social mix. She was bringing her marvelous taste to bear on a budding new vocation.

At a time when there were few interior designers and only limited advice about home décor from architects and furniture makers, Helen carved a niche for herself as an adviser, critic and one of the first-ever professional decorators.

"The woman who essays this work should have great taste and ingenuity," Helen had written in *How Women May Earn a Living*, modestly omitting her qualifications for the job. She added:

> *On being called in the decorator surveys the drawing room with a critic's eye, knowing at a glance exactly what changes to make in order to transform an ugly apartment. She hangs rugs, drapes portieres, screens the piano, places lights and in many ways works magic. She even searches the house for old bits of furniture, has them refinished and makes happy use of them.*

Helen Candee never operated a shop or manufacturing business, and seldom in fact advertised her work. But she was the decorator of choice to several influential New York and Washington architects as well as numerous friends and acquaintances. Unlike her contemporary Elsie de Wolfe (Lady Mendl), the first commercial interior designer, Helen was a private consultant on furniture and artwork, working almost as an historian or curator, rather than as an antiques buyer or creator of furnishings and accessories. In 1907, President Theodore Roosevelt commissioned Helen to advise on the "purchase of a set of Louis XVI chairs for the First Lady's dressing room."

Although she didn't always supervise the arrangement of rooms she was commissioned to refurbish (as most decorators insisted on doing), Helen did at times demand contractual approval of the "assemblage and display of furniture upon initial presentation." This was the case with architect Nathan C. Wyeth's "show house" opposite the Willard Hotel that featured "interior appointments specially chosen by Mrs. Churchill Candee." Wyath and Helen worked on several subsequent building projects in Washington, including an expansion of the west wing of the White House in 1909. Wyath designed one of Helen's trio of Washington DC homes.

Another of Helen's homes was 1621 New Hampshire Ave in the swank Dupont Circle neighborhood, built in 1905 by Waddy B. Wood, the architect for Woodrow Wilson's nearby residence.

Helen's visibility in the capitol attracted other distinguished clients including Secretary of War Henry L. Stimson; Viscount Benoit d'Azy, naval attache to the French Embassy; Mathilde Townsend Gerry; the Marchesa Cusati, wife of the Italian Ambassador, and the architectural partnership of Donn & Deming, which built the third of Helen's Washington houses.

Despite her impressive clientele, Helen Candee's work as a decorator was intermittent. It was therefore as a critic and educator, through her later books and articles on the history of furniture, textiles and art, that she made an impact on early 20th century interior design.

Candee's first book on home decor was the profusely illustrated *Decorative Styles and Periods*, published by Frederick A. Stokes, Co. in November 1906. It was well received and quickly became a standard reference on period furnishings and their modern use. It also began a 25-

year publishing relationship with Stokes.

Readers of *Decorative Styles and Periods*, a deep green cloth-bound volume with an inset portrait of an Empire room on the cover, were treated to the warmly delicate prose that already distinguished Helen Candee as a novelist and journalist. The book was long and thorough, addressing all major trends and designs, but was also full of human interest and historical sidelights that made it as entertaining as it was instructional.

More than any other book she wrote, Helen's philosophy of design (and living) can be gleaned from *Decorative Styles and Periods*.

Authenticity was the prime principle of her credo. Candee was a purist in the extreme, insisting on genuine antiques and unswervingly faithful period atmosphere in the arrangement of rooms. The "perfection of the old," she declared, was all-important, adding that the "best is of the past."

She was very critical of manufacturers and department stores that sold cheap imitation furniture; she didn't even approve of upscale decorators like de Wolfe endorsing good quality reproductions of period pieces for modern interiors.

"The atmosphere of antiquity which is its charm is impossible to describe," Helen insisted. "It must be felt. By reading you may know its history, by studying you may know its detail but only by contact can you feel its full charm."

Her elitist standards of acquiring furniture were at odds with the income of average readers. But the educational bent of her writing, and the personal touch that permeated the historical sketches in her book, struck a note of commonality and even intimacy that set it apart from other studies on the subject. Indeed, there was no cold recitation of facts and dates in *Decorative Styles and Periods*, just amusing, intuitive anecdotes that brought the past to life, setting the standard for all Candee's future books on the decorative arts.

Her focus was primarily historical when describing period design but occasionally she dispensed practical advice to the homemaker, such as her suggestion of using old lace or other "time-touched" fabrics:

> *In rooms where a happy hodge-podge of harmonious objects prevails, instead of a strict adherence to one thought, a length of old stuff or embroidery helps wondrously with the walls in giving an effect of warmth and elegance.*

Helen Candee was perhaps alone as a stylist in appreciating period furniture more for its historical importance than its visual appeal. The influence of the great rulers of the past whose political and social impact changed fashion and decoration was what made period design fascinating for her: "Reducing the matter to individuals gives its interest a vitality not possible otherwise."

From Louis XIV's pomp and protocol at Versailles to the humbleness of artisan weavers bent over their worktables, Helen's writing stressed the human element in design, charting new ground in educating the public on decorative arts history.

Candee's interior design showing her Italian country taste – Early 1900's.

"The human touch revivifies history," she explained, "and unites humanity."

More than any other writer in the emerging genre of the decorative arts, Helen recognized the significance of humanity in accurately recording the historical worth of interior design.

"What is furniture without man?" she asked. "And of what use are decorations unless the eye of man rests on their loveliness? To give these things value they must be associated with those for whom they were made."

It's been written that Elsie de Wolfe "made America antiques-conscious." If so, then it was Helen Churchill Candee who made sure America was "antiques-educated." Through her lively word-pictures of past times, Helen enabled consumers to appreciate period furniture and treatments beyond their artistic beauty, to see and admire them in relation to history.

Helen's reputation as an expert on period interiors and the arts in general was spread through her broadening freelance repertoire. In addition to her usual work for *Scribner's* and *Century*, she was now contributing to *American Homes, International Studio, Metropolitan Magazine*, the *American Magazine of Art* and *Collier's Weekly*. One of her proudest assignments was not related to the arts. In November 1907 she served *Forum Magazine* as political correspondent to the ceremonies in Guthrie that inaugurated Oklahoma as America's 46th state.

As Helen Candee's career expanded, so did her social life. At 1718 Rhode Island Avenue NW she hosted dinner parties and teas that made her mansion one of the most fashionable salons in the capitol, frequented not only by politicians, diplomats, visiting foreign dignitaries and royalty but by artists, musicians and actors. A typical 1911 guest list included President and Mrs. William Howard Taft, Admiral de Lajarte, commanding officer of the French Squadron, the Duke and Duchess of Newcastle, and writer Natalie Clifford Barney.

As the *Washington Post* reported, Helen's home was "the center of a charming and continuous, though quiet, hospitality. Its gracious chatelaine rarely dines without a small company of guests. Herself an interesting woman, Mrs. Candee has gathered about her the most interesting people in Washington society."

Helen's son, Harold, or "Harry," as he was known by his friends, was growing into adulthood by now and was soon away at college in Denver. Returning to the capitol on break from school, he sometimes accompanied his fascinating mother on her trips abroad, such as in June 1908 when they visited family and friends in England.

World travel didn't prevent Candee's involvement in a number of committees at home, including the trustees for the Corcoran Gallery of Art and the board of directors for Wednesday Homes, an "open house" program and garden tour of representative Washington estates. In addition, Helen was active in organizations like the Archeological Society, the American Federation of Arts and the National Civic Federation. Finally, she was a board member of such charities as the Neighborhood House and the Children's Hospital, for which she organized plays, concerts, exhibits and an annual flower show.

She also publicly supported the Washington chapter of the National Woman Suffrage Association, assisting in the planning of meetings and rallies. Helen's connection to the cause of women's rights was questioned by some of her conservative friends, who warned her it might mean having her name dropped from White House guest lists. A negative reception for President Taft at a NWSA conference in 1910 may have fueled the fears of Helen's friends. Despite opposing views of the suffrage question, however, it seems Helen's friendship with the Tafts was solid.

Helen Candee's parties and benefits were regularly featured in the society columns of the *Washington Post*, which often mentioned her attendance at premiers, weddings and other events as well. The flower display and reception she organized for the Neighborhood House in 1908 was, according to the *Post*, "one of the most attractive charity fetes given at Washington this year."

The elegant attire of the "lovely Mrs. Churchill Candee" was frequently commented on in these notices. It seems she had a penchant for black velvet and ermine, wore a perfect size 5 shoe, preferred wide-sweeping, feathered hats and was among the increasing number of society women taking up the "sport" of cigarette smoking. Helen readily admitted (and lamented) her vanity, saying that while she wanted to be respected for her intellect, she had no intention of going around "dressed like the matron of an asylum."

In the summers (beginning in 1906), Helen vacationed at York Harbor, Maine, a popular resort for the Washington colony. Here she rested after so much hobnobbing and wrote her articles in the peace of the garden she loved:

> *The garden is, in fact, a room of the house, a gathering room, especially at the hour of afternoon tea on sunny days. Often I lunch in mine, throwing bits to the birds, and sniffing the flowers.*

Candee also enjoyed horseback riding with her son, Harold, now 19, at Warrenton, Virginia, where he kept stables. An enthusiastic member of both the Riding Club of Washington and the Chevy Chase, the sport was Helen's favorite, and she rode a number of blue-ribbon winners in local and national horse shows. Her habits were always chic, as the newspapers never failed to notice, and she was one of the first women in the east to ride astride.

When not mingling with the Washington elite, she spent time with her daughter Edith, now Mrs. H.C. Mathews, in New York. There she was content with quiet family life, helping Edith entertain at her

Park Avenue flat and looking after her grandsons Harold Chauncey and Schuyler.

Helen Candee also spent whole seasons abroad, sometimes traveling with Harold and Edith, visiting England, France, Germany, but especially Italy. "In my heart," she wrote, "was abundant love for Italy and her adorable wiles."

On her trips, she liked to go off alone on little jaunts. Whether boating, hiking or just sightseeing, she would "sneak away, taking a picnic lunch, books to read, and my easel to paint wildflowers."

When in London, Helen stayed with friends and attended meetings of the India Society. In Paris, she lived in the Neuilly house once owned by her late mother, participated in the gala affairs of Les Amis de l'Orient, of which she was made an honor member, and paid a round of visits to her wide range of friends. These included U.S. Ambassador to France Robert Bacon, stage star Julia Marlowe and sculptor Raymond Duncan (brother of dancer Isadora Duncan).

Her travels weren't always pleasant. In the summer of 1906, Helen contracted typhoid fever while on a tour of the Mediterranean with her son. Doctors expected the illness to prove fatal, but she lived, nursed back to health by nuns at a convent hospital in Florence. After recovering, she was true to form, choosing to continue her vacation rather than return home.

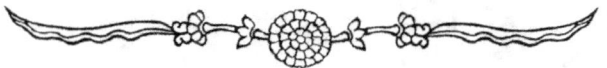

Six years later tragedy struck again. In January 1912 Helen went abroad to finalize research on a new book. In April, after spending time in Spain and Italy, she was returning to Paris via the Riviera, when she received a telegram from Edith, informing her that Harry had been seriously injured in a car wreck (some sources claimed it was a plane crash). She booked passage on the first boat out — White Star Line's brand new *Titanic*.

The legendary ship, largest, most technologically advanced in the world, laden with millionaires and emigrants, the famous and the obscure, modern ideas and outmoded methods, struck an iceberg and sank on the fifth night of its maiden voyage to New York, destroying lives, shaking up values and changing the world. Among the few survivors, Helen saw the sun rise on the residue of a fight that nature won:

> *Dawn showed the vast reaches of the sea, empty of big craft. But floating near, a swaying tangle of deck chairs and cushions, and a pale white babe rocked in the cradle of that fashioning. The sun lingered on coming on such a scene.*

The dawn illuminated more than the ruin of man's engineering triumph, or the deaths of 1,500 people, but the arrival of a new, uneasy era, a place that, like the once unassuming iceberg, was no longer innocent, gentle or safe.

The harrowing wreck of the super liner, though officially a footnote to history, has never lost its power to fascinate. In a pop-culture sense,

The *RMS Titanic* at Southampton before her maiden voyage – 1912.

Titanic never went down. Its tangibility struck a chord, and over the decades the public has thrilled to countless books, films and plays about the disaster.

It's unavoidable then that Helen Churchill Candee, despite her busy life as a hostess, decorator, writer, and political activist, should be best remembered for the part she played in one of the great dramas of history.

Making the great ship's maiden voyage wasn't as exciting as it might have been for Candee had she not been worried about her son. But friends en route, like Major Archie Butt, President Taft's military attaché, and artist Frank Millet, consoled her. Soon Helen attracted a flock of dapper admirers who kept her company wherever she went. When lounging or strolling on deck, playing bridge, lunching, or having a cocktail, she was cheered by the presence of these thoughtful men — "Our Coterie" they became known.

Two of Helen Candee's self-appointed cavaliers were Edward Austin Kent, 58, a New York architect, and Hugh Woolner, 45, a London investor. While Woolner was the more attentive, Helen and Kent had more in common, and the decorator and architect struck up a fond acquaintance. Yet Woolner succeeded in wooing Helen who was "divinely flattered" by the slightly younger man's devotion. They, too, formed an affectionate rapport, and it may have been romantic, to judge from a story Candee later wrote for *Collier's Weekly*.

"We all love a gentleman," she said some while later. "Time has nothing to do with effacing that."

Mr. Edward Austin Kent 1854-1912.

And she was right. Eighty-five years later it seems that the Oscar-winning motion picture *Titanic* borrowed this amorous incident from Helen's life with classic results. In one of the most memorable scenes in cinematic history, lovers Jack and Rose embrace on the bow of *Titanic* at dusk as the great ship plows toward destiny. Was the romantic coupling depicted by Hollywood true? Some historians believe so; in Helen Candee's recently auctioned, unpublished memoir there is a moment very much like that shown in the 1997 blockbuster film.

On May 26, 1931 the Woman's Titanic Monument was unveiled in southwest Washington DC by Helen Taft, President Taft's widow. It was designed by Gertrude Vanderbilt Whitney to honor men who died on the Titanic, sacrificing their lives to save the women and children who escaped. Both women were Helen's personal friends. The statue's pose evokes images from Helen Candee's story about her trip to *Titanic's* bow in 1912, a scene immortalized by the mythical Rose in the 1997 movie. It is unusual that Helen is, at present, not associated with this monument by any documents. The publisher invites readers to contribute any additional information.

Slipping unnoticed onto a deck restricted to crewmen, the adventurous Candee and an adoring beau head for the foremost point of the speeding behemoth. There they feel the power of nature and the majesty of man's achievement as they watch the liner's bow pierce the waves beneath them. According to the manuscript, Helen also savored the thrill on a separate occasion when she was (unlike mythical Rose) unfettered by male hands.

"I stood at the bow alone and absorbed her spirit," Helen is supposed to have said. "As her bow cut into the waves, throwing tons of water to right and left in playful intent, her

The New York Times, April 16, 1912.

indifference to mankind was significant. How grand she was, how superb, how titanic."

After *Titanic* struck the iceberg, Woolner rushed to Helen's cabin, assisted her into a lifejacket and accompanied her on deck. On their way up the grand staircase, they ran into Kent, who was just coming down to find Helen. She became emotional on seeing him, and in a singularly beautiful act, presented her tardy protector with tokens of her sentiment — a small gold flask, fatefully engraved with the Churchill crest and family motto "Faithful but unfortunate," and a locket with an ivory cameo of her mother Mary Churchill. Woolner, Kent and others of "Our Coterie" soon turned up and escorted Helen topside, handing her through the crowd into a lifeboat.

Helen's cameo portrait of her mother Mary, later recovered from Edward Kent's body after the *Titanic* sank.

In attempting to board the boat — No. 6 on the port side — Helen was frightened when she realized she would have to jump down into it. When she did, her feet became wedged between two oars stowed along the gunwale. As she lost her balance, one of her ankles twisted, fracturing it, and she fell into the boat. Despite the pain of her injury, Helen managed to row with the others, clearing the side of the sinking ship by a few hundred yards.

Titanic's Captain E. J. Smith put Quartermaster Robert Hichens in charge of the boat. He failed miserably and, in the absence of leadership, Helen and Margaret ("Molly") Brown, the feisty Denver millionairess and fellow suffragette, took control of the boat. Under Molly's direction, Candee and the other women rowed Boat 6 to the rescue ship *Carpathia* the next morning. Both women later testified to Hitchens' cowardice during the official Senate investigation into the disaster.

On landing in New York, Helen was taken by ambulance to a hospital where she was treated and kept under observation for a few days. After her release she visited her son in his hospital, remaining in New York with Edith until Harry recovered.

In following weeks, Helen was inundated with letters and cables from friends, congratulating her on her escape, including a personal note from the First Lady, relating her sympathy and that of the President. Strangers contacted her as well, asking questions about missing fellow passengers. One of these was Archie Butt's brother, who begged for news in a series of heart-rending telegrams.

Edward Kent's sister also wrote Candee. In mourning her brother, she found comfort in Helen's memories of his brave last hours. Kent's body was actually among those recovered and the two family heirlooms Helen entrusted to him before they said goodbye were found in his jacket. His sister returned these relics to Helen. In April 2006 the cameo sold for £58,000 while the flask fetched over £30,000 — two unique pieces of history that literally went down with the *Titanic* and resurfaced.

The press continued to pursue Helen. She gave an authentic account of her experiences in the disaster to the *Washington Herald*, but largely erroneous reports about her appeared in the *Washington Times*, in various New York papers and in syndication.

Her brief interview in the *Herald* revealed Helen's high emotions:

> *The action of the men on the Titanic was noble. They stood back in every instance that I noticed, and gave the women and children the first chance to get away safely. Major Butt was one of God's own noblemen. I saw him working desperately to get the women and children into the boats. What need can there be of recounting the heroic deeds performed by those men who remained on the Titanic? To dwell upon them only sickens the heart with the realization of how they perished.*

Yet she accepted an offer from *Collier's Weekly* to tell her *Titanic* tale in full. Appearing as a cover story in *Collier's* (Vol. 49, no. 7 – May 4, 1912) hers was one of the first in-depth eyewitness accounts of the sinking to be published in a major magazine. It was certainly one of the most widely read first-hand stories, *Collier's* circulation being the highest of American weeklies.

Written in Helen Candee's refined way, it was yet more personal than anything she ever published, and is considered a classic today. Depending on readers' tastes, Helen's long essay was either stirringly beautiful or excessively poetic. Called "Sealed Orders," the theme was the omnipotence of God

Collier's was one of the most read periodicals in the US when it published Helen Candee's account of the *Titanic* disaster.

and His orchestration of the convergence of three unwitting craft upon the sea — iceberg, *Titanic* and the rescue ship *Carpathia*, players in a game of life, hubris and death. Of *Titanic*'s terrible final moments, Candee wrote:

> *At last, the end of the world. A smooth, slow chute. Life went out on the big ship. The death call of 1500 units of divine selflessness spread its volume over the waters as a single cry to God. There was no shriek, nor wail, nor frantic shout. Instead a heavy moan as of one being from whom final agony forces a single sound.*

Helen's letters, telegrams, and her unique 36-page hand written account of the disaster, sold for £47,000 at the above-noted 2006 auction. A far cry from the 5 cent per copy price of *Collier's* in 1912 and far more than she would ever realize from her ordeal.

Helen recovered from her broken ankle, although she was forced to rely on a walking stick for a year, and Harry revived from his injuries after being confined to bed for three months. Helen never published another story about *Titanic* and was seldom interviewed about it. Even so, her name was released the following year as one of the survivors in a class-action lawsuit seeking compensation from the White Star Line. Helen's claim sought $10,000 for personal injury and $4,646 for lost possessions.

Helen tried to put *Titanic* behind her, and she mostly succeeded, though to some extent it haunted her professionally, being mentioned in official profiles, such as her entries in the *Woman's Who's Who of America* and the *Biographical Cyclopedia of U.S. Women*.

A welcome respite from the horror of *Titanic* was the successful release of Helen Candee's fourth and best-known book, a deluxe volume on the history of tapestries. Called simply *The Tapestry Book*, it was published by Stokes in New York in October 1912 and by Constable in London the following year.

The Tapestry Book, a lavish tome of 275 pages and 103 illustrations, was a true labor of love for Candee, whose chief interest in the decorative arts was period textiles. Thanks to the popularity of this delightful foray into the history of an under-examined art form, she became the foremost expert on the subject, writing further magazine articles and giving lectures at academies and universities.

The beautiful word pictures in which she specialized — of people, places and moments in time — were everywhere in this thick volume:

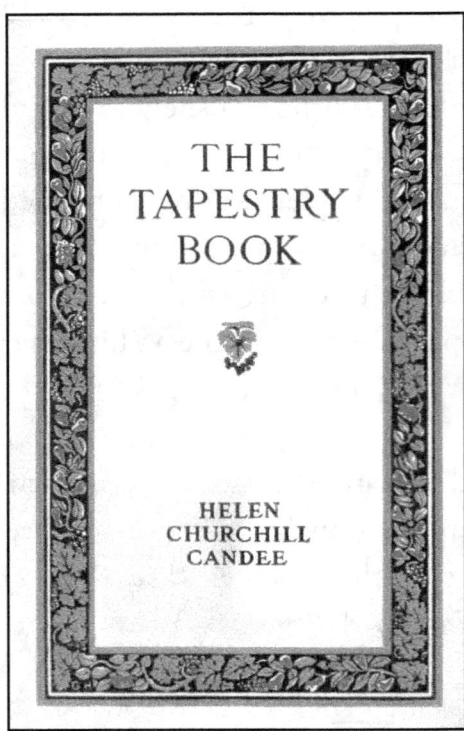

The Tapestry Book – 1912.

To enter a house where tapestries abound is to feel oneself welcomed even before the host appears. The bending verdure invites, the animated figures beckon, and at once the atmosphere of elegance and cordiality envelopes the happy visitor. To live in a house abundantly hung with old tapestries, to live there day by day, makes of labor a pleasure and of leisure a delight. In the big living room of the house, when the family gathers on a rainy morning, or on any afternoon when the shadows grow grim outside and the

Gobelin's late 19th century tapestry from The Tapestry Book – 1912.

> *tea-tray is brought in, whispering its sweet tune of friendly communion, the tapestries on the walls seem to gather closer, to enfold in loving embrace the sheltered group.*

The Tapestry Book was probably the most extensively researched of all her works. During her travels, Helen had visited museums and private collections all over the world, examining rich and rare tapestries, draperies, carpets and all manner of ancient materials, studying their construction, design and history. Her concentrated focus on such an obscure branch of the arts might ordinarily have been of interest only to connoisseurs. But The *Tapestry Book*, beautifully bound in natural cloth with an autumnal floral frame on the cover, was actually a bestseller, proving the decorating mania of the early 1900s, a time of developing, if confused, aesthetics, was at a peak.

Helen may have had to use a cane to walk now but her hurt ankle didn't keep her out of the saddle, literally and politically. In March 1913, the day before the inauguration of President Woodrow Wilson, she was chosen to ride her horse at the head of the National Woman Suffrage Association's "Votes for Women" parade down Pennsylvania Avenue, passing the White House and stopping at the steps of Capitol Hill. On that day, one of the greatest of her life, Helen and seven other dignitaries on horseback led over 10,000 fellow women from all over the United States in one of the largest female emancipation demonstrations to date.

Candee also continued in her civic and philanthropic duties. She was an organizer of fundraisers for the New York Home for Boys and for the Soldiers and Sailors Club, her loyalty to which increased with the outbreak of the First World War.

Privately, issues concerning her son caused Helen distress. Now in his mid-20s, Harry was leading an errant life, drinking excessively and losing a succession of lucrative jobs. The root of the problem, of which his mother may or may not have been aware, was the youth's struggle with homosexuality, of which there was little, if any, social understanding at the time.

Described by friends as "an attractive, brilliant young man," and "a very sophisticated, erudite fellow," Harry was nonetheless increasingly unhappy; companions recalled his attitude as "restless" and that he turned to alcohol more and more while indulging in a string of clandestine affairs. Even after securing a promising post as private secretary to philanthropist Edwin Coupland Shaw, Harry's "boy trouble" and drinking binges persisted.

Throughout 1915 and '16, perhaps to escape the worry of the troubled son she loved but was unable to help, Helen was busy as ever writing on home décor, art and design for the *International Studio, American Homes* and the *American Magazine of Art.* She also oversaw the re-release of her first book on house decoration, *Decorative Styles and Periods,* and the publication of a brand-new book, her fifth, entitled *Jacobean Furniture.*

Helen at the head of the National Woman Suffrage Association's "Votes for Women" parade in Washington DC.

Jacobean Furniture - 1916.

Devoted to one of the most popular "revival looks" of the moment, the 17th century English school of design, utilizing oak and walnut in furnishings and treatments, the small book of 56 pages and 43 illustrations was attractively bound in brown glazed cloth in a motif resembling Jacobean paneling. Of her eight books, *Jacobean Furniture* is one of the most delightful.

In it Helen Candee again shared romantic anecdotes, some of them her own:

> *I must confess to a thrill of delight when sitting at an old oak board, set out with lace and silver. Not only for its obvious beauty, but by the thought of the groups that have gathered there through 300 years, groups of varying customs, varying habits, varying fashions, yet human like ourselves, and prone to make of the dining table a circle of joy.*

She also spoke of the "subtle power of furniture to express the spirit of the times in which it was made," and touched on the innate sensitivity of expert antiques collectors and decorators:

> *Feeling is a word for the serious collector. Ability to read feeling amounts to a talent and is certainly an instinct. Those who possess it know without recourse where to place a piece of furniture.*

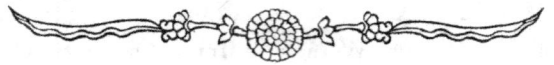

As the European conflict worsened, Candee's writing didn't sustain her spiritually. And with news of the hardships in Italy, a nation she had virtually adopted on her overseas jaunts, Helen knew she had to do something to help the cause.

Through friends at the Italian Embassy, she gained an appointment to the Royal Italian Red Cross, which she began serving in 1917, only a few months before the famous Battle of Caporetto in October, a crushing defeat claiming some 300,000 casualties. Helen was among a group of nurses dispatched to the front lines to try and save injured troops.

The scene was horrific, Helen recounted, and the task of treating the wounded enormous. One experience never left her memory. She and another nurse approached a young man lying near a dugout. While severely maimed, he was still alive. But when they tried to move him, his torso separated from his legs. "Drenched in blood," Candee wrote in a letter home, "we burst into tears and knelt in prayer at the boy's side."

Helen thereafter labored in hospitals in Rome and Milan well into 1918, proud to aid "the country I love as well as my own." While in Milan, she was astonished to find herself working alongside an elderly, fatigued nun whom she recognized as one who had nursed her at the convent in Florence over a decade earlier. When the old Sister realized who Helen was she exclaimed "God saved you so you may save us," and flew into her arms.

It was also in Milan that Helen assisted in the recovery of a young American ambulance driver, riddled with machine gun wounds. His name was Ernest Hemingway. The future renowned novelist would recount his wartime experiences in his *Farewell to Arms*, which also drew on his romance with another volunteer nurse, Agnes von Kurowsky, one of Helen's young coworkers.

Of course, Helen had more resources at her disposal than the average nurse, and she didn't hesitate to avail herself of them. In addition to endowing an emergency clinic in Italy, she purchased vehicles and supplies for a Belgian field hospital near the Swiss border.

Helen remained in Europe after the Armistice, settling in Paris, where she became a correspondent and eventually an editor for the cutting-edge New York design magazine, *Arts & Decoration*, contributing a stream of articles on a variety of subjects dear to her beauty-loving heart.

"When beauty assails," she once wrote, "reason has no part."

Before returning to the U.S. in 1920 she was decorated by the Royal Italian Red Cross "in honor of her heroic services and devotion to Italy."

Helen, now in her early 60s, was still active and vital, although her new job as editor for *Arts & Decoration* didn't work out; she found it too restrictive. Her abiding passion had always been travel, and she wasn't prepared to relinquish adventure for a desk job. As a journalist, she was much better suited to the life of a roving reporter, which she resumed, taking up her freelance pen with gusto. Still, she remained on the editorial staff of *Arts & Decoration* for several years.

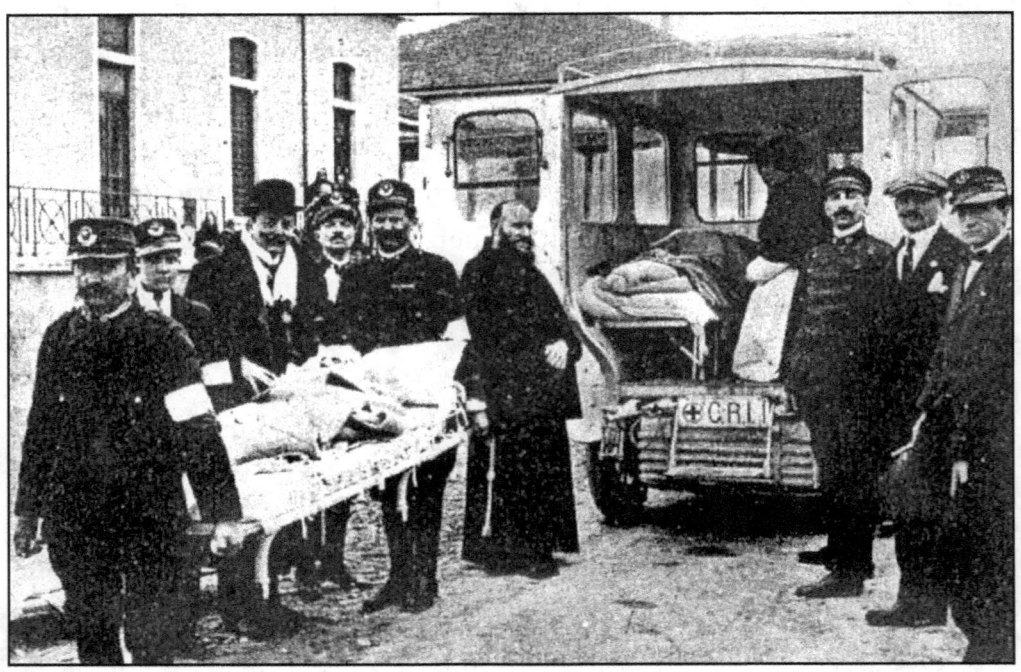

This March 1915 postcard from Bergamo's "Archivio Storico della Croce Rossa" shows one of the first ambulances of the Italian Red Cross, then simply called "carri da letto" (wagons of bed). Equipment and conditions were similar when Helen volunteered to serve in 1917.

Travel for Helen Candee in the early 1920s increasingly meant Japan, China and the exotic Far Eastern lands of Indonesia and Cambodia. The latter was a chief draw, and in her sixth book, *Angkor the Magnificent*, now a classic travelogue, Helen's facility for words found inspiration in the mysterious, half-hidden temples and palaces, hanging gardens, sculpture and stonework of the ancient "Wonder City."

In her book, the beauty and symbolism of the architecture of the temple of Angkor Wat came in for rapturous praise:

> *One can never look upon the ensemble of the Wat without a thrill, a pause, a feeling of being caught up to the heavens. Perhaps it is the most impressive sight in the world of edifices.*

The fascinating ruins of Angkor and their Eden-like environs had only been known to Westerners for 50 years, and weren't widely explored or photographed before Candee's ambitious study. Her book, published by Frederick Stokes in 1924, was the work Helen was most proud of.

Although *The Tapestry Book* was a greater popular success, *Angkor the Magnificent* brought her the most acclaim. She was commanded to give a private reading of her new book to King George and Queen Mary and was afterwards asked to Their Majesties' annual garden party at Holyroodhouse, one of only a few Americans invited. Helen was even decorated by the King of Cambodia in a native ceremony.

This passport photo would soon take Helen to her Asian adventures. Circa 1920. Photo courtesy of Phillip Gowan.

Holyroodhouse, where Helen gave a command reading of Angkor the Magnificent to King George and Queen Mary.

Captivated by the region, its riches and its people, Helen was pleased that the success of *Angkor the Magnificent* allowed her to focus on Asia in a series of articles and short stories for newspaper syndication the following year, as well as a special feature for *Art and Archeology Magazine*.

Her son Harry, who had relocated to England by 1922 — first to Wimbledon and then Birmingham where he was appointed president of the Working Boys Home — frequently joined his mother on her travels through Asia. The pair made an extended tour of Cambodia the following year, returning together to New York where Helen started research for a new book and Harry spent time with his friend and possible lover, poet Hart Crane, whom he presented with the gift of a jade Buddha from Ham Mountain.

Harold Candee

The Cambodian vacation was the last Helen was to enjoy with her son — in July 1925 Harry died suddenly of pneumonia at St. Chad's Hospital near Birmingham. He was only 39.

"It seems hard to realize that he's gone," Hart Crane wrote in a letter to a friend. For Helen, the grief of Harry's loss so devastated her she never spoke of it.

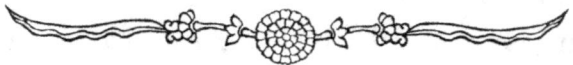

When not gallivanting across the world, Helen was with family and friends, commuting between her home in Washington and her daughter's house in New York.

In demand now as a lecturer on the Far East, she was active in

King Sisowath Monivong on his coronation day in 1928.

several new charities, notably the Boys Bureau and the Toc-H Club, funds for adolescent boys and young men employed on ocean liners. She was for some years on the organizing committee of Toc-H, hosting annual dinner dances aboard such famous ships as *Aquitania* and *Berengaria*. Candee was still involved with the Soldiers and Sailors Union as well, a high point in fundraising coming in 1925 when the group held a sold-out concert at Carnegie Hall.

Throughout the mid-1920s Helen traveled extensively in Asia, including a thousand-mile journey in Indochina. She also lived for a time in Peking.

The year 1927 brought further literary success with the publication of Helen's seventh book, *New Journeys in Old Asia*, a thorough treatment of her Oriental dreamland, touching on Bali, Siam, Java, Bangkok, Singapore and Thailand. *New Journeys in Old Asia* was the culmination of three years of traveling, accompanied by her friend, artist Lucille Douglas, who provided the book's etchings. In the course of that trip King Sisowath Monivong of Cambodia and the resident French government honored Helen for her earlier work, *Angkor the Maginficent*.

That year Helen witnessed the intrigues of Soviet Russia in the Far East, and she reported her opinion of the trouble in dispatches to the *New York Times*, saying among other things that "Russia is seeking to use the Chinese as a pawn in her ancient Asiatic struggle against Britain."

"Wherever (Mrs. Candee) went she found the people stirred up against the Europeans, and the people she talked with attributed the feeling among the natives to Russian propagandists," reported the *New York Times* on March 12.

Two years later, after receiving a commendation from the government of French Indochina for her latest work, Candee began to curb her international trips. She spent more time stateside — summers at her cottage in Maine, road trips to Palm Beach with friends, and housekeeping and occasional parties in New York with her daughter.

Life's Décor 313

The Mystery of the Beguiling Guide (pictured with The Authoress and Effie)

Helen's dedication of *Angkor the Magnificent* features "The Beguiling Guide," whom we first meet in Hong Kong. Her charming, knowledgeable traveling companion continues to play a role throughout her journey. The photo above shows Helen and the handsome "Beguiler" on an elephant at Angkor Wat. But *who* was her dashing companion?

Talented writer that Helen was, she knew how to promote a bit of intrigue in her accounts. But the facts suggest that her charming companion was none other than her son Harold, who frequently accompanied his mother on her journeys. A quick comparison with Harold's passport photo (p. 310) all but confirms the circumstantial evidence.

Helen Candee and The Society of Woman Geographers

As an adventurer and champion of woman's rights it was only natural for Helen Candee to join this group, founded in 1925 by four women ineligible for membership in similar "male-only" organizations. An October 2, 1926 article reporting on "the club of woman adventurers" identifies Helen as the member "who knows the most secluded spots of Siam and Indo-China." Future members would include Amelia Earhart, Margaret Mead, Jane Goodall and other prominent women.

Today, the International Society of Women Geographers remains a non-profit professional and social organization for women who love adventure. They define "geographer" in the broadest sense, and members continue contributing to the world's knowledge as anthropologists, geologists, journalists, biologists, archaeologists, oceanographers, geographers, economists, diplomats, explorers and ecologists.

For information please visit: www.ISWG.org

She also returned to her love of textiles for her eighth and final book, *Weaves and Draperies: Classic and Modern,* published in 1930. One of her longest books (at 300 pages), it was one of her most attractive, too, bound in gilt-lettered purple moire cloth with an Art Deco wrapper. Although some aspects of *Weaves and Draperies* were amply covered in *The Tapestry Book,* the new volume did address current, even avant-garde, design philosophy and principles, and was written in a slightly snappier style.

By 1934 Helen Candee, now 76, was restless for Europe and she set out again in search of new adventures, chronicling them in a series of *National Geographic Magazine* feature articles. These are the best of her travel essays, brimming with wit and romantic detail. The stories,

In 1934 and 1935 Helen "summered" at the Clock House in Stoke Poges, England. "A drapery of roses, wisteria and ivy, in which are hidden nests of robins, thrushes and merles for morning choruses, conceals its 200 years. Ivy over the gate spreads so thick that only hard showers spatter the visitor. From here a field path leads to the 'country churchyard' which inspired Gray's 'Elegy.' In her garden, Mrs. Candee entertained the late Clifton Adams, brilliant staff photographer of the National Geographic Society."

appearing in *National Geographic* between January 1935 and May 1936, included accounts of life in the English countryside, on the Italian Riviera and along the coast of Normandy.

Meanwhile Helen was preparing updates for a re-release of *The Tapestry Book* through Tudor Publishing. This elegantly boxed reissue, with a brighter binding and spiffy new dust-jacket, appeared in bookstores in 1935; a limited reissue of *Decorative Styles and Periods* also went to press in 1938.

Helen's years were catching up with her. By age 80, as she became physically weaker and her eyesight started to fail, she was increasingly dependent on her daughter, Edith, with whom she now lived permanently. Candee, one time party girl, seldom went out, but in 1938 she felt chipper enough to attend the opera in Washington. There she met up with an old friend, former First Lady Taft, and the two Helens posed for news photographers.

Over the next few years, despite deteriorating health, Helen made trips to her Washington house, maintained by the family, and visiting her old vacation home in York Harbor, Maine. There, her ever-faithful daughter Edith, and her equally loving granddaughter Mary Mathews, looked after her.

Her life had moved into the quiet, domestic realm of routine and simplicity.

Edith Matthews with Chauncey D. Mathews (born 1919) and Florence Mary Churchill Mathews (born 1921). Not pictured are her oldest sons, Harold Chauncey Mathews (born 1904) and Schuyler L. Mathews (born April 23, 1906). It would be most interesting to learn more about Schuyler; he was 18 years old when *Angkor the Magnificent* was released and Helen included him in her dedication. Schuyler is the only relative Helen ever dedicated a book to but the reason why and what influence that dedication had are a mystery. Photo and biographical information courtesy of Phillip Gowan.

But age and infirmity couldn't take away her imagination, or her love of beauty:

> *Each morning a perfect servant wakes me with a cup of tea left at my bedside. I look from my pillow at the three open windows, trying to decide which is preferable — red roses or pink, when thrust within the room and screening the sky outside?*

Mary, who graduated from college in 1941, married Allon Barker of the British Army in 1946. Helen attended the ceremony, which marked her last known public appearance.

In the summer of 1949, Helen, now 90, paid her usual visit to the cottage in Maine she had owned for half a century. There she used to recuperate after the grueling social round of Washington. It was where she used to write, where she dreamt of pending travels, and on August 23 where her valiant, tremendous life drew to a peaceful close.

In one of her last articles, about finding a perfect *pied-a-terre*, Helen wrote that "if I fail to obtain the house of dreams, I would say the quest alone had brought lasting joy."

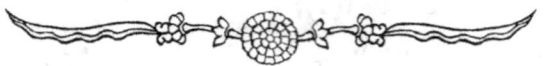

The parties, books and trips are in the past. But the fascinating woman who made them happen hasn't been entirely forgotten.

Yet it isn't as a globe-trekker, decorating maven or women's libber that Helen Churchill Candee is remembered. Her immortality has been preserved through the gallant role she played in the *Titanic* disaster, a human drama that continues to touch the generations.

Regularly mentioned in books about the sinking, Helen was even portrayed in cameo in the Walt Disney 3-D documentary, *Ghosts of the Abyss*, about filmmaker James Cameron's 2001 expedition to *Titanic*. In the movie, the tale of her sneaking out onto the bow at purple dusk, a lovely phantom in her flying scarves, was recreated.

Some may question Helen's communion with nature as the great ship sped towards its fate. But the image is indelible, too picturesque to defy, and blends too perfectly with the romance and daring of this unusual woman to dismiss.

As Helen herself wrote in 1912:

> "Everything is uncertain."

ಏ FINIS ಐ

ABOUT THE BIOGRAPHER

Randy Bryan Bigham is a journalist, historian and author. As an award-winning arts and entertainment journalist he has contributed to People magazine, Women's Wear Daily, The Times and other national and international publications.

As an historian, Bigham specializes in Edwardian era cultural history. He has provided documentary research for the National Geographic Channel, consulted for the Titanic Museum at Branson and provided images for numerous books, including Afternoon Tea by Jane Pettigrew and Century Girl by Lauren Redniss.

In 2005, Bigham released his first book, *Finding Dorothy*, a biography of silent screen star and Titanic survivor Dorothy Gibson.

Titanic Embarking – April 10, 1912

APPENDIX II

ઈ ✤ CB

Introduction to "Sealed Orders"
A Titanic survivor's classic tale of love and fate

by Randy Bryan Bigham

On her 1912 maiden voyage, the *Titanic* was the largest, most technologically advanced ocean liner in the world. She was laden with millionaires and emigrants, the famous and the obscure, modern ideas and outmoded methods. On the night of April 14th the massive ship struck an iceberg and sank, destroying lives, challenging values and changing the world. Among the few survivors, Helen Churchill Candee recalled her early morning thoughts upon seeing the residue of a fight that nature won.

She realized that dawn illuminated more than the ruin of man's engineering triumph or the deaths of 1,500 people, but the arrival of a new uneasy era — a place that, like the once unassuming iceberg, was no longer innocent, gentle or safe.

The wreck of the super liner, though officially a footnote to history, has never lost its power to fascinate. It was therefore unavoidable that Helen Candee, despite her busy life as an author, world traveler, design authority and political activist, should be best remembered for the role she played in one of history's greatest dramas.

Candee's strong *Titanic* connection is rooted almost entirely in a classic tale she penned for *Collier's Weekly* just days following her harrowing escape. Appearing as the May 4, 1912 cover story, hers was one of the first in-depth eyewitness accounts of the sinking published in a major magazine. It was certainly one of the most widely read first-hand reports, as Collier's circulation was among the highest of American weeklies.

Written in Helen Candee's refined way, the article was more personal than anything she ever published. Depending on readers' tastes, Helen's long essay was either stirringly beautiful or excessively poetic. Called "Sealed Orders," the theme was the omnipotence of God and His orchestration of the convergence of three unwitting entities upon the sea — iceberg, *Titanic* and the rescue ship *Carpathia* — players in a game of life, hubris and death.

Candee wrote from her heart, and it showed. Nothing about the ship or the people she met escaped her memory. A mother with her children standing in the breeze on the steerage deck as the ship set out. The enthusiasm of *Titanic's* athletics instructor as he bounced around the gymnasium, showing off exercise equipment to passengers. The glittering dinner scene on Titanic's last night afloat. The sad sight of the engine-room crew being turned away from lifeboats as the evacuation began.

Helen also paid homage to the ship's orchestra. As *Titanic* went down, the band's music was "freighted with a burden of love," she said, sending a message of "courage from man to man, cheering others while itself faced death."

But Helen held back on some aspects of her personal story, such as her reason for being aboard. It is now known that her son had been in an accident and she was hurrying back from a European business trip to be with him. She was also discreet — even tantalizingly vague — when referring to fellow passengers.

It has since become a sort of parlor game for researchers to identify the men and women to whom Candee refers anonymously in her narrative. The more famous of the travelers she describes — i.e., "the richest man," "the artist of renown," "the man of theatrical success," etc. — are fairly obvious to most readers but special insight, or at least an educated guess, is required to distinguish other characters in the story.

Who, for instance, is the "prettiest girl" she mentions? Who are "the handsome woman," her "fine son" and his "adorable wife?"

In that strange, lost rite of decorum called chivalry, a corps of gentlemen appointed themselves Helen's protectors on the voyage. These dapper heroes have all been identified. Known as "Our Coterie," the six-member international team, with Helen their gilded centerpiece, included three New Yorkers, Col. Archibald Gracie, playboy Clinch Smith and architect Edward Kent. Rounding out the suave group were E.P. Colley, an Irish civil engineer, Bjornstrom Steffanson, a Swedish military officer and Hugh Woolner, a British businessman.

Two members of "Our Coterie," Woolner and Kent, became especially fond of Candee, and her depiction of a romantic interest in "Sealed Orders" is likely an amalgam of these men, the "He of the Two" of her narrative. It was a fittingly feminine tribute to their self-sacrifice and devotion.

"We all love a gentleman," she said some years later. "Time has nothing to do with effacing that."

Neither has time effaced the appeal of her 1912 tale.

"Sealed Orders" is an engaging, if not entirely accurate, chronicle of *Titanic's* fatal voyage. But its emotion is genuine and, after nearly 100 years, it is still one of the most gripping survivor stories. Touching on more than the journey's nightmare end, Helen Churchill Candee provides a compelling, haunting glimpse of the beauty and power of a great ship, the elegance and fellowship of Edwardian travel, and the thrill of romance at sea.

Admitting that youth was the playground of love, Helen stipulated once that "no woman is so old that in her heart she has outgrown the habit of being a girl."

"Without romance," Helen Candee asked, "what would our lives be?"

☙ ❋ ❧

Sealed Orders
ঔ ✵ 08

By HELEN CHURCHILL CANDEE
Originally published in Collier's Weekly,
May 4, 1912 (Vol. 49, no. 7)

"Those who love them call them gone
                    but they live with a virility immortal."

Mrs. Candee was a passenger on the Titanic, returning to America after a winter of literary work abroad. She has written impersonally a narrative so vivid that the imagination cannot escape from it.

When all the lands were thrilling with the blossoming month of shower and sun, three widely differing craft crept out upon the sea.

One sailed from the New World's city of towers, plowing east. Another coquetted with three near ports of Europe and then sailed west. The third slipped down unnoticed from the glacial north.

The first was a little ship, and modestly glided down the bay and took her place on the ocean highway.

But across, on the other side of the world, the triumph of shipbuilding was starting her maiden trip — challenging the sea, men said. But a challenge is given to those who have rivals. The mammoth had none. She was the largest ship man had ever made; in her construction and in her finish, from keel to topmast, she was the ultimate note of talent and skill and invention. Triumphant was the word that best told her imperial progress.

And the third, a sinister craft, set out from the north with an insolent indifference that transcended even the magnificence of the greatest ship afloat.

And to all three of these craft the power that is greater than man gave sealed orders. All three, though they knew it not, were bound for the same unmarkable spot on the shifting surface of the deep.

The titan's departure was the one men noticed, for power and riches cannot be obscure.

Three days out the ship knew she was Queen of the Seas. Not only was she the largest, the most beautiful, but she was hour by hour discovering herself a possible fleetest. And that way came destruction.

There had been delays in detaching from the shore; at one port a too close touch with another ship, a stop of hours at another for heavy bags of mail. But when free of the land, at last on the high sea, day followed day with the weather in which ships make time. When the run went on the board it astonished, and there was a light laugh of pleasure from smoking room, deck and lounge. Each man felt it a credit to himself. The ship was to make a record trial run.

RMS Titanic **sea trials April 2, 1912**

The oldest captain of the fleet had the crowning honor of his sea life in his assignment, and the head man of the line was on board. From stokehole to bridge the men had been picked with care from among their fellows on lesser boats, that the crew might be worthy of their trust.

It almost seemed that passengers had been picked, too. The richest man was there, and he who by striving had nearly reached him. About the decks strolled the artist of renown and the great writer, the man of theatrical success, the giant in the world of trade, the aid of a nation's president, the prettiest woman, the woman who represented social prominence, the indispensable American girl, presidents of railways, aristocrats of Europe — all these to add to the glory of the first sea-crossing of the biggest ship.

Two days to try her wings, to prove herself, and she was off for the saving of time. And the passenger for whom the keel had been laid and the magic wrought looked over the side at the flying water and laughed as a child.

A blond woman on the steerage deck stands like a viking's daughter, facing the wind. Her hair is golden bright in the sun, her long lines of grace show bold where the wind passes hard their draping. Around her is her little brood, shouting and leaping in the wild free air. All have their faces set on the new Land of Possibility, whither the ship is taking them smooth and fast, day to night. Over the child asleep in her arms, the woman's wide eyes are directed forward with the look of the emigrant, the look of courage, which has conquered fate since the days of Columbus and the colonies.

A first-class cabin aboard the *RMS Titanic*.

"Let us wander over the ship and see it all," said she of the cabin de luxe to him of the bachelor's cabin. So they mounted the hurricane deck and gazed across to the other world of the second class and wondered at its luxury, and further across to the waves and wondered at their clemency.

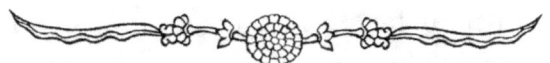

A door along the starboard side was open, there were clicking sounds within and a cheery English voice sang out.

"Come in, come right in, and try your strength," cried the exhibitor of this particular booth in Donnybrook Fair. "Have a race with me on the wheel, sir, while the lady takes a trot in the saddle. Or, here is a camel for you, sir — good for the liver."

His own could not have needed it, so rubicund and clean of tint was he, this powerful five-feet-five of white flannels. He bounded about the place, pulling weights with a smooth finish, slipping into a sliding seat and begging him of the Two to take the other boat and beat him with a Cambridge stroke. He was up again like a cat and gave a hard hand to the lady's foot to mount her into the saddle and to turn on the appliance for the trot.

And so they played an hour with the toys in this wonderful retreat, never thinking of the sweet waters that lay so far away.

"I expect you'll be having a plunge in the pool after all this exercise, sir," said the white flannels. "I'll see you in the morning for another go with the wheel and the oars."

It was getting cold, biting cold, the cold that makes you glad to be alive, with air and water clear and clean as young blue eyes. The acres of decks were free of loungers, even those whose chairs were set well behind the plate-glass weather screen. It was a time for activity, and a scattered parade was on.

"You are flirting with the prettiest girl," she accused, laughing.

"Man is omnivorous," he admitted, laughing back. "One of the women I most admire is this one," and he signified an elderly figure, soberly dressed, walking arm in arm with her husband. With no parleying you knew they were people who had gained and accepted the sweets of success without intoxication. Sobriety and modesty were theirs; strength and calm showed in their faces.

"They, too, have been using one of the ship's appliances," explained he of the Two. "They have just finished a Marconi chat with their son, whose east-bound ship is talking to ours. I see the glow on their faces — the same parental glow of the woman on the steerage deck. And there it is again — that handsome woman over there. See, it is for her son who is beside her with the admirable young wife. I have noticed them all the way over."

Then they went inside to escape the cold sparkling in the water and snapping in the air. And snugly in a green bay of the saloon, a bay of velvet and wood in furniture shapes, they settled down before a glowing grate as one settles down before the home fire after a frosty afternoon ride over the fields. And servants brought tea and toast, and a general feeling of well-being brought content. The old couple came in and settled nearby; the lady with the fine son drifted in and showed her pride to the world, her loving care for him. The quiet hour was on, the hour when the sun grows sleepy.

At dinner, two hours later, the scene might have been in London, or New York, with the men in evening jackets, the women shining in pale satins and clinging gauze. The prettiest girl even wore a glittering frock of dancing length, with silver fringe around her dainty white satin feet.

And after dinner there was coffee served to all at little tables around the great general lounging place, for here the orchestra played.

Some said it was poor on its Wagner work, others said the violin was weak. But that was for conversation's sake, for nothing on board was more popular than the orchestra. You could see that by the way everyone refused to leave it. And everyone asked of it some favorite hit. The prettiest girl asked for dance music, and clicked her satin heels and swayed her adolescent arms to the rhythm.

He of the Two who had walked the deck asked for Dvorak, while she asked for Puccini, and both got their liking, for the orchestra was adroit and willing.

At eleven, folk drifted off to their big cabins, with happy "see-you-in-the-mornings," until a group formed itself alone, and the only sounds the musicians made were those of instruments being shut in their velvet beds.

The Two had all their friends about them. It was early yet. There was the restaurant above, a more cozy place for a little crowd — and things to drink were there on the end of a word of order. So they all

**A view of the Grand Staircase with the crystal dome and the clock.
Photograph taken at the boat deck level.**

strayed easily up the regal stairway — refusing this time the lift — and arrived at the littlest place that one might eat, and took a table large enough for the six. The only other table was made gay by the party of a president's aid.

"But how cold it is, how arctic!" and she of the Two drew close her scarf.

"Something hot, then," said he to the waiter and the steam savored of Scotch and lemons.

How gay they were, these six. The talkative man told stories, the sensitive man glowed and laughed, the two modest Irishmen forgot to be suppressed, the facile Norseman cracked American jokes, the cosmopolitan Englishman expanded, and the lady felt divinely flattered to be in such company.

Half-past eleven came. Even the last parties were breaking up, and only a handful of men strayed ladyless into the smoking room and fell to cards or reminiscence. Except for those and the night watch, the ship's company had settled in for another night of repose.

Silence and emptiness were all the illumination shone in the public rooms and corridors of the great vessel. And in this soft silence the titan was flying like an arrow on the trackless sea, whither sealed orders were sending her.

But she was not the first to arrive at the tryst.

Down from the north that other sinister craft had slipped into her destined place. No wireless equipment, no port or starboard lights, no lines of cabins showing bright, no compass, no captain. But the power that is greater than man has no need of man's methods.

The craft stretched its low, uneven length over miles of smoothest sea, shooting up peaks of dazzling white in lieu of sails, and her escort was the sleek, black seal and the wide-winged gull.

With implacable patience the white craft awaited the coming of the greatest ship on earth, a virgin running to the unknown bridal across a starlit sea. It was nearly midnight when she shuddered with horror in the embrace of the northern ice. Twice, from bow to stern, she shook with mighty endeavor to crush beneath her the assailant. And it seemed she had succeeded.

A great calm at once fell upon the ship, such a calm as falls in port, and solitude reigned along the wide halls. A sleepy head or two were thrust from cabin doors, but seeing nothing went back to bed. Stewards were reassuring, gay and idle. In the smoking room men went on bidding for the trump.

But the Two went for a walk in the keen cold air of the decks, "because I was startled," so she apologized.

They mounted the hurricane deck again and stood by the closed door of the gymnast's chamber. They looked up at the violently roaring steam escaping by the mammoth funnels.

"It's all right," he said. "That is always a precaution when machinery stops."

"But why are not the other engines doing the same?"

He could not answer; he did not know the bottom had been torn from the ship beneath him. They walked aft and looked down where the mother and children of the steerage had been playing, and where the prosperous second class passengers had reveled in their comforts — solitude, desertion, not a human being in sight.

"There is a list to starboard," said she.

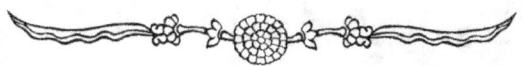

He was grimly silent. They went forward to make sure. There the list was worse — the deck leaned as a man leans with a sword in his side. On the deck below they found the same desertion as everywhere, the deck where all the chairs were spread, where folk displayed themselves and criticized others. The Two now seemed all the people in the world, and because of the cold, and because each was facing sorrow back home, they walked about for warmth of body and cracked jokes for warmth of heart.

"If I had had a wireless — if I knew that my child was no longer living…" she left him to imagine the rest.

"I don't mind going either," he said, grim for a moment.

"Nevertheless," she laughed. "I'd fight death to the last if it came. I'd be Mrs. Lecks and put on black stockings to scare sharks. Why are we so calm?"

"We are Anglo-Saxons," said he.

The cold drove them into the big green velvet room with its glowing grate, empty in its blaze of light.

The first-class smoking room.

A young man — he of the adoring mother and adorable wife — sprang across the wide floor, holding cuplike hands together as he approached the Two.

"Ice!" he laughed. "Have some iceberg. Take a piece! That's what happened — we struck an iceberg. This is what was left on deck." And he flew away.

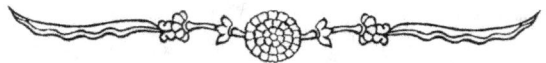

She took the bit, wondering in awe, until he of the Two dashed it from her and chafed her cold, small hand until it glowed again. Turning the chafing into a caress, he never let her hand go. And in that minute they looked into each other's faces, acknowledged the presence of death and accepted it. But neither spoke a word.

After that, people began to come about, some dressed, some not, some alarmed, all quiet and curious to learn the cause of the disturbance. They took the seats about the companionway and talked low.

Women still in sweeping dinner gowns drew wraps about them as the deck door opened. People talked in conventional groups, and all waited, knowing not for what they delayed.

The Two went again outside. The list had terribly increased as they viewed it from the deserted deck.

"Listen!" said she, holding his arm. "That noise over our heads — it is the sound of lifeboats being put out?"

His answer was to force her to the scene above. Scarce a passenger, but the port side filled with a growing crowd of wiry men, black alike in face and dress, crowding in orderly fashion about the strong, quiet figure of the captain.

The firemen had been ordered up from the engine room and that black crew huddled together, awaiting the order to man the lifeboats, the order that would put life again into their hands, for they knew, these hard-faced toilers, that only little boats could save from death at sea. She smiled on them as she walked through the iron crew, and they looked, startled at the smile, thinking it lack of wit, not excess of courage.

But he was uneasy and again took her downstairs and within, in search of less grim scenes.

Lifeboat 6 with Helen Candee and Molly Brown upon rescue.

Different, but was it less grim? Up the sweep of the regal staircase was advancing a solid procession of all the ship's passengers, wordless, orderly, quiet and only their dress told of tragedy. On every man and woman's body was tied that sinister emblem, the life preserver, as each one walked to await the coming horrors. It was a fancy-dress ball in Dante's Hell.

Another glance between the Two. He caught her by the arm and forced her to a cabin, threw over her shoulders the white and bulky pack, saw that she was warmly wrapped, seized a rug, and said, briefly, "Come."

They passed those who huddled within the ship and mounted again to the topmost deck. A line of boats swung on davits at deck level; the black cloud of firemen, faces set, still waited for the command to jump in. The order came on clear, cold air: "Down below, men. Everyone of you, down below!"

And without a sound they willingly turned from life and went to death, no protest, no murmur, no resistance, a band of unknown heroes.

Then it was that the captain ordered: "Put the women in the boats. No men are to go." He spoke hard words in a quiet voice, that none might disobey.

Now for tragedy; all the horrors of separation had begun:

A little lady made her appeal: "See, captain, my arm is broken. My husband must go with me or I am helpless."

"No men allowed in the boats, madam," and the captain turned away.

Another tried: "I am not young, and need my son; may he not come?"

"Only women."

And the young man in gay courage gave his mother and wife to the care of the swinging boat.

Others got in; the captain, who knew he was living his final hour, stopped a number, augmented it, then ordered the little craft lowered. In the boat, twenty-five silent women descended nearly a hundred feet. They were filled with hope, sure that those on board were better off than they, sure that all would be reunited either on the big ship they were leaving, or on the other vessel whose far white light showed just over the port quarter.

The Marconi man was hard at work; the second biggest ship was in near waters, and hope was high.

Terrible was the artillery of the rockets. The great ship seemed to shriek in despair. Before that was a dignity of self-confidence, but in that wild cry to heaven went up all the horror of death.

Titanic Sinking by Willy Stöwer 1864-1931.

Then it was that the women in the lifeboats agonized over what love had coerced them into doing. What was life but love, and what was life without loved ones? The weight of the discovery can never be told. Women of courage had been tricked by noble heroes into saving their own lives. It was an easy ruse — "get into the boats; obey because it helps me; we will soon be together again; do it for my sake, or the children's." By these sophistries of love were the women put into the boats at a time and in a place where theirs seemed the harder part to do.

But when each boat reached the water, the women knew. They saw the salt flow sloping over the lighted ports of the third deck and knew the vessel was already sunken forty feet into oblivion.

"Keep all the boats together and pull away from the vessel," the captain had said in a strong, calm voice. Why pull away? Because presently the great palace of light would be following the lead of her diving bow, and in the final plunge would draw everything after her.

On the ship the bravely competent still loaded boats with protesting women and wailing children.

"Take her from me, take her!" cried the men from whom wives refused to part, and it was done.

In a corner against the cabin stood the aged couple, calmly resolute. "Come into this boat," the rescuers said to her. "I stay with my husband," she said simply. It was not the frantic protest of the younger women, but the firm will of the seasoned soul. And in death these two were not divided.

What can one whose profession is to amuse do in a time of tragedy? They, too, have a part in the great play of courage. Over the crowds, quiet, inactive, anguished, there flowed a flood of music, such music as was never before heard — a gay march, a two-step, light operatic airs, all freighted with a burden of love, that love which lays down its life for a friend. The ship's orchestra was sending out courage from man to man in its peculiar expression, cheering others while itself faced death.

Men of courage and resource who had been loading and lowering boats from the very first came at last to a stop. The last boat was ready for the launching. Two who had held together in the work went a deck below to see if any stray women were there unrescued. All was brilliant desolation. The lights were beginning to burn low. Water — soft, noiseless water — was creeping up the slanting deck so fast that in another minute they would have been imprisoned under the deck's roof. They leaped to the railing and mounted it.

At that moment the last boat floated before them, three yards away, with vacant room in the bow. Surely they had the right! They looked in each other's faces to ask the question, and each nodded to the other, "yes." They leaped the space and caught the side of the boat, the last to leave the ship by boat, and almost the only rescuers who were saved.

The hundreds that were left drew closer. The beaten bow was hidden underwater, the only uncovered stretch of deck sloped high toward the stern, and on this diminished point huddled a close pack who awaited death with the transcendent courage and order and quiet that had been theirs for the horrible two hours.

And over them trembled the last strains of the orchestra's message: "Autumn" first, then "Nearer, my God, to Thee."

Down on the sea, the little lifeboats were following the captain's orders to pull away from the ship in water as calm, as full of stars, as the pool in a Moorish garden. All awaited the end, transfixed. Window after window of the ship became dark as the water covered it in slow descent; less and less became the stern where the hushed crowd waited.

At last, the end of the world. A smooth, slow chute. Life went out on the big ship.

The death call of 1500 units of divine selflessness spread its volume over the waters as a single cry to God. There was no shriek nor wail nor frantic shout. Instead a heavy moan as of one being, from whom final agony forces a single sound.

And with this human protest against stifling arctic waters was a muffled sound from within, the groan of the dying ship, as if she, too, were sensate and joined her agony with man's.

The mass in the dark waters was thrown hither and thither, and one or two caught rafts and boats. In the human instinct to preserve life, one man had drawn himself upon a raft.

He was white-haired and bearded, but short and strong, and had much to live for. At last the raft had rescued so many she endangered all, and then began the horrid task off fighting off the swimmers.

Those who looked for the gray beard on the raft saw him no more. Seeing the crush of men, he had seded his place and slipped into the sea.

"Don't get on. You'll swamp us!"

"All right. God keep you all. Good bye." And the waters closed over him. It was the little gymnast.

After that, silence on the surface of the deep, and awe on the faces of the stricken freight in the scattered lifeboats. Where had been the glowing lights from the luxurious cabins of the mammoth ship was now a soft, impersonal sheen of silver starlight, the implacability of nature.

And how futile were the little boats. Where were they going? Why were they there?

The distant light that some had followed from the first scudded away into the aurora as fast as the first breath of breeze rippled over the glassy waters.

Why live now, to die miserably of cold and starvation and drenching? And always with the horror of that death groan sounding in ears and soul. It was then that those in the boats who had been picked up from the water gave up the spirit. It was then that the mother of the fine son began to call for him in the unmeaning repetition of the mind which has snapped. It was then that the emigrant woman of the many babes sent screams for them ringing to the stars in maniac baby-talk. It was then that the ghostly gulls swung and cried in the icy air.

Three hours before, the Marconi man had been at his post on the ship. Out over the oily sea, out in the clear, crisp air, as far as the twinkling canopy of stars, trembled a soundless cry from magic wires: "Ship is sinking fast!"

Fully 60 miles away a faithful wire had trembled in response.

And thus the third craft that went a-sailing on an April day learned of her sealed orders and their import, and turned flying to the trysting place.

All night she was preparing to help the proud, big ship, happy to serve so great a supplicant. She would be small and shabby beside the greater vessel, but would humbly do her best, and so she pounded the engines and kicked the waters and strained the boilers.

The latitude and longitude given by the cry for succor were attained, yet the keenest glass could find no lights other than the stars. Darkness brooded on the face of the ocean, and terror in the faces of the relief.

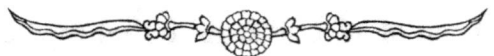

Dawn showed the vast reaches of the sea, empty of big craft. But floating near, a swaying tangle of deck chairs and cushions, and a pale white babe rocked in the cradle of that fashioning. The sun lingered on coming on such a scene.

The rescue ship lay still and watched it. The aurora in the north was paled by steaks that looked like rosy chiffon scarfs, waving over the sun's east. Close down in the warm glow perched an impertinent crescent moon.

Toward the sun rose sinister points of ice, dark against the light. Struck by the morning rays were these wondrous glistening sails of frozen white and pearly pink — ice mountains glorified into celestial beauty. And as far as the eye could see, the limitless level of the ice pack, purer and whiter than man's imagining.

The woman crying for her babes because they were not, the moan of the mother calling her son — these were almost the only sounds from the rowboats that showed like shells on the water, a limping, chilled, sorrowing fleet to whom the rescue ship brought salvation.

But a few hours more and the modest ship of gentle aim was turning back to port, heavy with the hundreds saved, its flag at half-mast. The burden of sorrow in the widows' hearts was to be read in the dark shadows of their eyes, the wail of the mothers was heard in the closed chamber of the sick.

For every life on board, three braver ones had surrendered theirs in God-like selflessness.

The icepacks lay for miles, dazzling in the sun, peaks rising proudly here and there. Seals, black and shiny, showed in the waters, gulls flew and cried — active white against silent white.

Superb, thrilling, dominant, the ice held the region with nature's strength. The power greater than man's had prevailed, the crushing force against which there is no defense, no pity, no sparing. It was the power that is of God, which is the divinity of noble men.

Those who love them call them gone, but they live with a virility immortal. The courage of 1500 souls who quietly gave their lives for others floods an entire world and makes us humbly eager to give tribute by living nobler lives.

And as long as man lives the uplifting tale will be told, showing the divinity which is man's and his kinship to God.

ᛞ THE END ᛣ

The Women's Titanic Memorial in southwest Washington, D.C. honors the men who died on the *RMS Titanic*. The thirteen-foot-tall figure is of a partly clad male figure with arms outstretched. The statue was erected by the Women's Titanic Memorial Association.

The memorial is located on P Street SW next to the Washington Channel near Fort Lesley J. McNair. It was designed by Gertrude Vanderbilt Whitney, who won the commission in open competition, and sculpted by John Horrigan. It was unveiled on May 26, 1931, by Helen Herron Taft, the widow of President Taft. (also see page 296)

Titanic's bow today, as seen from the Russian MIR I submersible.

BIBLIOGRAPHY

PRE-1924 WORKS ON CAMBODIA

Angkor the Magnificent was a significant contribution to Cambodian literature for Anglophones worldwide. In the early 20th century, French scholarship eclipsed everything available in the English language. Helen Candee's proficiency in English and French gave her a broad selection of works to draw from. Her book preceded many early Khmer scholars such as Victor Goloubew, Sappho Marchal, Guy Porée and Phillipe Stern who were as yet unpublished in 1924.

As an aid to readers, the editor compiled the following bibliography to suggest books that Helen Candee *may* have consulted in her research on this topic. Descriptions of the actual editions below are provided, when available, to help scholars identify original editions.

Selected Pre-1924 Books and Pamphlets about Cambodia

Adams, W. H. Davenport. *In the Far East: A Narrative of Exploration and Adventure in Cochin-China, Cambodia, Laos and Siam*. Book 208, [8] p.: ill. ; 17 cm. London: T. Nelson and Sons, 1879.

Agostini, Jules. *Au Cambodge*. Book 32 p. illus. 22 cm. Paris: Plon, Nourrit, 1898.

Aymonier, Etienne. Aymonier, E. *Le Cambodge*. Book 3 v. front. (port., v. 3) illus. (incl. facsims.) maps, plans. 28 cm. Paris: E. Leroux, 1900.

—*Histoire de l'ancien Cambodge*. Book 198 p.; 22 cm. Strasbourg: Impr. de Nouveau journal de Strasbourg, 1920.

Bois, George. *Les danseuses cambodgiennes en France*. Hanoi: Extrême-Orient, 1913.

Bouillevaux, C. E. *L'Annam et le Cambodge; voyages et notices historiques*. Paris: Victor Palmé, 1874.

Bouinais, Albert Marie Aristide, and A. Paulus. *Le royaume du Cambodge*. Book 76 p.; 25 cm. Paris: Berger-Levrault, 1884.

Boulangier, Edgar. *Un hiver au Cambodge; chasses au tigre, à l'éléphant et au buffle sauvage; souvenirs d'une mission officielle remplie en 1880-1881*. 400 p. illus., maps, plates. 30 cm. Tours: A. Mame et fils, 1887.

Bowring, Sir John. *The Kingdom and People of Siam: with a Narrative of the mission to that country in 1855*. Book 2 v. plates (part col.), fold. map, fold. facsim., ports. 23 cm. London: J. W. Parker, 1857.

Branda, Paul. *Ça et la: Cochinchine et Cambodge, l'ame Khmère, Ang-Kor*. See Paul Émile Marie Réveillière.

Delaporte. Louis. *Voyage au Cambodge: L'architecture Khmer*. Book 462 p. incl. front., illus., plates (part mounted, part double) map, plans (part double) 28 cm. Paris: C. Delagrave, 1880.

Dieulefils, P. *Indo-Chine Pittoresque & Monumentale, Ruines D'Angkor Cambodge = Indochina Picturesque and Monumental Ruins of Angkor (Cambodge) = Indochina Malerisch Und Monumentalisch Ruinen Von Angkor Cambodge*. Book 67 plates, each with descriptive letterpress: ill. ; 28 x 36 cm. Hanoi: P. Dieulefils, Photo Publisher, 1907.

Filoz, Auguste Achille Hippolyte. *Cambodge et Siam voyage et séjour aux ruines des monuments Kmers*. Book 190 p. 19 cm. Thonon: A. Dubouloz, 1876.

Fournereau, Lucien. *Les ruines khmères, Cambodge et Siam: documents complémentaires d'architecture, de sculpture et de céramique*. Book [10] p., 110 plates: ill. ; 40 cm. Paris: Berthaud Frères, 1890.

Garnier, Francis. *Chronique royale du Cambodge*. Book 336-386, 112-144 p. map. 23 cm. Paris: Impr. nationale, 1871.

Gervais-Courtellement, Jules, and Augustin Challamel. *Empire colonial de la France: l'Indo-Chine: Cochinchine, Cambodge, Laos, Annam, Tonkin*. Collection Courtellemont. Book xv, 195 p.: ill., col. map; 33 cm. Paris: Firmin-Didot, 1901.

Groslier, George. *Danseuses cambodgiennes anciennes et modernes*. Paris: Albert Challamel, 1913.

—*A l'ombre d'Angkor; notes et impressions sur les temples inconnus de l'ancien Cambodge, avec 16 photographies inédits d'après les clichés de l'auteur et une carte itinéraire*. Book 4 p. l., [3]-190 p. 1 l. 16 pl., map. 20 cm. Paris: A. Challamel, 1916.

—*Note sur la sculpture khmère ancienne*. Book p. [297]-314. illus. 28 cm. Hanoi: Imprimerie d'extrême-orient, 1920s.

—*Recherches sur les Cambodgiens d'aprés les textes et les monuments depuis les premiers siècles de notre ére*. 432 p. illus., XLVIII pl. (incl. front.) fold. map 32 cm. Paris: A. Challamel, 1921.

—"Royal Dancers of Cambodia." *Asia*, 22, No. 1 (Jan. 1922), pp. 47-53, 74.

Hammerton, J. A. *Manners and Customs of Mankind*. New York: Wm. H. Wise, n.d. Vol. II.

Herz, Martin Florian. *A Short History of Cambodia from the Days of Angkor to the Present*. Book 141 p. illus. 22 cm. New York: F.A. Praeger, 1900.

Jeannerat de Beerski, Pierre. *Angkor: Ruins in Cambodia*. London: G. Richards, 1923.

Julien, Félix. *Doudart de Lagrée au Cambodge et en Indo-Chine*. Book 221 p.: port., folded map; 19 cm. Paris: Challamel Ainé, 1886 (2nd edition).

Knox, Thomas Wallace. *The Boy Travellers in the Far East: Part Second, Adventures of Two Youths in a Journey to Siam and Java, with Descriptions of Cochin-China, Cambodia, Sumatra and the Malay Archipelago*. Book 446 p.: ill. ; 23 cm. New York: Harper & Bros, 1881.

Leclère, Adhémard. *Cambodge. Contes et légendes*. Book xxii, 308 p. 22 cm. Paris: Librairie Émile Bouillon, 1895.

—*Cambodge; fêtes civiles et religieuses*. Book xii, 660 p., XIII pl. incl. front. 21 cm. Paris: Imprimerie nationale, 1916.

—*Histoire du Cambodge depuis le 1er siècle de notre ère, d'après les inscriptions lapidaires, les annales chinoises et annamites et les documents européens des six derniers siècles*. Book 3 p. l., [ix]-xii, 547, [1] p. 26 cm. Paris: P. Geuthner, 1914.

—*Les livres sacrés du Cambodge*. Paris: Ernest Leroux, 1906.

—*Le théâtre cambodgien*. Book [1], 26 p. illus., 4 pl. 28.5 cm. Paris: Ernest Leroux, 1911.

Loti, Pierre. *Siam*. Book xi, 182 p. : ill. ; 23 cm. London: T.W. Laurie, 1900.

—*Un pèlerin d'Angkor*. Paris: Calmann-Levy, 1912.

Lunet de Lajonquière, E. *Atlas archéologique de l'Indo-Chine. Monuments du Champa et du Cambodge*. Book 24 p. incl. tables. 5 double maps. 67 x 38 cm. Paris: Imprimerie nationale, E. Leroux, éditeur, 1901.

—*Inventaire descriptif des monuments du Cambodge*. Book 3 v. illus., fold. plates, plans (part fold.) and atlas of 2 fold. maps. 28 cm. Paris: E. Leroux, 1902.

Monod, Guillaume Henri. *Légendes cambodgiennes: que m'a contées le Gouverneur Khieu*. Book 148 p.: ill. ; 17 cm. Paris: Bossard, 1922.

MacGregor, John. *Through the Buffer State; A Record of Recent Travels Through Borneo, Siam and Cambodia*. Book xv p., 1 l., 290 p. 8 pl., 2 port. (incl. front.) map, plan. 20 cm. London: F.V. White and Co, 1896.

Marchal, Henri. *Angkor. La résurrection de l'art khmer et l'œuvre de l'École française d'Extrême-Orient*. Book 32 p. illus. 21 cm. Paris: Office Français d'Édition, 1900.

Maspero, Georges. *L'empire Khmèr: histoire et documents*. Book 115, [29] p.; 33 cm. Phnom-Penh: Imprimerie du Protectorat, 1904.

Meyer, Roland. *Saramani danseuse khmère*. Fiction 238, [2] p. plates. 32 x 24 cm. Saigon: A. Portail, 1919.

Monod, Guillaume Henri. *Ruines d'Angkor*. Book 207 p.: ill.; 23 x 31 cm. Saigon: Édition photo Nadal, 1920.

Mouhot, Henri. *Travels in the Central Parts of Indochina (Siam), Cambodia, and Laos, During the Years 1858, 1859 and 1860*. Book 2 vol. (303, 301 s.): ill., kartor. London: John Murray, 1864.

—*Voyage dans les royaumes de Siam, de Cambodge, de Laos et autres parties centrales de L'Indo-Chine*. Book, viii, 335 p., [28] leaves of plates: ill., map (fold.), ports; 23 cm. Paris: Librairie Hachette, 1868.

Moura, J. *Le royaume du Cambodge*. [Author's true name was Simone Lévêque Louvet] Book 2 v. illus. (incl. ports., facsim.) 2 pl. (1 double) fold. map, 3 fold. plans. 29 cm. Paris: Ernest Leroux, 1883.

Pannetier, A. *Notes cambodgiennes au cœur du pays Khmer*. Book 159 p.; 19 cm. Paris: Payot, 1921.

Parmentier, Henri. *Vat Nokor*. Book 38 p. v pl. (incl. fold. plans) 28 cm. Hanoi: Imprimerie d'Extrême-Orient, 1917.

—*L'art Khmer primitif*. Paris: G. Van Oest, 1927.

Pavie, Auguste. *Contes du Cambodge*. Book 262 p. illus. Paris: Leroux, 1921.

—*Recherches sur la littérature du Cambodge, du Laos et du Siam*. Book 2 p. l. xlvi p., 367 p., 1 l. illus., pl., maps. 29 cm. Paris: E. Leroux, 1898.

—*Mission Pavie Indo-Chine: 1879-1895. Geographie et voyages*. Book v.: ill.; 28 cm. Paris: E. Leroux, 1901.

Pavie, Auguste, and M. Schmitt. *Recherches sur l'histoire du Cambodge, du Laos et du Siam*. Book [V], XLV, 494 p.: ill.; in-8. Paris: Leroux, 1898.

Réveillière, Paul Émile Marie. *Ça et la Cochinchine et Cambodge; L'ame khmère; Ang-Kor*. Book 451 p. 19 cm. Paris: Fischbacher, 1886.

Salaun, Louis. *Indochine*. Paris: Imprimerie National, 1903.

Tessan, François de. *Dans l'Asie qui s'éveille; essais indochinois*. Book 370 p. illus.; 19 cm. Paris: La Renaissance du Livre, 1922.

Testoin, Édouard. *Le Cambodge, passé, présent, avenir*. Book 191 p. fold. map. 26 cm. Tours: Impr. E. Mazereau, 1886.

Thouvenot, Maurice. *Une idylle au pays Khmer; roman de moeurs cambodgiennes*. Book 273 p. 19 cm. Paris: Jouve & Cie, 1913.

Tissandier, Albert. *Cambodge et Java: ruines khmėres et javanaises 1893-1894*. Book vi, 160 p., [25] leaves of plates: ill., map, plans; 31 cm. Paris: G. Masson, 1896.

Vincent, Frank. *The Land of the White Elephant: Sights and Scenes in Southeastern Asia. A Personal Narrative of Travel and Adventure in Farther India, Embracing the Countries of Burma, Siam, Cambodia, and Cochin-China. (1871-2)*. New York: Harper & Bros, 1874.

Zhou, Daguan, and Paul Pelliot. *Mémoire sur les coutumes du Cambodge*. Book 1 v. (unpaged) 27 cm. 1902.

INDEX

A

Ambassador. *See* Zhou Daguan.
Angkor, 5, 9-10, 54, 114, 166.
    See also Khmer; temples
    by name
    best season to visit, 50
    disappearance of civilization, 6,
        115, 163, 168, 181, 262, 264
    discovery of, 6, 266
    religion of, 270
    roads, 190
    stone type used, 268
    temple style, 70
    trees, destructive force of, 258
    water, 190, 239
Angkor Thom, 54, 115, 127
    barays, 241-242, 244
    Bayon, 118, 127
    Banteai Kedei, 224
    Baphuon, 122
    Bridge of Giants, 124-125, 158
    Civa, faces of, 118
    Civism, 230
    entrance, 115
    founding of, 272
    south gate, 115-116
    Gate of Victory, 124, 158
    kings who built, 120
    moat, 115, 240
    Phimeanakas, 122, 165
    population, 132
    Ta Prohm, 224
    the Terrace, 122
    Terrace of the Leper King, 158,
        163-164
    Yasovarman, 272
    Zhou Daguan, 116-118, 166
Angkor Vat, 62, 81
    Apsaras, 100. *See also* Tevadas
    arch, science of, 72
    bas reliefs, 88-96
    best time to visit, 50
    bonzerie, 86
    central tower, 77
    cruciform terrace, 70, 87
    dance presentation at, 103-112
    discovery of, 6, 266
    enciente, 68, 81-82
    entrance, 240
    first view of, 62-63
    flower patterns, 74, 96
    French acquisition of, 7, 266
    galleries, 72, 87, 236
    gate for elephants, 84
    General Joffre visit, 84
    gopura, 82
    hotel, 60-61. *See also* Bungalow

libraries, 68
military scenes, 92-94
moat, 64, 66, 81
myths, depiction of, 95
Naga at, 68, 86, 91
perrons, 66
portico, 82
rinceau, 82. *See also* flower patterns
Sea of Milk, 91-92, 268
second gallery, 74, 76, 77
tevadas, 74, 98, 100
third level, 77
Vishnu, 77-78
water, 239
western orientation, 266
windows, 84
animals. *See also* elephants, horses, lions, monkeys, tigers
apes, 115, 254
caiman, 142
gibbons, 222, 245
rhinoceros, 102, 154
Annam, 23, 30, 90, 137, 261, 264
Annamite, 35. *See also* Cham
women, 40, 42, 44-45
Apsaras, 92, 206
origin, 92
relation to *tevadas*, 100, 174
arch, 72, 115, 124-125
army
Chinese, 12
Khmer, 6, 90, 92, 94, 176, 262
Aryvat, 144
asuras, 92, 125, 158, 220

B
Babylon, 208
Bak-Keng, 196-198, 272
Bali, 95, 200. *See also* Ramayana
bamboo
elephant bell, 156
for administering punishment, 238
house construction, 6, 50, 86, 182, 192, 222, 226
Banteai Kedei, 224-226, 232, 241
entrance, 224
gopura, 224
Baphuon, 198, 200, 241, 272
barays, 241, 242, 244, 272
barattement. *See* Sea of Milk
Barye, Antoine-Louis, 207
bas-reliefs
Angkor Thom, 150
Angkor Vat, 72, 88-96
Baphuon, 198
Bayon, 135
depicting dance, 174
depicting everyday life, 176-177, 264, 268
depicting war, 261
validating Zhou Daguan, 174
bathing
as ceremony of maidens, 236
bathing suits in Saigon, 40, 42
Cambodian affinity for, 179, 239
in Siem Reap, 190
Battle of Tsushima. *See* Russian fleet
Bayon, the, 118, 120, 127
age of, 130
Civa, 230
construction of, 120, 130, 134-135, 230, 272
discovery of, 266
entrance, 134, 240
four faced towers, 228, 230
galleries, 134-137
golden tower, 118, 136
illustrations of daily life, 132
power of the Trimurti, 127

Sea of Milk, 92
Yasovarman, 272
bibliotheques. See libraries
Birmans, 234
boats, 22
    ancient boats, 207, 241, 257, 264
    Canton boat, 14, 16
    gunboat, 21
    in carvings, 132, 134
    Mekong riverboats, 44, 46
    Messageries Fluviales, 56, 59
    on the Tonlé Sap, 57-58, 104
    the Pak Hoi, 22
    pirates, 18
    rice boats, 12, 23
    Russian fleet, 32-34
bonzerie, 86, 137
bonzes, 68, 86, 130, 134, 136, 137, 197
Brahm, 127, 250, 252, 268
Brahma, 86, 88, 116, 128, 260
Brahmanic religion, 127-128, 228-230
Brahmanism, 76, 77, 78, 95, 116, 118, 127, 137, 148, 176, 184, 196, 200, 202, 209, 220, 228, 230, 246, 254, 268, 270
Bridge of Giants, 92, 124-125, 149, 158
Buddha, Buddhism, 90, 137, 202, 252, 270
    at Angkor Vat, 100
    at Tep Pranam, 200, 202
    defacement of carvings at Prah Khan, 252
    in the Bayon, 137
    in Néak Pean, 257
    monks similarity to, 130
    palace statue, 52
bullock cart, 104, 190, 192, 226, 252
Bungalow, The, 60-61, 150, 210
    bedding, 212
    dress style at, 63
    on the terrace, 192, 194, 213
    proximity of Bak-Keng, 196
    staff involved in WWI, 218, 220

C

Çakti, wife of Civa, 209
Cambodia, Cambodian
    daily living, 226, 238
    dancers, 111
    features, 164, 176
    French influence, 183, 275
    as French Protectorate, 6-7, 54
    house construction, 6, 50, 86, 182, 192, 222, 226
    Khambu, 140, 272
    kings of, 52, 54, 166, 186
    legends, 158
    museum, 56
    Phnom Penh, 52
    races of, 5, 6
    temples, 237
    travel to, 12
    warfare, 92, 137, 261-262
Cam Ranh Bay, 32, 34
Canton, 12, 19
    rice cargo boat, 14
carts. *See* bullock carts
caryatides, 124, 144, 145, 148, 152
Champas. *See* Chams
Chams, 42
    envy, 262
    Khmer enemies, 90, 137, 220
    victory over the Khmers, 264
chariots, 134, 177
    at Angkor Vat, 70, 84
    laws restricting use of, 238
China, Chinese, 5, 23
    ambassador. *See* Zhou Daguan
    army, 12

Chinks (slang), 18
Cochin China, 10, 50
   people, 24, 26, 28, 30
   pirates, 18, 20
   relationships with Khmers, 260-261
   travel, 24, 37
China Sea, 56
Chinese Ambassador. *See* Zhou Daguan
Christian, 237
Cholon, 24
Civa, Civaism, 95, 116, 118, 125, 127, 128, 130, 132, 134, 135, 176, 177, 209, 228, 230, 236, 252, 256, 270. *See also* Brahmanic religion
Civil War, 60
cocoanut, 45, 182-183, 190
   cocoanut palm, 193
   vendors, 45
Cointreau, 194
Commaille, Jean, 164
concubines, 172, 174
cruciform terrace, 70, 87
   dance show, 108-110
cumsha, 18

D

dagoba, 90
dance, dancers, 104-112
   Apsaras, 92, 100-108, 174, 206
   costumes, 107
   at Cruciform Terrace, 108-110
   dancers (ancient), 100, 107, 110, 111, 174, 175, 226, 234, 235, 236, 238
   dancers (modern), 52, 104, 106, 107, 172, 178
   depicted at Angkor Wat, 98, 100
   hands, 106, 111
   headdresses, 100, 134, 161
   jewels as adornment, 107, 110
   premières, 106, 110, 107
   rope-dancers, 204
   sacred dancers, 7,
   tevadas as sacred dancers, 98, 100, 111, 174
Delaporte, Louis, 275
Devas, 92, 125, 158

E

Eastern Baray, 242, 272
l'Ecole de l'Éxtrème Orient, 275
elephants
   ancient, 84, 86, 90, 94, 115, 116, 122, 145, 152, 156, 158, 163, 170, 175, 176, 177, 206, 207
   Aryvat, 144
   Effie, 115, 116, 122, 124, 125, 195, 196
   for hunting, 154, 156
   for transportation, 114-115, 118, 125, 155, 196, 198
   Ganesa, 144
   gates for, 84
   howdah, 84, 134, 154, 156, 195
   royal, 52
   stairways for, 64
   wild, 32, 34
enceinte, 66, 235
   at Angkor Vat, 68, 77, 81, 82, 87, 88, 96, 200
   at Banteai Kedai, 224
   at Mébon, 242
   at Prah Khan, 248, 250
   at Ta Keo, 208
   at Ta Prohm, 228, 230, 237, 238, 240

F
Florida, 50
Ford, Henry, 60
    automobile, 180, 202, 218, 220, 246
France, French
    architecture, 40, 52
    at the time of Angkor, 5
    colonial attitudes, 40, 44, 46, 78
    discovery of Angkor, 6-7, 266, 275
    exploitation of colonies, 45
    Franco-Siamese 1907 treaty, 7, 266, 275
    Indochina, 6, 40
    influence on Phnom Penh, 52
    in Siem Reap, 183, 190
    King Sisowath visit, 54
    language in Cambodia, 218
    penalties for antiquity theft, 225
    WWI, 218
French Protectorate, 38, 44, 52, 50, 54, 172, 266, 275

G
Garnier, Francis, 275
Garuda, 145, 150, 270
    at Angkor Vat, 91
    at Terrace of Honor, 148, 150, 163
Gate of Victory, 92, 124, 145
gharri, 40, 47
godowns, 12
gopura, 82, 208, 224, 235, 250
Grand Lac. *See* Tonlé Sap
Groslier, George, 56, 81
    interpreting the Khmers, 234-235

H
Hanuman, 95, 146, 220.
    See also Ramayana

Harshavarman, 166
Hindu, Hindus, 5, 95, 100, 150, 164, 260, 270
Hong Kong, 10-23
horses
    ancient, 94, 102
    modern, 40, 94, 213,
houris, 160
howdah. *See* elephant

I
India, 163, 164, 183, 260, 261, 268
Indochina, 6, 266
    colonists, 40, 186, 261
    in Khmer times, 84
    priest's attire, 48
Indra, 70
Indravarman, 120

J
Jayavarman II, 272
Jayavarman V, 272
Jaya-Varmediparamecvara, 170
    jewels as adornment, 79, 100, 107, 110, 116, 134, 161, 164, 168, 174, 177, 235, 236, 261, 262
Joffre, Gen. Joseph, 84, 108

K
Kama, 95, 200. *See also* Ramayana
Kashmir, 86
Kellermann, Annette, 40
Khambu, 139, 140, 260, 261, 272
Khmer
    architecture, 72, 76, 77, 87, 135, 158, 206, 208, 222, 228, 237, 250
    art, 54, 68, 70, 132, 138, 145, 146, 163, 164, 166, 226
    disappearance of, 6, 115, 163, 168, 181, 262, 264

discovery of (by the West), 6-7, 266, 275
historical records of, 88, 90, 92, 95, 122, 132, 158, 168, 174, 176, 234, 268, 270
hospitals, 234
hunters, 154
interpreting the mysteries of, 8, 9, 10, 56, 66, 88, 139, 162, 228, 259
kings, 54, 79, 120, 128, 166, 170, 174, 175, 176, 230, 272, 274
origins of, 70, 139, 140, 260-261
race, 5, 6, 260
religion, 136, 137, 150, 200, 228, 230, 234, 237, 238, 252
rice, 51
temple guardians, 54, 66, 77, 125, 142, 144
warfare and enemies, 42, 78, 90, 92, 95, 137, 220, 261, 262, 264
water, 239-244
wealth, 6, 7, 84, 134, 138, 235, 262
women, 100, 111, 172, 174, 175, 182, 236
Khmer Museum, 54, 56, 81.
See also Groslier, George
King of Cambodia, 54
King of the Giants, 111, 112
Kublai Khan, 166.
See also Zhou Daguan

L
Lagrée, Commandant de, 275
Lajonquière, Etienne-Edmond Lunet de, 275
Leper King, 158, 160, 163, 164, 183
  lack of jewelry, 164
libraries, 68, 76, 86, 134, 200

lions
  guardians of Khmer temples, 66, 142
  origin of Khmer lion, 144
  sacred animals, 144
  royal throne covering, 175
Lolei, 238
lotus, 64, 74, 90, 98, 106, 111, 125, 152, 158, 177, 194, 202, 206, 256, 257

M
Mahabarata, 88
Maricha, 90. *See also Ramayana*
Mébon, 242
Mekong, 37, 42, 46, 48, 56, 57, 142, 244, 260, 275
Messageries Maritimes, 10, 56, 57, 59, 213
moats, 208, 240, 242, 248
  at Angkor Thom, 115, 124, 158, 272
  at Angkor Vat, 63, 64, 66, 68, 70, 79, 81, 82, 103, 239, 240
  at Banteay Kedei, 224, 225, 241
  at Prah Khan, 240
  at Ta-Keo, 240
  at Ta Prohm, 228, 232, 240
  at The Bungalow, 181, 223
monkeys, 95, 110, 146, 196, 197, 221, 222, 245, 254, 268
Mouhot, Henri, 6, 266, 275
Mount Mandara, 92
Mowgli's Song Against People, 274
mukuta, 125, 158, 176
museum. *See* Khmer Museum
Mytho, 47

N
Naga, 54, 68, 70, 125, 139-140, 142
  at Angkor Thom, 139-140, 158

at Angkor Vat, 64, 68, 86, 91
caiman as inspiration for, 142
at Néak Pean, 256, 257
at Pimeanakas, 147, 148, 150
Néak Pean, 221, 241, 256-258

O
Onco, 275

P
palanquins, 145, 172, 175, 177, 207, 236, 264
Pearl River, 16, 20
Pelliot, Paul, 270
Père Chévreuil, 275
perrons, 66, 77, 87, 89, 122
    Phimeanakas, 122, 147-148, 165, 166, 179, 237, 272
    entrance, 166, 175
    gallery, 147
    in writings of Zhou Daguan, 166, 168, 170, 172, 175-178
Phnom Penh, 44, 52, 54, 56, 104
    museum, 54, 81
    palace, 166, 168, 178
Pimeanakas, 122, 147-148, 165, 166, 168, 170, 172, 179, 237, 272
pirates, 16-21
pottery, 45, 132
Prah Khan, 165, 208, 214, 216, 220, 226, 232, 240, 241, 246, 248, 250, 252, 254, 272
    enciente, 250
    entrance, 248, 250
    galleries, 250, 254
    gopura, 250
    moat, 240
Prah Pithu, 206-207
premières. *See* dance
Protectorate. *See* French Protectorate
punishments, 225, 238

Q
Quiroga de San Antonio 274

R
Rama, 90. *See also* Ramayana
Ramayana, 88, 200, 220, 262, 268
    Bali, 95, 200
    Hanuman, 95, 146, 220
    Kama, 95, 200
    Rama, 90
    Ravana, 200
    Sita, 95
    Sugriva, 95
Ravana, 200. *See also* Ramayana
rinceau, 82, 98. *See also* Angkor Vat, flower patterns
Rishis, 115
Rockefeller Institute, 234
Roi de Cambodge. *See* King of Cambodia
Russian Fleet, 32
Russo-Japanese War, 32-34

S
Sacred Sword, 52, 168, 177, 261
Saigon, 10, 37-46
    Rue Catinat, 40
sampot, 77, 107, 134, 161, 176, 183, 190, 197, 236
Sanctuary, 77, 168, 181, 206, 209, 235-236, 266
    Angkor Vat, 63, 66, 77, 78, 79, 87, 113
    Bak-Keng, 197
    Banteai Kedei, 225
    Neak Pehn, 256
    Pimeanakas, 177
    Prah Kahn, 250
    Ta-Keo, 209
sandalwood, 179

Sea of Milk, 92, 268
Siam, Siamese, 137, 260, 262, 266
    Franco-Siamese 1907 treaty, 7, 266, 275. *See also* Thais
    war with the Khmers, 6, 78, 90, 264, 274
Siem Reap, 60, 98, 103, 181-183, 190, 192, 196, 239, 244
Sisowath, King, 54
Sita, 95. *See also* Ramayana
Sra Srang, 241
Sugriva, 95. *See also* Ramayana
Suryavarman II, 274

T
Ta-Keo, 208, 240
    gopura, 208
Ta Prohm, 224, 226-238, 240
    entrances, 232
tea, 26, 28
Terrace of Honour, 142, 147-148, 150, 152, 165, 272
    hunting scene, 154-156
Terrace of the Leper King, 158, 183. *See also* Leper King
Tevadas, 74, 98, 100, 111, 152, 174, 179
Thais, 90, 137, 262, 264. *See also* Siamese
Tibet, 50, 56
tigers, 32, 34, 37, 50, 144, 150, 252
    as inspiration for Khmer lion, 144
    danger from, 37, 60, 164, 192, 208, 222-223
    Garuda with head of a tiger, 150
Tonlé Sap, 56-58, 190, 206, 242, 244, 275
Trimurti, 77, 118, 127, 128, 230, 236, 257

U
umbrellas
    as signs of rank, 90, 94
    in ancient China, 90

V
varmans, 240
Vasuki, 92
Vishnu, 77-79, 91-92, 116, 117, 136, 228, 230, 236, 270. *See also* Brahmanic religion
    at Neak Pean, 256-258
    Garuda, mount of Vishnu, 150
    Vishnuism, 270
Vishnuloka, 90
volutes, 98, 206, 225, 252

W
Western Baray, 242, 244
World War I, 218, 220

Y
Yasovarman, 120, 174, 272

Z
Zhou Daguan, 136, 166, 168, 270
    Angkor Thom, 116, 118
    Baphuon, 200
    Khmer king, 170, 176-178
    Kublai Khan, 166
    palace of the king, 178-179
    Phimeanakas, 166, 168, 170, 172, 175-178
    Terrace of Honour, 124, 158
    wives of the king, 172
    women of the palace, 174-177

Cambodian Dancers
Ancient and Modern
by George Groslier

ISBN 978-1-934431-11-5

It is my pleasure to introduce new generations of readers to this classic account of Cambodia's royal dance tradition.

H.R.H. Princess Norodom Buppha Devi

George Groslier's pivotal artistic study of Cambodia's ancient dance tradition, in an expanded English language edition of the author's rare 1913 publication.

This deluxe hardcover volume includes more than 250 photos, all of Groslier's hand-drawn illustrations, his original French text, extensive background materials, a bibliography and index.

The book also features the first detailed biography of the author: **Le Khmérophile - The Art and Life of George Groslier** by historian Kent Davis. Working with the author's daughter Nicole Rea Groslier, her family, and previously unseen family archives, Davis recounts the epic tale of the man who committed his life to serving Cambodia and her people.

www.CambodianDancers.com

DatAsia

Earth in Flower
The Divine Mystery of the Cambodian Dance Drama
by Paul Cravath

ISBN 978-1-934431-28-3

The most comprehensive analysis of Southeast Asia's most esoteric female performing art: the ancient Cambodian ballet.

Since the dawn of recorded history, Khmer royalty have nurtured a dance style unique to their Asian kingdom, yet instantly recognizable throughout the world. Spiritually, these graceful dancers act as a living liason with the gods as they embody the essence and strength of the Khmer race.

Earth in Flower examines the art, culture, origin and spiritual relevance of this sacred dance tradition. A wartime twist of fate made Dr. Paul Cravath one of the only Westerners in history to gain full access to this formerly sequestered troupe of royal dancers, their archives, theater and teachers. In *Earth in Flower* he gives new insights into this beautiful art, its long-hidden mysteries, the dancers themselves, and how they balance the Khmer relationship between heaven and earth.

www.EarthInFlower.com

DatAsia

Daughters of Angkor Wat
Unlocking the Secrets of Asia's Ancient Khmer Goddesses
ISBN 978-1-934431-17-7

Lost in the jungles of Southeast Asia for centuries, the Khmer temple of Angkor Wat is the largest religious structure ever built by humankind. Inside, it protects an extraordinary treasure unlike any on Earth: detailed portrait carvings of nearly 2,000 ancient women immortalized in stone.

Today, their identity and purpose remain a mystery. Were they wives of the king? Servants and dancers? Imaginary angels rendered by skilled sculptors? Or do these women represent a storehouse of knowledge beyond anything previously imagined?

Daughters of Angkor Wat begins unlocking their secrets with surprising theories, hundreds of original photos and insights from leading experts including:

**Paul Cravath - Kent Davis - Madeleine Giteau - George Groslier
Trudy Jacobsen - Julie Mehta - Peter Sharrock - Krishna Srivastava
...and other enlightened observers.**

www.DEVATA.org

DatAsia

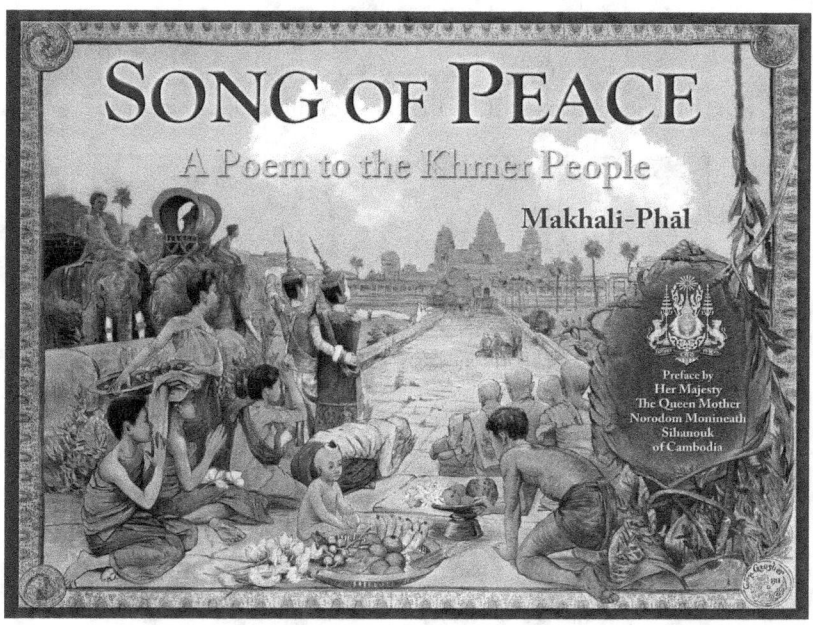

Song of Peace
A Poem to the Khmer People
ISBN 978-1-934431-77-1

A timeless poem of the mythical years...inspired by an ancient era of conquest and meditation, yet still capable of touching the great grandchildren of today's children. To be understood by them, and retained, and recited.

EDMOND JALOUX ❁ The French Academy

In 1898, Makhali-Phāl was born a Franco-Khmer child in Cambodia, her very blood blending the wisdom of two diverse cultures. As an author and poet, she devoted her life to expressing the conflict, harmony and hope inherent in the powerful forces of East and West that lived within her body and mind.

Song of Peace is the author's ultimate literary bequest to her people, with a clear message of purpose and enlightenment in our materialistic modern world. Her Majesty The Queen Mother Norodom Monineath Sihanouk introduces this special first edition presenting this monumental poem in French and English, with a Khmer language edition now in preparation.

www.Makhali-Phal.org

DatAsia

Under the Royal Patronage of
HRH Samdech Reach Botrei Preah Ream Norodom Buppha Devi

 **NKFC CONSERVATOIRE**
Preah Ream Buppha Devi
Chhouk Sar — Banteay Srey

This unique school within the Angkor Heritage Park in Banteay Srey district teaches traditional Cambodian dance and music. The school provides rural children with rigorous training in these arts, based on the strength and discipline of Khmer heritage. The goals of the foundation are to enrich each child's life while preserving and expanding Cambodia's cultural legacy.

A portion of the proceeds from *Angkor the Magnificent* supports this effort. We invite you to participate in this cultural revival by sponsoring a young dancer or musician at the conervatoire.

www.NKFC.org

the Nginn Karet Foundation for Cambodia

www.ingramcontent.com/pod-product-compliance
Lightning Source LLC
Chambersburg PA
CBHW051359070526
44584CB00023B/3218